DATE DUE

NO 20 '92	AG 1 '96		
MR 28 '93	NO 21 '96		
AP 23 '93	AP 7 '97		
JY 7 '93	JY 23 '97		
JE 11 '93	DE 1 '97		
AG 6 '93	AP 23 '99		
OC 15 '93	AP 1 '00		
NO 5 '93			
NO 19 '93			
AP 1 '94			
JE 10 '94			
JE 23 '94			
AG 18 '94			
SE 23 '94			
MR 31 '95			
MR 1 '96			
MR 22 '96			

DEMCO 38-296

200 LETTERS FOR JOB HUNTERS

by
William S. Frank
President, CareerLab®
Denver, Colorado

Ten Speed Press

Excerpt on page 14 from Tested Advertising Methods copyright ©1974 by John Caples. Used by permission of Prentice-Hall, Inc., Englewood Cliffs, New Jersey.

Text from Boeing advertisement on page 14 used by permission of the company.

Bloop cartoon on page 20 copyright ©1990 by Roy J. Wilson. Used by permission, all rights reserved.

Ten Speed Press
P O Box 7123
Berkeley, California 94704

Library of Congress Cataloging-in-Publication Data
Frank, William S.
     200 letters for job-hunters / William S. Frank.
        p.   cm.
     ISBN 0-89815-363-8 : $14.95
     1. Job hunting. 2. Letter writing.
  3.   Employment references. 4. Applications for positions. 5. Thank-you notes. I. Title. II. Title: Two hundred letters for job-hunters.
HF5382.7.F72   1990
650.14—dc20   89-20652
                              CIP

3 4 5 6 — 95 94 93 92 91

Printed in the United States of America

For my family

My parents, Scott and Ruth
My brother and sister, Brad and Sherry
My young-adult children, Kenny and Brandon
and especially for
My sweet wife, Beverly.

CONTENTS

PART ONE

WHAT TO DO FOR A QUICK JOB-SEARCH

What to do for a quick job-search

If you're in a hurry—and most job-hunters are—you'll make the best time if you do things in exactly this order:

1. Get stationery, envelopes, and business cards printed on white or off-white paper. No "parchment." Five hundred of each should be plenty. Use an "executive" looking type style, like a lawyer might have—nothing fancy and no large computer fonts.

2. Get set up with a secretarial service, or with your own word processor. Don't try to type correspondence on your dad's old Underwood, unless that's your only choice. Don't do your own letters unless you're a good typist. Even then, make only six to twelve originals. (Don't force your spouse to type for you, either, unless he or she really loves the idea.)

   If you can afford it, use a secretarial service for mailings of twelve or more pieces. Repeat letters normally cost about $1.00-1.50 each which is cheap compared to the value of your time. Your time is better spent on the telephone or in face-to-face meetings.

3. Read the section in this book called "The most important letter you will ever write," page 6. Take great pains remembering the names of everyone you've ever met.

4. Send a "friendship letter" like Dale Kreeger's to close personal friends (see page 12), and include a resume. (Since 75 percent of all good jobs come from friends—or friends of friends—this is the single most important strategy you can follow.)

5. Call your friends after they've had a chance to review your letter. Ask them if they got it and what they think of it.

   You'll be amazed at how many "have been meaning to call you," but didn't quite get around to it. You'll also be amazed at how many are actually glad to hear your voice. Begin to set face-to-face informational meetings with anyone who seems interested or especially helpful. Follow up on every lead you get, no matter how "silly."

   Don't pre-judge what others will say before you call them.

6. Write a series of tailored "friendship letters" to the most powerful and influential people you know: your banker, your stockbroker, your former employers, your spouse's friends and soon. (See pages 76-90.)

7. Contact search firms (recruiters and headhunters).

8. Write to members of your professional association(s) or organization(s). (See pages 87-88.)

9. Develop a generic letter and begin to answer want ads. Customize the letter for important ads, but only devote 5 percent of your effort to answering want ads—not 95 percent, as is all too common.

10. Select a mailing list and write a high-powered sales/marketing letter. Mail 50-100 pieces as a

test, with no resume included. Mail on Mondays, telephone late in the week, after the letter is received. Record your results, then adjust the letter and the list and mail again if necessary.

11. Send a thank-you letter after *every* marketing contact and social occasion, telephone call, and personal visit—no matter how insignificant. Job-hunting is a public relations campaign, and you're trying to build goodwill.

12. Look through this book to find clever ways to introduce yourself to companies, and begin some one-shot, highly targeted mailings. Follow as many letters as possible with phone calls.

13. Make sure your telephone is always answered. Get an answering machine (about $50), use an answering service, or subscribe to an electronic voice mailbox (about $13 per month). Put a businesslike message on your recorder or voice mailbox (no cute messages featuring your kids).

   If you're based at home, you might want to consider adding a second line for your business calls.

14. Once the calls from your mailings start pouring in, keep meticulous records to be certain nothing falls through the cracks. Review your records occasionally to be sure you haven't missed anything.

15. Continually reprioritize, and see the most important people first. As management expert Peter Drucker says, "Do first things first, and second things not at all."

16. Spend as much time as you can talking on the phone or visiting with others. Letters are useful, but it's not wise to try to conduct an entire job-search through the mail. Real opportunities come in face-to-face meetings, because, as theologian Martin Buber said, "All real living is meeting."

17. The letters in this book are available as IBM-PC software called **INSTANT Job Hunting Letters**. If you're really in a hurry to get a job, this is the fastest way to go. For information about **INSTANT Job Hunting Letters**, turn to page 320.

PART TWO

HOW TO WRITE A GREAT LETTER

How to Write a Great Letter

Why this book?

Most job-hunters want a job *fast*, few have the luxury of time. Even senior executives with large severance packages are often panicked at the thought of being unemployed, no matter how briefly. There's something inside us that says, "I have to be working."

Interviews produce job offers, but letters produce interviews. Well-worded letters will get you talking to more people quicker than any other method. That's why no job-search campaign is complete without them.

A sales or marketing letter is the quickest, surest way to reach a decision-maker, short of calling that person on the telephone.

A letter is fast. It goes right into the employer's office and requires less courage than the telephone. Most importantly, it's efficient. Letters can be sent out by the hundreds. You can't call two hundred people per day, but you can mail to that many.

Best of all, a well-written letter gets results. I have never seen a job-hunter with a superb letter fail. Even if a manager doesn't need you immediately, a really good letter will usually be kept, or passed to another decision-maker. Your letter may have long-term effects you never imagined.

Most job-hunters don't write well

Most job-hunters have trouble writing; they dislike it and agonize over it. Either they didn't learn the craft in school, or they're rusty.

Executives and professionals don't write well, either. In fact, they often write poorly, because they haven't had to do it themselves. Their secretaries write for them, their spouses help them, or they delegate writing to subordinates. No one seems to like to write.

Think about it. It's rare to receive a polished, well-thought-out letter, isn't it? Most business letters are routine: unimaginative and dull.

If you send an exceptionally good letter, you stand out. If your letter is excellent, it will be read. And if it's especially good, or if it's timely, you'll get a phone call.

The most important letter you will ever write

All job-hunting correspondence is important, but the letter you send your friends is absolutely critical. Here's why:

When you're in a job-hunt you're selling personal services—what you can do—something intangible. People buy services based on trust. Marketing personal services is not like marketing a product—shoppers buy a product knowing full well they can return it if dissatisfied. But how do you return an executive who doesn't pan out? You can't. The stakes are vastly different, so buyers of services are much more cautious.

Crucial hiring decisions are generally made by committee. Key managers get together and decide what sort of person they want. Then one of them says, "Who do we *know* that could fill this slot?" Most of the time, someone in the group knows someone. That candidate is interviewed first and usually hired. The moral of the story is that we hire our friends—known quantities, not shots-in-the-dark. No one likes to hire strangers—there's too much at stake. One bad hiring decision can ruin a manager's career.

What does this mean to you?

It means your next job is probably going to come from one of your friends—or else from one of their friends. Not from a recruiter. Not from a newspaper ad. Not from knocking on doors or pounding the pavement.

Your friends are your strongest marketing allies. That's why it's important to involve them in your campaign not just notify them. Most job-seekers simply call and say, "I've lost my job. Let me know if you hear of anything." The friend says, "Sure I will." And that's the end of it. The phone never rings. Friends want to help, but they have to know exactly what kind of help you need. Tell them in a "friendship letter."

Who are your friends?

When I say "friends," I mean "everyone you know." Not just your closest friends, but anyone who knows your name. I mean your contact network, both personal and business—especially people you've worked with on projects. Begin your marketing campaign by making a list of your friends. Use the following checklist to help you remember names.

Record all names. Don't prejudge people, guessing which ones can help you (you'll often be wrong). Don't rule anyone out prematurely.

THE FRIENDSHIP CHECKLIST

- ❑ Family (uncles, aunts, cousins, distant relatives)
- ❑ Your significant other's family and friends
- ❑ Close personal friends
- ❑ Builders, plumbers, electricians
- ❑ PTA members
- ❑ Students, fellow classmates, former college professors
- ❑ Parents of your children's friends
- ❑ Organizational groups
- ❑ Professional societies
- ❑ Club officers
- ❑ Hobby groups
- ❑ Social groups
- ❑ Headhunters
- ❑ Church groups
- ❑ Religious leaders (pastor, priest, rabbi)
- ❑ Current and former employers
- ❑ Fellow jurors
- ❑ Fellow employees (your peer group)
- ❑ The staff, editors and reporters of your local newspaper
- ❑ Professionals
    - ❑ Dentist
    - ❑ Doctor
    - ❑ Attorney
    - ❑ CPA
    - ❑ Financial planner
    - ❑ Psychologist
    - ❑ Banker
    - ❑ Veterinarian
    - ❑ Realtor
    - ❑ Insurance agent
- ❑ Fellow vacationers or travelers
- ❑ Former clients, customers, buyers, suppliers, and sales representatives
- ❑ Librarians
- ❑ Consultants you've used
- ❑ Chamber of Commerce members
- ❑ Store owners
- ❑ Former cellmates (just kidding)
- ❑ Ex in-laws
- ❑ High school buddies
- ❑ Fraternity brothers/sisters
- ❑ Friends of your parents
- ❑ Favorite waiters, bartenders, and hosts
- ❑ Secretaries
- ❑ Security guards
- ❑ The person at the dry cleaners
- ❑ Your hairdresser
- ❑ Neighbors
- ❑ Parents (yes, *your* parents!)

Go as far back as high school, even grade school. List your old college classmates and roommates. Look at your Christmas/Chanukah card list. Write names until your mind goes blank. Then stop and rest, and begin again later.

Common objections

Many job-hunters resist doing this exercise. They don't see the point. They find it time-consuming and come up with a variety of objections, like these:

Objection	Answer
I don't want to use my friends.	Contact them and give *them* something: a journal article, an idea, an invitation to lunch, a compliment, a good listening. Find out how they're doing.
All my friends are in Chicago and I want to work in Dallas.	People in Chicago have family and friends in Dallas.
I hate to call people and ask for favors.	Read answer number one, above.
I can't remember all these people.	Yes you can. You just don't want to.
I would be embarrassed to say I'm unemployed.	Say something like "I have some great news. I'm finally leaving HighTek—it's about time. Their accounting system is snarled up, and I want to get into a company where I can bring the latest computer solutions into the picture. This is great! I've never been more excited in my life. I can't sleep at night. I feel like a kid again."
I would feel funny writing a letter to people I see in person all the time.	Don't write them a letter. Talk with them face to face.

The following stories show the importance of collecting the names of friends, even if it doesn't make logical sense.

It doesn't matter where your friends live

Ken Grange was a senior data processing manager in Denver. He wanted to relocate to Dallas because his wife had family there. I asked Ken to list his friends so he could send them something. He resisted doing the assignment.

His reasoning went like this: "All my friends live in Chicago. I want to work in Dallas. Why should I write to people who can't help me?"

Finally, after three weeks, Ken made his list. We sent a letter, and guess what? One of his contacts in Chicago had a brother who was president of a data processing company in Dallas. Ken flew down to interview and was hired.

That's the kind of thing that often happens in networking.

"You never know how many friends you have until you rent a place at the beach."

quoted by Wayne Norris in
You Don't Have to Be Crazy to Work Here . . . But It Sure Helps (Price/Stern/Sloan).

Don't guess who your friends are

I've seen hundreds of people go through this process of contacting their network and asking for help, and I see two patterns.

First, friendship letters *always* work. You get *some* positive response from *some* of your friends. That's a big boost when you're feeling down. Second, it's impossible to accurately predict who will help you and who won't. You'll be wrong 50 percent of the time—maybe more.

It's interesting, and sometimes disconcerting, to find out who can be counted on when you need a helping hand. Some of your "dearest friends" will let you down, and some people you have written off will come out of the woodwork and shower badly needed love and attention on you.

Your friends will always help

I contacted my friends—especially former clients—in writing this book. I was announcing the project, asking for permission to use their materials, and looking for advice and ideas. I was reaching out for support.

I was surprised at the positive responses. They really lifted me and made me feel the whole project was worthwhile. There was one letter I will never forget. Kay Tubbs said, "My advice: Go for it! It's perfect. I would buy it (and recommend it) in a heartbeat. It would also solve a personal problem I have, of not being physically close enough to utilize your services. (It's probably a good thing—I'd be tempted to mortgage the house to hire you as a permanent 'life consultant.')" That felt really good.

But I was also disappointed at the results. Some people whom I had given a great deal of support either didn't answer or wouldn't let me use their materials. And that hurt.

All I can say is, I'm glad I sent the letter, because those who helped really offered a great deal. You'll find that most of your friends will help you, too, and their heartfelt response may surprise you.

The world's greatest letter

I've always encouraged clients to contact their friends to ask for advice and ideas. They used a variety of letters, and I'm certain many of them worked. But one day in a workshop, I found the ultimate "friendship letter." It was a work of art.

The tone was right: It was warm and friendly, and not too pushy or boring. It made you want to help.

I began distributing Dale Kreeger's letter in my classes. Students used it as a guide. (As you will see, many of the letters in this book take off from Dale's.)

Dale was an accountant in a large oil company. At age 55 he was asked to take early retirement before he was ready. Here is what he wrote:

DALE M. KREEGER
6950 South Olive Way
Englewood, Colorado 80112

March 5, 19--

Mr. Mike Roberts
Arthur Andersen & Co.
717 Seventeenth Street, Suite 1900
Denver, Colorado 80202

Dear Mike,

As friend to friend, I want to let you know that I plan to
accept the voluntary early retirement package offered by
Worldwide Oil Company as of March 31, 19--; however, I do not
plan on moving out to pasture for at least another five to
ten years. Consequently, I have put together a current
resume in order to begin marketing myself for what I believe
will be the most productive and exciting years of my life.

I am totally open not only to an industry change but also to
relocating if necessary--naturally Thelma and I both prefer
to remain in Denver!

Should you be aware or become aware of any of your business
associates, friends, etc. who may be in the market for new
blood and innovative thinking, I would truly appreciate your
slipping them the attached copy of my resume or giving me
their names for me to contact personally.

Any assistance or advice that you can give me at this special
crossroads period of my life will be greatly appreciated.

Very best regards,

Dale M. Kreeger

DMK:df
Enclosure

What makes this letter work?

It's warm.
It's friendly.
It's interesting.
It's not begging.
It's enthusiastic.
It's light-hearted ("not ready to be
 put out to pasture yet . . .").
It's short.
It's everything a great letter should be.

But as good as it is, it can still be improved. The letter doesn't specify exactly what kind of job Dale wants. Friends can't help very well unless they know exactly, clearly, and specifically what kind of help you need. The more specific, the better. As an example, here's a "what I want" paragraph another career counselor wrote:

"I'd like to work for outplacement firms coaching their consultants in career counseling and marketing techniques. I'd like to live somewhere remote and travel to major cities—but no more than 25 percent travel. I want to spend 50 percent of my time consulting and selling, and 50 percent writing and researching." That's a lot to ask, and maybe he won't get it. But on the other hand, maybe he will.

Some job-seekers object to being specific. They want to keep their options open. They reason this way: "If I tell people exactly what I want, I might miss out on other things I might like."

That's true. But, on the other hand, if you tell people exactly what you want, you might get your ideal job. Wouldn't that be better?

The anatomy of a friendship letter

If you write a letter to your network, you can use Dale's letter as a model, or you can invent your own. If you do your own letter—and I recommend that—here are five steps you should take:

1. *Establish rapport*
   Rebuild old fences. Make your reader feel good. Make them glad you're writing.
   "I can't help remembering the fun we had last time in Atlanta."
   "Denver has not been the same since you left town. We have missed you."

2. *Explain the situation*
   "I was just laid off. The company is downsizing."
   "I've decided I need more responsibility."
   "Sally's health is not good, and we feel we must leave Wisconsin to find a warmer climate."
   "The new chairman and I don't see eye to eye."

3. *Tell them what you want*
   "I want a team environment. I've proved I can do it all myself, and I'm tired of my Lone Ranger act."

4. *Ask for advice and ideas*
   "Your words of wisdom have always meant a great deal to me over the years."
   "I've always counted on you to spark my creativity."
   "Would you mind reviewing my resume and letters and giving me some honest opinions? Could you call me or jot some notes in the margins?"

5. *End on a warm, friendly, enthusiastic note*
   "Should you be free in the near future, Jim and I would like to have you come to dinner."

Writing to strangers

After you've mailed to your friends, you'll be mailing to "strangers," and that's a much tougher sell. To many of them, you're just a number, an interruption, a salesperson.

In trying to reach outsiders, you have a lot of competition. In Denver, for instance, there are 35 commercial television channels, 60+ radio stations, 2 major metropolitan dailies, billboards, and ads on shopping carts all vying for attention. You may have a similar situation in your city.

Americans spend $34 billion a year on advertising (more than $400 per household). Network television features 600 commercials per day. There are at least 1,500 advertising messages sent directly to you. That's a lot of hype.

During a recent recession in Denver, the Colorado Association of Realtors spent $250,000 to promote only three words: Take Another Look. (Meaning, the real estate market may be better than you think.)

When you market or advertise yourself (that is, when you try to find a job), you're competing for attention with well-capitalized corporations. So you and your message may easily get lost.

The only marketing lesson you'll ever need

Right after college I had a "marketing lesson" I've never forgotten; it has shaped much of my business success. Here's what happened: I decided to teach a personal growth workshop, printed several hundred flyers, and passed them out like handbills.

After about an hour of walking, I faced a dilemma: should I continue putting out flyers or go home to answer the phone? I knew it would be ringing off the hook.

When I couldn't wait any longer, I raced home, and guess what? The phone never rang. Not even once. I call that my "Marketing 101" lesson: customers (employers) don't really care about our great stuff and nifty ideas. They're busy people. In marketing—the job-hunt—we have to grab their attention.

Drawbacks to letter writing

A well-written letter can break through the "communications jungle" and lead to interviews, but there are definite pros and cons to writing sales and marketing letters. Here are just a few:

Plus	Minus
They're fast.	They're hard to write. They take brain power. They take time.
They're personal.	A letter must be extremely well-written or it will fail.
They take less guts than a cold call.	They're somewhat costly (versus the telephone, which is virtually free.)
Once you have a letter that works, you can send it out hundreds of times and multiply your efforts enormously.	A bad marketing letter can make you look like a real loser or egomaniac, and, therefore, blow your future chances.

The letter can be selling while you are doing something else.

If you write a good letter, you may be perceived by the recipient as extremely creative.

A well-written letter *always* gets responses.

If you send a poor marketing letter and don't get any response, it can be quite depressing.

The average letter gets between three and ten seconds on the way to the trash can. (How fast do you open your own mail?)

My world famous junk mail lecture

Do you save the junk mail that comes to your house? Perhaps you should. Businesses spend hundreds of millions of dollars each year designing direct mail pieces and testing the results. Obviously, some of it works or they wouldn't keep using it. In direct mail, nothing is sacred—results are the only thing that counts. If a mailing doesn't pay for itself, it's discontinued.

Years ago, I started collecting junk mail and advertising gimmicks: door hangers, table top tent cards from restaurants, all kinds of direct mail—especially letters. And I learned to write letters that always get results.

My own letters have landed major corporate accounts, built a thriving consulting business, gotten me interviewed on television, collected delinquent bills, and secured a publisher for this book—plus much more. With a little research and planning, yours can do the same.

Look at a few direct mail letters from your mailbox. What do you notice about them? For one thing, no two are alike. Sure, there are similarities, but each letter is essentially one of a kind. Some are amateurish, some are great. Some turn you off, some pull you in.

Examine the format and you'll see a lot of white space on the page. That's visual appeal—the letters look good. Also, they're fun to read—not dull, boring, or routine. They offer something. They're loaded with benefits for the reader. They tell you exactly what you're going to get—and precisely how it will help you.

The words and sentences are short and easy to understand. You seldom see jargon or buzzwords—unless the offer comes from a specialized industry source.

Here's a project that will help your letter writing:

Collect your junk mail for a week. Look at it. Study it. Critique it. See how you could improve it. Rewrite it. Play with it.

Try to incorporate some of it in your writing. If you can, most of your letters will be winners. (You don't want your letters to seem to be "junk mail," though.)

What is "advertising appeal"?

I once noticed a restaurant billboard that said, "We welcome tour buses." Why do they want tour buses? I wondered. And then it dawned on me: Tour buses are full of hundreds of customers. I watched the signs. They changed slightly, but most sounded alike: "Bus Drivers Welcome." That sort of thing.

Then I saw a sign that accomplished what all the other signs had merely tried to do. It stopped the buses. What did it say? "Bus Drivers Eat Free." That's advertising appeal: Finding the right message for the right crowd.

Why write emotional copy?

John Caples, author of *Tested Advertising Methods*, says, "If you write with the prejudices and preferences of other people uppermost in your mind, you will produce copy as correct as a school child's essay, but utterly lifeless . . .

"Get excited! Get worked up! . . . Then start to write. Write fast. Write furiously. Write as if you had to catch a plane. Write as if you had to put all your thoughts on paper in the next five minutes or lose them forever . . .

"Action—that's the vital quality that emotional copy possesses and that 'reason why' copy lacks . . .

"Everybody knows that you can tame a wild horse and make the animal useful. But it is impossible to put life into a dead horse. The same is true of advertising copy. An advertisement that has been pounded out in the white heat of enthusiasm can be tamed and

made effective. But it is impossible to put life into dead copy."

The best emotional copy I ever read

It appeared in an ad for Boeing. Picture this: an empty beach, white sand, bright sunlight. A young couple—no children around—walking away arm-in-arm.

Then the words:

"SOMEDAY"
We'll take off. Just the two of us.
No kids. No pets. No worries. We'll
lie on a lonely beach. And plan
another 100 years together.

"Remember the first time you mentioned going away? How many somedays ago was that? Is your warm and wonderful someday really ever going to happen? Right now, your travel agent or airline can arrange especially good values in air travel on Boeing jetliners. To anywhere in the world. So go. Before your someday slowly slips away."

BOEING

Isn't that wonderful? Nothing logical about it—it's all emotion, all persuasive. Doesn't it make you want to go to the beach?

Show your excitement and enthusiasm

A big part of letter writing is attitude. If you have a positive attitude that comes through in your words, you shouldn't have any trouble getting the right response.

The best letters are "heartfelt"—not academic or strictly logical. They have feeling; they move you.

Be brave. Yes, if you're too aggressive you run the risk of turning them off, but if you write too carefully, you run the risk of being totally ignored. And being ignored is the fate of most job-search letter writers—I can tell you that from experience.

If you like people, tell them so. Don't be afraid to show honest feelings. Here's an excerpt from one of my own sales letters: "Great meeting you! You sound like a very positive, upbeat, helpful person—just the kind I like to work with."

Here's something else I used: "You really got me off to a great start last week. I think Saturday was the most exciting day of my life. Almost too exciting."

Make your letters electric. Don't hide your feelings, and don't play "hard-to-get." Your words should feel fresh and alive. Interesting and intriguing. Different, creative, and thought-provoking. Let the reader feel your emotions. Does that seem like a tall order? It is, but you can do it.

How to collect your ideas

When you begin to write, your mind may give you random, disjointed thoughts. Ideas probably won't come out logically or sequentially, but write them down as they appear, without worrying about order or logic. Don't judge or evaluate, simply collect them. Later you'll evaluate, judge, sort, and organize them. At this stage you just want to get them down—on paper, on tape, or on disc.

It is easier for most people to write this way, because the creative part of your brain isn't very logical, and the logical part of your brain isn't very creative. Don't expect your mind to perform both functions at once (although some can).

Use the "card trick" to organize your thoughts

Sometimes it helps to put all your thoughts on individual index cards, exactly as they come to mind. Later, you can sort the cards to get a finished product, eliminating cards that don't fit.

This is also a beautiful way to write a magazine or journal article with very little stress—and very little "writer's block," because nothing you write down has to be said perfectly or accurately. Everything can be sharpened up later.

Your first goal has to be simply to collect your rough thoughts. Once you've accomplished that, here's what to do next:

1. Spend some time on your letter. Someone once said, "With part-time effort, you get part-time results." This is especially true in letter writing. You can expect to spend several hours, or even several days, on a letter.

2. Write a draft of your letter, then let it cool off overnight.

3. Rewrite if necessary.

4. Be sure you use a strong close, like these:
   "After you have had a chance to review this letter, I will call you to get your reactions."
   "I will call your office next week to arrange a time when we might be able to get together. If you have any questions before that, please call me at (303) 771-4357."
   Avoid weaker endings like these:
   "Please call me at your earliest convenience."
   "I believe that a meeting could prove to be mutually profitable, and ask, that if you agree, you contact me so that we can arrange a convenient time."
   "Thank you for your consideration. I am available for a personal interview at your earliest convenience and look forward to hearing from you."
   "In the next week or two when your schedule permits, let's meet and discuss my aspirations in more detail. Please give me a call."
   "I look forward to your reply."

5. Ask for opinions, advice, and feedback from friends, and from sales, marketing, and advertising experts.

6. Mail a small sample to test your letter. This is important. A consultant friend once mailed 76,000 brochures at a cost of nearly $15,000, and only got three responses. What a shame! The material was poorly written and poorly tested. Test your letters before you roll them out on a large scale.

7. If you're getting the kind of response you want, mail larger numbers.

8. Enclose a *response form* to increase your results (see page 183).

9. Remail the same letter to the same people two or three times. Repetition often helps.

10. Don't mark letters "Personal and Confidential," unless there's a solid reason why they can't be opened by a secretary. If the letter is persuasive enough, it will probably get through.

Give yourself time

You can't expect to produce an exceptional document overnight. Letter writing is actually harder than resume writing because you're starting with a clean slate. In resume writing at least you have your background—which is definite—to work with. In letter writing, you start with nothing. Letters can be about anything, and that's why they're so difficult.

I once took a class called "How to Market a Book." The class focused on writing query letters to publishers in order to get a book contract. The course lasted six weeks and met for two hours each week. I spent several hours per week on homework—staying up all night several nights—and the end product was a one-page sales letter to publishers.

Lots of work for just one letter.

I mailed the letter to about 30 publishers and got 13 responses. No one bought the book, but one publisher did offer to publish it for royalties only (no advance), which I declined. That book was the forerunner of this one.

Writers often say, "I don't like writing, but I like having written." That's how many of us feel. Writing can be hard work. Don't take it lightly, and don't feel bad if you can't compose a zippy marketing letter in half an hour. Writing is a profession, like rocket science. Don't expect to learn or perfect it overnight.

Don't copy someone else's letter

Take these letters as samples and modify them to fit your needs, but don't copy them verbatim. I've found that people who copy someone else's letter seldom get a good response, regardless of how good the letter is. Be original.

It *would* be easy to take the letters in this book and use them word-for-word. That would be quick, but probably not effective. Your letter has to be "you." It should sound like you, feel like you, read like you—because *you* have to follow it with a phone call, or answer questions about it. So, don't send a really "hot," aggressive letter if you're introverted and laid-back. You'll have trouble following up on the letter and you may not come across well. Send a letter that mirrors your style—and only you can write that letter.

Get professional help

If you're a skilled writer, fine. The letter may be easy for you. But if you're not, you may need some help. Consider hiring a professional freelance writer to help you compose and edit your letters (not to do them for you).

Where can you begin to look? Call your local ad club for the names of direct mail freelance writers. Read the classifieds in *Writer's Digest.* Check the Yellow Pages under "Writers." Contact your local writers' guild. Check with local advertising and PR firms. They use lots of freelancers. Newspaper and magazine editors know writers too.

Thirteen common mistakes

If you've ever seen a batch of letters sent in response to a want ad, you know they can be hysterically funny. A random sampling usually demonstrates every mistake in the book (like sending the letter to the wrong company). Here are thirteen common errors to avoid:

1. Crowded and cluttered copy (300-word paragraphs), and amateurish format.

2. Handwritten letters. One psychologist I heard from actually turned the paper sideways and filled the right-hand margin when he reached the end of a page. It looked awful.

3. Mailing the letter to a job title like "Director of Personnel" or "Vice President of Marketing." You wouldn't send a love letter to "Dear Occupant," would you? It's too impersonal.

4. Addressing correspondence to "Dear Sir/Madam." Try to learn the name of the person you're targeting, and don't use "To Whom It May Concern." Find out whom it does concern and send the letter to *that person.*

5. Misspelling the recipient's name. Even popular names like "Smith" have several spellings (Smythe, Smithe). I recall prejudging a letter addressed to "Bill Frank Accociates," because it was so badly misspelled. Always verify the spelling of names, even common ones.

6. Talking mostly about yourself (I this, I that). Minimize the word "I" in your letters. Selling is about "you." Focus on the recipient's

needs. Here's an actual bad example that came to my office:

"Dear Sir: I would like to relocate to your city in January. This move would depend solely upon my ability to obtain a job with your company . . ."

That made me feel like his future was my responsibility, not his. I thought he might always be looking for someone to take care of him. Remember, the most important word in advertising is "you."

7. Talking down to people or insulting the reader.
     Having heard one of my speeches, a consultant wrote:

"You are obviously very knowledgeable in selling and perhaps are an excellent salesman in a one-on-one situation . . . but a dynamic, charismatic speaker, you are not . . . To make your program better, you simply need a better speaker. Who, you say? Ah, that should be obvious."

She meant *herself!* It *wasn't* obvious, and I didn't like being insulted.

8. Cliches. Avoid cliches like the plague.

9. Typos. One personnel director told me that he throws out any resume if he sees even one drop of white-out on the cover letter. That's terribly short-sighted, but it's exactly what he said.

10. Arrogance or flippancy.

11. Trivializing a serious subject.

12. Lack of focus. The letter should be like a karate blow: all the body's energy focused on one small point.

13. Promising too much. Don't promise what you can't deliver.

Try using stamped reply envelopes

If you're doing a small mailing to a carefully selected list of important contacts, say to thirty recruiters in your targeted geographic area, it might be worthwhile to include a self-addressed stamped envelope. It's a convenience to the reader, and it may increase your response dramatically. I would try this tactic with any important letter where I definitely want an answer.

Advantages of the plain white envelope

I always open envelopes with no return name or address. I'm afraid not to. Who knows what's in them?

I once received a mailer that looked like junk mail. It was one of those envelope-like packages you pull apart at the seams to expose the contents, like the things your bank sends at the end of the year for tax purposes. I opened it on the way to the trash can. And surprise! It was a $5,000 check for a consulting assignment. Since that time I seldom throw away unopened "junk mail." There may be some real treasures in there.

I never throw plain envelopes away unopened, either— especially if the name and address are handwritten or typed onto the envelope (mass-produced labels and bulk postage are a tipoff that this could be junk mail). Try some different approaches for your mailing and see what results you get.

Personal and confidential

Never mark an envelope "personal and confidential" unless it really is. Yes, you may fool the secretary and get the letter to the right person. But if they open it expecting something extremely urgent—perhaps an emergency—only to find a job-seeker, the results can be negative. Most people don't like to feel they've been tricked or outsmarted.

It's like getting an executive on the phone by saying his house is on fire. It works. You do get the targeted person on the phone, but the rest of the conversation can only be disastrous.

There are times when "personal and confidential" is appropriate, such as when security would be breached, in an emergency, when time is of the essence. In these cases, use the notation without worrying. That's what it's for.

How to select a mailing list

List selection is critical to a successful mailing. It just doesn't make sense to send a sales letter to someone who couldn't possibly be interested.

Where do you get the right names? First of all, you compile them yourself. Begin with your own contact network. That's the most important list you could ever get your hands on, because those people know and trust you. You're a known quantity to them. (Remember, the world is suspicious of "strangers.") Your friendship list will be your biggest ally in your search for new employment.

Get other lists from:

Professional organizations (names of their members)

Telephone directories

Contacts Influential

Your city directory

The newspaper (business section, special inserts)

Chambers of Commerce

Directories In Print (a directory of directories)

Lists you can buy

I've found the best lists are those you create and verify yourself, but if you're in a hurry, or want to do a mass mailing—say 1,000 pieces—you can buy or rent names.

These list compilers will send you free catalogs:

1. Dun & Bradstreet/American Executive Registry, Market Data Retrieval, P.O. Box 2117, Shelton, Connecticut 06484; 800-624-5669.

2. Hugo Dunhill Mailing Lists Inc., 630 Third Avenue, New York, New York 10017; 800-223-6454.

3. PCS Mailing List Company, 125 Main Street, Peabody, Massachusetts 01960; 800-532-LIST.

4. Ed Burnett Consultants, 99 West Sheffield Avenue, Englewood, New Jersey 07631; 800-223-7777.

Be a list-monger

Be on the lookout for lists and directories. Get your hands on them and don't let go. If they're affordable, buy your own directories so you can mark them and reuse them.

Some directories are free. Get them. Some cost as little as $5 or $10. Grab them. Some cost $25-$35. Buy them if you will need them often. Borrow expensive directories from the library.

Copying names and titles from the library is the worst-case scenario because it's slow and boring. I prefer to find smaller directories I can buy and own—usually those under $25. I have a filing cabinet full of them.

Don't forget that some associations sell their membership lists on pre-printed labels, so you can buy the labels and skip the data entry—a big time-saver, although labels tend to look like "mass mailings."

Some lists come on computer disc, a great idea if you need a lot of names—and if the list is current. Some list services offer their names "on line" so you can access them over a modem.

Where to get the names of executive recruiters

1. Buy a copy of *The Directory of Executive Recruiters*, published by Kennedy & Kennedy, Inc., Templeton Road, Fitzwilliam, NH 03447; 603-585-2200, $30.95. All listings in the directory are available on pressure- sensitive labels (but look mass-mailed).

2. Contact Ken Cole, publisher of "The Recruiting & Search Report," and author of *The Headhunter Strategy*. P.O. Box 9433 Panama City Beach, FL 32407; 800-634-4548 or 904-235-3733. Ken sells updated search lists by industry, functional specialty, and geographic location. You can get a custom geographic printout of all the recruiters in your area. General lists are now $9.00 each, a real bargain.

Verify all names, titles, and addresses

My definition of a directory is "something that's obsolete the day it comes off the press." Why? Because people move so often.

Every time you use a list, verify names and titles. Call the company and ask, "Is Joe Green still in charge of manufacturing?" Five times out of ten they'll say, "No, Joe has left the company. Ron Black is now in charge of manufacturing. Shall I ring his office?"

Verifying names is a lot of work, but I think it's worth it. Letters that don't go to an identifiable person are useless to you. People don't like to receive mail addressed to someone else, especially their predecessor. Readers like their mail personalized. I think you're better off sending fifty letters to the right people than mailing five hundred pieces to an outdated list.

Follow up. Follow up. Follow up.

An extremely well-written and timely letter will get response automatically. People will call you. But, you'll improve your odds dramatically if you follow your letters with a phone call. (Even a great letter can sit unanswered on the reader's desk for weeks.)

In nineteen years as a marketer, I've followed dozens of letters with phone calls. It's not at all uncommon to hear something like this: "I've got your letter right here. I've been meaning to call you."

Yes, they've been meaning to call me, but there's a 98 percent chance they never would have called, had I not called them first. Why? Because they're too busy.

How to follow a letter with a phone call

It took me years, and lots of calls during which my hands were shaking, to decide what to say after I'd sent a letter. (I always use first names when I phone, but you may prefer Mr. or Ms. for those one or more steps above you in a business setting.) The script I settled on after a decade of agony goes something like this:

"Hi Tom, this is Bill Frank calling you from Denver. I sent you a letter last week and wanted to find out if you've received it."

Simple, isn't it?

I've found that once I ask this question, two things happen. Number one, they say they've received the letter, and they launch into a fifteen-minute response to it. They tell me everything I need to know, and then they let me ask questions.

Number two, they haven't seen the letter or the mailing. If they haven't seen the letter, I tell them I'll send another one immediately and that I'll follow up after they've received it.

If they want to know what the letter is about, I don't tell them, unless I feel absolutely confident I can sell myself over the phone. Usually, I don't try it. That's why I wrote the letter in the first place. I needed an icebreaker. I want them to have some background infor-

mation—exactly the right information--before we talk.

I loaded the document with crucial information. It has exactly the right appeal. It's concise and well written. It's polished. It creates a highly favorable impression. It makes me something of a known quantity instead of a complete stranger, so it's usually to my advantage to wait until the reader sees the letter before trying to sell myself.

To repeat: if they ask what the letter is about, I say, "If it's okay with you, I'd rather let you see the letter. It's complicated. There's a lot in it. I'll give you a call in a few days after you've received it. Is that okay?"

Usually it is. Callers seldom press me to tell them immediately "what this is about." They're too busy. Life is too short.

By the way, most people are friendly on the telephone. I've made hundreds of calls, and all my worst fears about being attacked, sworn at, or hung up on have never materialized. Most people are supportive. They like to help, if given the opportunity. On the other hand, I'm not pushy on the telephone. I'm friendly and helpful myself. For instance, I treat secretaries like "helpers," not like "barriers" or "obstacles to progress." I don't try to "get through them." I ask for their help and advice, and they usually cooperate.

Measure your results

How can you tell if you've truly communicated? You get a positive response. Therefore, if you don't get the results you want, you don't have the letter right yet. Work on it some more.

Avoid mass mailings

I'm not a big fan of mass mailings. By "mass mailings" I mean mailing letters by the thousands. I believe in targeted mailing, writing to clearly identified groups for a specific purpose. I can see sending 100 letters to selected search firms. Or 250 letters to targeted companies. Or 300 letters to the members of your personal contact network. I can't see mailing to one thousand companies. To me that means you haven't done your homework and you're really shooting in the dark. Yes, maybe there's a chance *one* of those letters will hit, but at what cost? Fifteen hundred dollars? Job-hunters are typically budget-conscious, making every dollar count. I think you're better off writing an excellent letter and mailing it to fewer people than writing a mediocre letter and mailing it to thousands.

"WE COULDN'T IGNORE YOUR AGGRESSIVE LETTER CAMPAIGN."

What are "formula letters?"

They are letters that are easy to use, because you simply fill in the blanks. Let's take a look at two examples: the problem-solver letter and accomplishment-oriented letter.

1. *The problem-solver letter*

Here you introduce yourself as the solution to a difficult business challenge. It could be lack of personnel policies and procedures, low employee morale, or lack of inventory control. It can be *anything*. The important thing is that it's the kind of problem you love solving.

To write this letter, first decide what kind of problem(s) you want to solve. Then ask companies if they have that particular problem—and if they want it solved. (Some companies like their problems.)

Isn't that simple?

The formula for the letter looks like this:

1. Do you have_____problem?

2. If so, I might be able to help (I'm the solution).

3. Here's why (list your accomplishments).

4. Here's how you're going to benefit by having me around (go heavy on the benefits).

5. Close the sale: After you have had time to review this material, I'll call you to get your reactions.

A real-world example

Nancy Thomas came to see me after graduating from law school. She had written to 250 Denver law firms, and had called the senior partners in all 250 firms. The net result of her effort was two courtesy interviews and no job offers.

Nancy was upset. She had tried everything. She had answered ads in legal journals and newspapers and done extensive networking, and nothing was working. (Imagine having spent five years and $23,000 on an advanced degree, only to find no job waiting.)

We analyzed the situation. It wasn't that no attorneys needed help. They did. Show me a major law firm that isn't swamped. The real problem was the economy: We were in a recession, and lawyers were afraid to add new staff—and $20,000 to $30,000 in overhead—in uncertain times.

We pictured our ideal "problem situation" graphically, even humorously. This was the "perfect" work environment for Nancy to walk into. And here's what it looked like:

- It's midnight.
- An attorney sits at his desk, still working.
- He's bleary-eyed. He had a couple of drinks at dinner and has now consumed a pot of coffee.
- He has a headache.
- The office is a mess—he's disorganized.
- His tie is loose, sleeves rolled up, shirt wrinkled.
- The desk is stacked with papers.
- His wife has called him three times for help with the kids.
- Tomorrow he has the biggest court case of his life, and he's going up against F. Lee Bailey.

To this imaginary attorney, we sent the following letter:

O V E R W O R K E D ?   N E E D   H E L P ?

Wouldn't it be fantastic to be able to hire a part-time lawyer when you need help in emergencies?

<u>Nancy Thomas</u> . . .

    -- Was admitted to the Colorado Bar on October 17, 19--.
    -- Has a commitment to law.
    -- Deals well with clients.
    -- Is eager to learn . . . likes to be "taught."
    -- Turns out quality work, and
    -- Is unhappy cutting corners.

<u>She is heavily experienced in</u> . . .

The field of Estates and Trusts;

and is <u>very interested</u> in (1) Real Estate, (2) Natural Resources, and Tax and Corporate matters.

Y O U R   F I R M   W I L L   G A I N

-- <u>Expert help</u> without the cost of a full-time salary.

-- Flexibility in your scheduling.

-- Relief from <u>pressures and deadlines</u>.

-- A co-operative, interested colleague.

I ' M   A V A I L A B L E   T O   H E L P   Y O U   N O W

Call 893-7989 and ask for Nancy Thomas
388 South Monaco Parkway
Denver, Colorado 80219

The letter produced instant results. Apparently, we found the right appeal. Within a week, Nancy had two or three part-time legal jobs. She chose her own hours and decided which assignments she wanted to accept. She became the first freelance attorney in the country, and she still continues as a freelancer today. Nancy has had opportunities to accept full-time assignments, but declined them. Freelancing is too much fun.

Nancy solved her problem—not by focusing on her own needs and frustrations—but by focusing on ways to help others. It was truly a win-win situation. And there's an answer like this to every career problem. The answer may not be obvious at first. It often takes several hours— sometimes weeks—of wrestling with the problem to see the solution. But it's there. And it can often be implemented with a well-planned letter.

Take action

Think about yourself for a moment. Do you want to solve accounting problems? If so, exactly what kind? Do you want to solve marketing problems? If so, where?

List some of the kinds of problems you'd like to solve, and be as specific and detailed as you possibly can.

1.＿＿＿＿＿＿＿＿＿＿＿＿＿＿＿＿＿＿

2.＿＿＿＿＿＿＿＿＿＿＿＿＿＿＿＿＿＿

3.＿＿＿＿＿＿＿＿＿＿＿＿＿＿＿＿＿＿

4.＿＿＿＿＿＿＿＿＿＿＿＿＿＿＿＿＿＿

5.＿＿＿＿＿＿＿＿＿＿＿＿＿＿＿＿＿＿

6.＿＿＿＿＿＿＿＿＿＿＿＿＿＿＿＿＿＿

7.＿＿＿＿＿＿＿＿＿＿＿＿＿＿＿＿＿＿

8.＿＿＿＿＿＿＿＿＿＿＿＿＿＿＿＿＿＿

9.＿＿＿＿＿＿＿＿＿＿＿＿＿＿＿＿＿＿

Now, picture a company badly in need of your services. What does it look like inside? What's happening? Exaggerate the situation greatly so that everything seems larger than life. Write down the particulars.

1.＿＿＿＿＿＿＿＿＿＿＿＿＿＿＿＿＿＿

2.＿＿＿＿＿＿＿＿＿＿＿＿＿＿＿＿＿＿

3.＿＿＿＿＿＿＿＿＿＿＿＿＿＿＿＿＿＿

4.＿＿＿＿＿＿＿＿＿＿＿＿＿＿＿＿＿＿

5.＿＿＿＿＿＿＿＿＿＿＿＿＿＿＿＿＿＿

6.＿＿＿＿＿＿＿＿＿＿＿＿＿＿＿＿＿＿

7.＿＿＿＿＿＿＿＿＿＿＿＿＿＿＿＿＿＿

8.＿＿＿＿＿＿＿＿＿＿＿＿＿＿＿＿＿＿

9.＿＿＿＿＿＿＿＿＿＿＿＿＿＿＿＿＿＿

10.＿＿＿＿＿＿＿＿＿＿＿＿＿＿＿＿＿

Next draft your letter. You'll be on the way to some well-deserved interviews (where you'll often be the only candidate for the job).

2. *The accomplishment-oriented letter*

The word resume means "summary," and resumes began as biographical sketches. They listed hobbies and interests, and things like your height and weight.

Today, resumes are more sales and marketing-oriented. They have become *sales tools*. Some are so accomplishment-oriented ("at my last job, I worked a miracle") that they bear almost no resemblance to the modest resumes of the past.

If you have an accomplishment-oriented resume, it's easy to cut and paste a marketing letter. The two-step formula for this letter is:

1. I hit home runs at my last job, so . . .

2. I can hit home runs for you.

Here is the text of an excellent accomplishment-oriented letter that was sent to me:

Steven K. Richards
4421 Oak View Road
Sioux Falls, South Dakota   57103

May 24, 19--

William S. Frank
President
CareerLab
7700 East Arapahoe Road, Suite 275
Englewood, Colorado   80112

Dear Mr. Frank:

For some time my wife and I have been discussing a move from the South Dakota prairie to Colorado, and my research shows CareerLab to be active there. In eleven years with Northern Bank, I have developed skills in managing people, budgets, products, and services. These skills work well in any organization or profession.

Here are some of my accomplishments:

o   As Director of Consumer Loans, I successfully managed 20 loan officers in 8 locations. In four years we tripled our outstandings ($15,000,000 to $45,000,000) and profits, while keeping our delinquencies at the same low of 1.0%-1.3%.

o   As Retail Manager of our largest branch, my staff was motivated to increase deposits 30% ($73,000,000 to $90,000,000) over the last three years. I accomplished this with measurements, rewards, and enthusiastic training sessions.

o   In the last three years I reduced my branch staff from 30 to 23 (23%) by implementing automation and reorganization. This saved us $70,000 annually.

o   I developed our large line revolving credit product and also developed new fee income which is now 20% of total fee income.

Since my training has been in the banking profession, that is where I will concentrate my search. However, I think you will agree that the skills I have developed are adaptable to other situations. I will be home for two weeks beginning May 24th. I would like to visit with you and look forward to hearing from you some time then.

Sincerely,

Steven K. Richards

Steven crafted a thoughtful, persuasive letter. I could tell by reading it that he got some phone calls. Well-written letters always do.

To summarize

As a general rule, a marketing letter is:

1. addressed to a specific person by name and title;

2. brief, short, and direct—seldom more than one page;

3. intriguing, never boring;

4. written by you, never canned;

5. tailored to the audience;

6. warm and personal, not cold and analytical, and

7. infused with energy, excitement, and enthusiasm.

What do conservative people say?

Some conservative businesspeople resist writing "sales letters." They say, "That's fine for salespeople, but it really wouldn't work for me. I'm an accountant (or a lawyer or an engineer . . . or whatever) and we're very conservative."

That's true. Some businesspeople are conservative, but not all of them. If you're an executive or a professional, all this means is that you have to tone down your sales letter to meet your market. You have to tailor your approach to your recipient (choose the right appeal).

There are at least five kinds of letters:

1. Hot
2. Warm
3. Neutral
4. Cool
5. Cold

When you draft your thoughts, think about who will receive them. A doctor? A lawyer? A union steward?

If you're conservative, you can still use a marketing letter, but cool it off to match your audience. It's still a sales letter, because it's selling, but it's a subtle soft-sell. It's less obvious, but it's loaded with benefits for the reader.

As you page through this book, you'll find examples of soft-sell letters that any professional could feel comfortable sending.

About the examples that follow

This book consists of letters I wrote myself, letters that were written to me, and letters my clients and I created for their job campaigns. I know the reactions they got; I know they worked. These are the best job-search letters I've seen. So if you read and study them, you'll know everything you need to know about letter-writing. You'll open doors that have been closed to you before.

And that's a promise.

Anonymity and fictitious names, places, and companies

I've printed the real names of friends who wanted to see themselves in print. All other names, companies, addresses telephone numbers, situations and events in this book are fictitious to preserve the privacy of the contributors. Any similarity to any real person, living or dead, or any company or business unit is strictly coincidental.

How the letters are arranged

The letters which follow are organized by "main theme"—their central idea. However, many letters have several themes in them. This has made organizing difficult.

For example, reply letters are really a form of self-introduction. So are sales letters. Thank you letters are often sales letters in disguise. Announcements and thank you letters are also PR/relationship-building letters. You get the idea.

Therefore, don't look for letters in only one place. Browse through the material. The letter you want may be filed elsewhere in the book.

If you're an accountant, read letters to and from marketing people. If you're an engineer, read letters by geologists. You'll miss a lot if you confine your reading to only examples from your own profession or specialty. Read all through the book. See what you can discover.

You may want to cut and paste to get the letter that's ideal for you. By the way, that's how I wrote the query letter for this book.

Why I break my own rules

In the letters that follow, I've occasionally broken my own rules. For example, some of them lack a date, telephone number, return address, secretarial initials, or enclosure notations—or they are crammed onto the page. Usually, that's because I've condensed a two-page letter onto one page to save space. Normally, a long letter would go onto the next page, and all the proper data would be included.

How to read the page notations

The bottom of every page lists the section number, the page number, and the kind of letter you're looking at. For example:

15.1	Sell Your Accomplishments	**244**
Section Number	Kind of letter	Page Number

What the symbols mean

You'll notice symbols at the bottom of some pages.

Here is what they mean:

✍️ Easy to adapt for quick job-search

☞ Produced interview

✌️ Resulted in job offer (or desired result)

❤️ One of the author's favorites

✱ Discussed in "Notes and comments" section

I'm sure many other letters in the book produced interviews, job offers, and other desired results. I've just highlighted the ones which certainly did.

PART THREE

200 OF THE WORLD'S BEST LETTERS

Announce Job Changes

The world's economy is increasingly uncertain, and for many people job-hunting is becoming a lifestyle. Try to let your network know where you are and what you're doing. Don't forget about them just because you've landed a great job. Things can change drastically overnight. The best time to find a new job is when you don't need one, and the best time to cultivate business friendships is when everything is going smoothly.

GEORGE L. OCHS
6031 West Rowland Place
Littleton, Colorado 80123
(303) 979-9293 (H)
(303) 629-6653 (W)

November 14, 19--

William S. Frank
7700 East Arapahoe Road, Suite 275
Englewood, Colorado 80112

Dear Bill:

After spending nearly three years consulting for Urban
Investment and Development Company, I will be moving on to a
new assignment. Effective December 2, 19-- I will be
consulting for The Prudential Insurance Company, Denver Real
Estate Investment Office. The past three years were very
exciting, being part of a team which managed the
construction, lease-up and tenant build-out of City Center 4.
Your support throughout these past few years is greatly
appreciated. Please keep in touch, as I'm not moving out of
town. I'll be just a few blocks down the street.

Starting Monday, December 3, 19-- I can be reached at:

    The Prudential Insurance Company of America
    Denver Real Estate Investment Office
    1050 17th Street, Suite 2501
    Denver, Colorado 80265

    (303) 629-6653

Sincerely,

George L. Ochs

/cb

Mark D. Espinoza
18 West Princeton Place
Lakewood, Colorado   80227
October 27, 19--

Mr. William S. Frank
CareerLab
7700 East Arapahoe Road, Suite 275
Englewood, CO 80112

Dear Bill:

As a follow-up to our earlier networking conversation, I
wanted to let you know that, as of November, I will be
working for Amoco Production Company as Senior Vice President
of Human Resources for one of their two international
divisions. Although the position is based in Houston, my
area of responsibility will be Africa and the Middle East, so
I'm glad I have quick reflexes.

Thanks again for your assistance and please give me a
call before your next trip to Houston--or Africa or the
Middle East. Lunch is on me.

Sincerely,

Mark D. Espinoza

MDE: sl

Neil B. Stein
Agent
Michael L. Johnston and Associates
1872 South Bellaire Street, Suite 600
Denver, Colorado 80222
(303) 691-5150

June 13, 19--

Mr. William S. Frank
President
CareerLab
7700 East Arapahoe Road, Suite 275
Englewood, Colorado 80112

Dear Bill:

I'd like to share some very exciting news with you.

As of June 1st, I've established an insurance practice
affiliated with Connecticut Mutual Life, a highly-respected
"blue chip" company for the last 142 years.

Although I firmly decided before going to work for
Connecticut Mutual that I would never use friendship for
business purposes, I feel that it would be appropriate to at
least make you aware of my career change and to offer my
services should your situation warrant it. I would be happy
to make an objective appraisal of your present life or
disability insurance situation at some time in the future.

I'm sure you'll agree that because we are friends, you would
receive a more accurate appraisal of your insurance situation
from me than you would from a total stranger who may not have
your best interest at heart. I realize the mere fact that we
are friends is no reason why you should buy insurance from
me. On the other hand, it's no reason why you shouldn't,
either.

I'll be moving into my new office by the time you receive
this letter. My new address and phone number are above. If
you're in the neighborhood, please stop in and say Hello.

Sincerely,

Neil B. Stein

NBS/daf

BIG CHANGE!

Please note the following change of business address:

    FROM: James L. Rasmus
             Manager, Communications and Human Resources
             United Technologies Microelectronics Center
             1575 Garden of the Gods Road
             Colorado Springs, Colorado 80907

      TO: James L. Rasmus
             Manager, International Personnel
             United Technologies Automotive
             Avenue Du Tribunal Federal 34
             1005 Lausanne
             Switzerland
             Telephone: 041-21-208614

Thank you for noting this change. Please update your
mailing lists and stay in touch.

Jim Rasmus

FROM:
Norman A. Newton
4505 South Yosemite
Denver, Colorado 80237
Daytime: (303) 771-4357

STARTING DATE: NOW

ENDING DATE: JAN. 31, 19--

NEWS RELEASE

Norman Newton has joined McDATA Corporation as Vice President of Manufacturing. In this capacity, Newton will be responsible for overseeing all manufacturing operations for McDATA's network communication product lines. Prior to joining McDATA, Newton worked for Samsonite Corporation as Vice President of Operations. Other positions at Samsonite included Director of Special Projects and General Manager of the El Paso/Juarez operations. Newton has also worked for Atari Inc. as Managing Director of European Operations. Newton brings 25 years' experience in managing industrial manufacturing operations to McDATA Corporation.

Clarify Your Direction

The first part of any job-hunt is figuring out where you're going. As Dick Bolles, author of *What Color Is Your Parachute?,* says, "The more time you spend in preparation, the less time you spend on the pavement."

Your friends and acquaintances can give you some valuable information about yourself and about the business world in general. If you feel uncertain at all, ask for their ideas. Ask them what they think your strengths are, and where they see you fitting in. You might be pleasantly surprised by some creative ideas.

Few of us can go it alone these days—it's a networking world. I've seen a number of highly successful businesspeople fail in the job-search because they were afraid to utter four little words: "I need your help."

*

Sandra M. Collins

May 18, 19--

Carol Shannahan
655 Redwood Highway
Mill Valley, California 94941

Dear Carol,

My present position with the National Management Association
is part-time, and I'm trying to define my career goals. I
have a clear idea how I would like to proceed, but I'm not
sure what position or department within a company that fits.

Enclosed is a scenario of how I want to spend the next five
years. It is obviously idealistic. (The scenario was an
exercise of envisioning what my future might look like if I
"had a magic wand.") I seek your help to make it realistic.

Following the scenario are two lists--one telling what I've
done, and one telling some of what I can do--as well as a
letter describing how some people perceive me. I am asking
you to respond to some or all of the following questions:

1.   How can I make this scenario more realistic?
2.   What beginning position in a company am I describing?
3.   Who, if not the CEO, is the logical person for me to
     report to?
4.   What is the career path to move to external and
     international areas?
5.   Is it appealing to a company to have me on retainer?
6.   Where are the holes in my logic?
7.   What training do I need to support these goals?
8.   Is there someone else you think might help me clarify
     these goals?
9.   Do you have suggestions as to what company/industry
     might have such a position, and/or at what level I
     should make contact to pursue such a position?
10. Any other suggestions/direction?

I realize every organization is different, but I respect your
insight and experience, and believe your suggestions would be
applicable.

As with anyone in the job market, my internal time line is
short, so a quick response would be greatly appreciated. A
self-addressed envelope is enclosed for that purpose, or if
it's more convenient for you to call me, please do.

You have my sincere gratitude for helping me to pursue my
career goals, Carol.

                    Sandra

                              Douglas P. Arnold, Jr.
                              295 Treetop Lane N.W.
                              Ft. Collins, Colorado 80521

                              January 15, 19--

Mr. Richard R. Nelson
President
REMAX
P.O. Box 255
Ft. Collins, Colorado 80522

Dear Mr. Nelson:

     Because you are a visible leader in the Ft. Collins
business community, your advice and ideas are of value to me.
After 13 productive years here (summary of accomplishments
enclosed), I am seeking to make contact with other
Ft. Collins business executives who may be in a position to
provide me with advice regarding my next career step.

     I will call you next Thursday between 3:00 and 4:00
p.m., and I would appreciate hearing your thoughts about
where you think someone with my skills and abilities might be
needed. Please note, I will not be asking you for a position
in your firm. I ask only for five minutes of your valuable
time, and the benefit of your experience.

                         Sincerely,

                         Douglas P. Arnold, Jr.

Enclosures

Mr. Richard P. Riley, Jr.
4353 Roswell Road
Atlanta, Georgia 30342
(404) 342-9865

December 1, 19--

William S. Frank
President
CareerLab
7700 East Arapahoe Road, Suite 275
Englewood, Colorado 80112

Dear Mr. Frank:

I am interested in entering the outplacement field and would
appreciate any assistance you might be able to offer.

As my enclosed resume outlines, I have had considerable
experience in the Human Resources function. I have done
extensive training of managers in the job search process and
have lectured on the subject before university groups and
professional associations. It is my intent at this time to
devote my career to this area.

If your professional practice involves activities in which I
might be of assistance, I would welcome the opportunity to
speak with you. I would be interested in working with you on
a permanent or contract basis if your workload requires
additional professional assistance.

I have attached a copy of my resume and an article I wrote
which appeared in the Wall Street Journal's "National
Business Employment Weekly."

I look forward to hearing from you.

Sincerely,

Richard P. Riley, Jr.

RPR:sh
Enclosure

Richard E. Hart
2700 Valley Drive
Hermosa Beach, California   09254
(213) 376-3897

November 23, 19--

PERSONAL AND CONFIDENTIAL
Nancy K. Turner
Pacific Bell
11882 West Olympic Boulevard
Los Angeles, California   90064

Dear Ms. Turner:

Since you are legal counsel to one of the largest corporations in California, I am writing you hoping to obtain some information pertaining to practicing law as an "in-house" attorney. You are ideally situated to help me gain some insights into corporate practice.

I am writing you this letter because, after seven years of building a law firm from three employees to twenty, I have rethought my lifetime objectives, and have decided to change the direction of my career. I am not writing you seeking employment from Pacific Bell, as it is my understanding that you are not currently hiring; however, I am seeking any information which you might have regarding my job search.

In this effort, I am enclosing my resume, from which you can see that I have had my share of successes, not only in contributing to the building of a $1 million-plus-a-year business, but also in the practice of law. For a variety of reasons, I have decided to make a career change and have determined that I shall move into an "in-house" corporate practice.

I would appreciate the opportunity to discuss with you several questions which I have about corporate practice. I will be calling you in the next few days. For obvious reasons, I must request absolute confidentiality.

Thank you for your attention.

Very truly yours,

Richard E. Hart

Jory L. Laine

October 24, 19--

Mr. George McLean
10 South Riverside Plaza
Chicago, Illinois 60606

Dear Mr. McLean:

As I mentioned, I recently discussed my career
development plans with Bill Frank and he highly recommended
you as someone who was very knowledgeable and who may be
willing to provide advice regarding opportunities in your
industry, and other industries as well.

My goal is to locate a management position in which I
direct business resources in support of short and long-term
business objectives. I want to investigate a variety of
industries and locate an organization which requires a goal-
oriented financial and administrative manager. Thus far, I
have directed my efforts at industries such as real estate
development and management, recreation, legal services and
health services. Although these industries offer challenge
and opportunity, my intent is to achieve the widest possible
exposure to the marketplace.

My qualifications are comprised of a broad background in
financial management ranging from controllership and treasury
responsibilities, in a fully-automated environment, to design
and implementation of manual accounting systems. I have
increased the scope of my business knowledge by assuming
administrative management responsibilities in areas such as
property management, human resources, contract administration
and data processing. I am an effective resource manager who
utilizes an intuitive and participatory management style to
direct staff efforts toward the realization of business
objectives.

When you are reading the enclosed resume, Mr. McLean,
I ask that you consider my background and experience relative
to your organization and its current and future needs.
Moreover, I would appreciate your mentioning my
qualifications to your business contacts and associates.

I would like to call you within the next week and
request that you suggest the names of people who could
assist me. In that discussion, I would also like to
explore potential opportunities within your organization.
I sincerely appreciate your efforts on my behalf.

Very truly yours,

Jory L. Laine

B R U C E   R .   V A N D E V E N T E R

Mitchell Dunhill
Senior Geologist
Rocky Mountain Petroleum
5800 South Quebec Street
Englewood, Colorado 80111

October 10, 19--

Dear Mitchell,

As you may be aware, I am a consulting petroleum geologist with over 11 years of experience in the Rocky Mountain basins. Most recently I was affiliated with Ladd Petroleum for almost 6 years, and had approximately 25 wells drilled with 6 new discoveries in several different areas. I have good, broad Rockies experience, and feel I can provide a valuable service for your company if given the opportunity.

Until specific consulting or other opportunities come my way, I plan to actively generate [oilfield] prospects out of my home, predominantly in areas where I have past experience. These areas include the Williston, Paradox, Central Kansas, Uinta, Greater Green River, and Piceance Basins. I will concentrate on one or two of these areas, but have not yet decided which ones.

I would appreciate your input in this matter, primarily in terms of your company's needs for prospects or specific interest level in particular areas. I would like to generate plays [discoveries] in areas where you have a strong interest, hoping that you will want to see these prospects when completed. Your input will guide me to these areas with minimal waste of time and effort.

I am planning to follow this letter with a phone call to you in a few days to hear your thoughts and suggestions. Your input will be greatly appreciated. Also, should you have specific needs for a consultant or a possible full-time geologist, I would appreciate your interest for that as well.

Thanks for your help and consideration.

Sincerely,

Bruce R. VanDeventer
Consulting Geologist

*

Bud Inzer
237 Acoma Street
Denver, Colorado 80223
(303) 771-3548

March 18, 19--

Mr. William S. Frank
CareerLab
7700 East Araphoe Road, Suite 275
Englewood, Colorado 80112

Dear Bill:

Four years ago I attended one of your seminars and your presentation made a distinct impression on me. Your certainty and belief that it is not only possible but practical to pursue work that is fulfilling validated my own convictions. Your success over the years encourages me to seek you out, for the purpose of learning more about the career development field today. As someone who followed your heart and stayed with it, your experience and opinions are very valuable to me.

Like you, my own career frustrations became a motivation for educating myself in the process of career change. Although, for several years, I developed and led a number of successful workshops and consultations, I became frustrated with the financial position. I am presently running my own small promotions business but am interested in returning to the career development field. My purpose is not to look for a job, but to gain more information.

I would like to call you shortly to arrange a meeting. I know that your time is valuable so please be assured I won't ask for more than 30 minutes.

Sincerely,

Bud Inzer

3

Find Part-time Employment

Inactivity during unemployment can be depressing. Usually, the longer you are unemployed, the lower your self-esteem falls. Never let yourself be "unemployed" in your mind, even for a day.

Always find something productive to do. If necessary, volunteer for a few hours a week. Work part-time for a friend. Don't let yourself say, "I'm out of work. I have nothing to do. No one wants me." That's not only ridiculous, but terribly damaging to your sense of self worth.

You also want potential employers to perceive you as busy and active, not bored and depressed. Tell them, for instance, "I've got several things going while I'm in the market. I work part-time for Hewlett Packard on a new product launch, and I'm helping Memorial Hospital set up their SIDS department." Action! Movement! Momentum!

May 6, 19--

Mr. William S. Frank
Principal
CareerLab
7700 East Arapahoe Road, Suite 275
Englewood, Colorado 80112

Dear Mr. Frank:

          Is your company under <u>PRESSURE?</u>

          Are your employees <u>OVERWORKED?</u>

          Are <u>DEADLINES</u> difficult to meet?

          Wouldn't it be great to have:

               *   Experienced   *
               *   Efficient   *
               * Part-Time Help   *

          to alleviate the stress!

                    <u>Nancy Austin</u>

     -- has ten years' experience in accounting
     -- maintains a high level of productivity and accuracy
     -- uses superior verbal and written communication skills
     -- listens effectively
     -- is self-directed
     -- likes to learn
     -- has a valuable ability to organize
     -- is adaptable
     -- is cooperative

     Nancy enjoys:

     -- team problem solving and development
     -- coordinating
     -- client relations
     -- staff development
     -- instructing
     -- promoting a growth-oriented environment

Let's discuss how we could work together. Call 771-4232.

Sincerely,

Nancy Austin

BRUCE D. ROBERTSON, CPA
Assistant Professor
ROBERTS WESLEYAN COLLEGE
2301 Westside Drive
Rochester, New York 14624-1997
(716) 594-9471 X324 (W)
(716) 594-2766 (H)

December 8, 19--

Mr. Bill Frank
President
CareerLab
7700 East Arapahoe Road, Suite 275
Englewood, Colorado 80112

Dear Bill:

Thank you for your support during my recent job search. As
you know, I have accepted a job as Assistant Professor of
Business at Roberts Wesleyan College, a small Christian
Liberal Arts college founded in 1866. I am really enjoying
teaching in the college setting. This semester, my favorite
course is Income Tax. Next semester, I will be teaching
Micro Economics, Cost Accounting, and Beginning Accounting.
I am also involved in developing international courses and
working them into the existing curriculum.

I will be expanding my consulting practice in accounting and
international business in Denver during breaks from school.

I plan to be consulting in Denver on the following dates:

> --Friday, December 18th through Sunday, January 10th
> --Friday, February 12th through Monday, February 22nd
> --Thursday, March 31st through Monday, April 11th
> --Monday, May 16th through Friday, August 18th

If you know of companies that might need tax, accounting,
international or financial help, I would like to know about
them.

Thank you for your continuing help and support.

Sincerely,

Bruce D. Robertson, CPA

BDR:bl

BRUCE D. ROBERTSON, CPA
3182 South Holly Street
Denver, Colorado 80222
(303) 756-7434 (H)
(303) 779-1417 (W)

March 6, 19--

Ms. Loretta B. Hazen
Vice President Administration
The Weyerhauser Corporation
6000 Stewart Street
Seattle, Washington 98101

Dear Ms. Hazen:

<u>Do you have a one-time overload project</u>?

    -- An accounting crisis?

    -- A new computer system?

    -- A new European operation?

<u>Would you like to hire a part-time financial expert</u>?

Someone who . . .

    -- Established an international consulting firm.

    -- Was number two man in a European operation which grew
       from $5 million in sales to $55 million in sales in
       two years.

    -- Has 17 years of experience in administration and
       finance.

I'm in the process of a full-time job search, <u>but I would be
interested in helping you part-time in overload situations</u>.

Please call me at your earliest convenience at
(303) 779-1417, or return the enclosed postage-paid
questionnaire.

Sincerely,

Bruce D. Robertson

BDR:bl
Enclosures

Richard P. Ruby
P.O. Box 267
Boulder, Colorado 80306
(303) 440-9876

January 11, 19--

Bill:

Congratulations!

By re-entering the workplace you certainly have
rewritten the book on great ways to retire!

Despite its many problems, steering the university
battleship through choppy waters has got to be more
satisfying than running a major bank--and trying to
collect from all the countries south of the border.

I have ended my Lone Ranger counseling act, and am
negotiating on a corporate-finance job back in Peru
and I'm also talking to one of Denver's larger law
firms. Neither idea is going to crystallize for a
while, however, so I've got several weeks of time
on my hands.

Could you use any emergency help from a local
citizen--who also served time in Missouri?

Best regards,

Dick Ruby

ARE YOU UNDERSTAFFED?

Do you have full time secretarial needs,
but only a part-time budget?

Wouldn't it be great to have a part-time secretary with all
the skills and experience of a full time secretary? Here are
some of my skills and abilities:

- Get things done and handle a variety of tasks EFFICIENTLY.
- Organize my time and complete tasks quickly and ACCURATELY.
- Work very well independently--am an ambitious SELF-STARTER.
- Have extremely good PEOPLE SKILLS.
- Am super CONSCIENTIOUS.
- Will turn in work that is neat and PICTURE PERFECT.
- Am a skilled typist--90 WORDS PER MINUTE.
- Am thorough in RECORD KEEPING.
- Show painstaking attention to DETAIL.
- Am attractive and WELL-GROOMED.
- I have a STRONG and very COMPETENT secretarial
  background, as well as experience in SUPERVISION.
- I have worked as a secretary/administrative assistant in
  a variety of areas, including STOCK BROKERAGE FIRMS, OIL
  AND GAS, LAW and CONSTRUCTION MANAGEMENT.
- I have two years experience as a legal secretary, having
  done bookkeeping, payroll, journal and general ledger
  posting, quarterly reports, client billings, as well as the
  typing of all legal documents.
--BONUS: I love to be BUSY.

I AM LOOKING FOR PART-TIME SECRETARIAL WORK AND WILL PROVIDE
YOU WITH TOP-NOTCH, QUALITY SERVICE. IF YOU ARE LOOKING FOR
THE BEST, WHY NOT GIVE ME A CALL?

Bobbi Winston
100 Reed Street, Lakewood, Colorado 80215

You can reach me weekdays at 231-4765.

Sally Butler

May 21, 19--

William S. Frank
President
CareerLab
7700 East Arapahoe Road, Suite 275
Englewood, Colorado 80112

Dear Mr. Frank:

I would like to provide your firm with a convenient, high
quality, low-cost training alternative. I excel in this work
and enjoy offering training:

    -- as short-term or long-term repetitive assignments
    -- as a substitute for unavailable staff (vacation,
       illness, travel)
    -- to enhance current staff temporarily for special
       projects
    -- <u>without adding to your headcount or benefits costs</u>

As head of a management consulting firm, are your talents
needed more for marketing and directing? Are you and your
staff of consultants less inclined to do the daily grind of
standup training? My interest and expertise <u>is</u> stand-up
training for all areas of business management from new-hire
orientation to outplacement. I specialize in flexibility,
short notice, and teaching those basic, repetitive courses
frequently requested by new or smaller firms.

My training expertise focuses in the areas of management and
professional development. I've had over 10,000 adult
classroom training hours in business. I'm a highly
experienced trainer with top-notch group facilitation skills.

My background includes start-up companies, large
multi-national and high tech firms, as well as the public
sector. With my word processing equipment I can tailor my
materials (or yours) to meet client needs.

Keep me in mind. Don't turn down a strategically important
or profitable opportunity because it's too basic for your
firm to handle. When you need some temporary help, I'm
available. I bet a need will arise soon. Thank you.

Sincerely,

Sally Butler

*

Clinton D. Jones
1330 Marion Street
Denver, Colorado   80218
(303) 861-7356

November 3, 19--

Mr. William S. Frank
CareerLab
7700 East Arapahoe Road, Suite 275
Englewood, Colorado   80112

Dear Bill,

I have begun to market myself as a personnel manager on a permanent part-time basis to small firms (25-75 employees) in the greater metro area. I am open to any type of organization or industry, but I prefer professional firms such as:

        Law
        Medicine
        Engineering
        Accounting
        Financial Planning
        Dental
        Architecture

Should you be aware or become aware of any of your business associates, friends, or acquaintances who may be considering the need for a part-time Personnel Manager, I would appreciate your giving me their names for me to contact personally.

Any assistance or suggestions that you can give me will be appreciated.

Sincerely,

Clinton D. Jones

CDJ/

Enclosure

Douglas P. Arnold, Jr.
295 Treetop Lane N.W.
Ft. Collins, Colorado   80521

January 25, 19--

Ms. Pat Jones
Robert Half, Inc.
2000 College Parkway
Ft. Collins, Colorado   80522

Dear Ms. Jones:

    Having completed the financial turnaround of Ft. Collins Manufacturing, I am now seeking a regular full-time position. I'm sending you my current resume and a summary of my recent significant accomplishments as an accounting, finance and computer systems manager.

    I would like to call your attention to the fact that I am particularly strong in working with computerized accounting systems.

    Having been a resident of Ft. Collins since 19--, I am aware that locating a suitable full-time position may take some time. I would appreciate being considered for appropriate Robert Half temporary assignments. I am available to interview at your convenience and can begin work immediately.

            Very truly yours,

            Douglas P. Arnold

DPA/
Enclosure

When Caught Without a Resume

Everyone knows it's a good idea to keep an updated resume, but few people actually do it. We're just too busy.

Here's how to summarize or update your work history in a letter when you haven't yet had time to prepare a current resume. Of course, you'll want to follow up quickly with a full-length, accomplishment-oriented resume.

*

Michael D. Burns
Two Thousand Oaks Towers
2000 West Federal Street
Boston, Massachusetts   02110
(617) 765-9898

September 4, 19--

Mr. William T. Dewar
Executive Vice President
U.S. West, Inc.
7800 Orchard, Suite 200
Englewood, Colorado   80111

Dear Mr. Dewar:

    I understand that you are looking to fill a key
management position in your Controller's department. I would
like to be considered for that position.

    The enclosed excerpt from Fortune magazine describes
what I am doing now and how I got there. My investment
advisory practice is successful and growing, but it does not
use enough of the skills and competencies I have spent a
lifetime building.

    My background is in finance. I earned an MBA in finance
from Stanford in 19--. Upon graduation, I went to work for
Amoco in a small group that did strategic planning, capital
budgeting, and merger and acquisition work. Amoco, at that
time, was a leader in this area, and we completed some very
significant acquisitions during this period.

    From this position, I went to Collins Chemical, Amoco's
fertilizer subsidiary, where I was a principal architect of
the strategy that brought the company from an $11 million
loss to profitability. Then in 19--, I moved to Denver to
take charge of the administrative, financial and later, the
domestic and international acquisition areas, for Amoco's
Minerals department.

    After Amoco was acquired by Dow Chemical Company, I
became Executive Assistant to the Chairman of Bender Coal,
where I worked on problems in the capital expenditure and
cash flow areas that arose from the merger. In late 19--, I
left Amoco to join InTek as Executive Vice President in their
troubled oil and gas operation. Later, I became President of
this company. The Fortune article sets out the rest.

My experience in finance, organization and business has been both extensive and varied. I am a "pro." My background is finance, but my success has been due to my ability to work well with people, whether negotiating with officials of foreign governments or leading management teams in turnaround situations.

I have a lot to offer, and would like to put it to better use. Even if my information is wrong about the position in your Controller's department, I would like to meet you and get your advice. I will be in touch with you in the next few days to ask if I might schedule a few moments with you.

Yours truly,

Michael D. Burns

Enclosure

Todd R. Robertson
2 North Park East
Dallas, Texas 75201
(214) 374-4858

April 24, 19--

Thomas Blackman
Russell Reyonlds Associates
320 Grand Avenue, Suite 4200
Los Angeles, California 90071

Dear Mr. Blackman:

Confirming our telephone conversation of this date, I am
including my resume which is current up until 19--. In April
of 19-- I resigned my position with Texaco Oil Company to
accept a position as Vice President of Supply and
Distribution with Gulf Oil (U.S.), Inc., in their San
Francisco office. In addition to being responsible for all
of Gulf's crude oil activities, I was Vice President of Gulf
Pipeline, Inc., a subsidiary company for Gulf's pipeline
activity.

In November 19-- I resigned my position at Gulf--along
with seven other employees--to set up a crude oil purchasing
and gathering operation for a company, Petrol, Inc.,
operating out of Houston, Texas. By March of 19-- Petrol,
Inc. had a change of heart, shut down the Houston operation
and I was laid off.

During my employment at Texaco, the natural gas sales
function reported to me and I supervised a gas sales contract
person.

Hopefully, the foregoing will be a sufficient update of
my resume to acquaint you with my background and experience
in the oil industry.

My contacts and associations throughout the oil and gas
industry are strong assets. I'll call you Monday.

Sincerely,

Todd R. Robertson

TRR/dl
Enclosure

Get Help From Friends

Most good jobs come from friends and friends of friends—by word of mouth. The higher the level of the job, the more that rule applies. At the senior executive and professional level, for example, as many as 90 percent of good jobs come through personal friends.

Therefore, it's urgent to *involve* your friends in your job search, not just *notify* them of your plight ("I'm out of work. Let me know if you hear of anything").

Job campaigns often stall because job-hunters leave their networks too quickly and go off into the world of "strangers." Make sure you get your job-hunt strongly established with friends before you spend a lot of time answering ads, working with recruiters, or contacting companies cold.

7105 Algona
Elgin, Illinois   60120
(312) 878-3827

March 19, 19--

Michael Gold
President
Gold & Associates
613 Poplar
Elmhurst, Illinois   60126

Dear Michael,

As you may be aware, I recently left Texas Instruments as
Vice President of Operations. Since leaving T.I., I have
been spending most of my time away from home. Because of the
lengthy travel required, I am now looking to find a permanent
chief executive or senior management position with a small to
medium-sized company in which I can acquire an equity
position.

I am totally open to the type of industry since I have dealt
with such diverse items as luggage, toys, consumer
electronics and automobiles during my business career. While
preferring to remain in the Chicago area, I would consider
relocating for the right opportunity.

As you may know, I have certainly enjoyed and have been
acknowledged for my accomplishments in startup operations and
turnaround situations over the past several years, as well as
the results I have achieved in the international
manufacturing arena. These are areas which continue to hold
strong interests for me as well as being able to again
develop results-oriented management teams.

Should you be aware or become aware of any of your business
associates, friends or acquaintances who may be in the market
for someone with my background and abilities, I would truly
appreciate your slipping them the attached copy of my resume
or giving me their names to contact personally.

Any assistance or advice that you can give me at this time
would also be greatly appreciated.

Kindest regards,

Charles A. Miller

John H. Norris
2894 S. Lima Street
Aurora, Colorado 80014
(303) 755-8880

April 14, 19--

Mr. Jory Laine
MGA Incorporated
1125 17th Street, Suite 2070
Denver, Colorado 80202

Dear Jory:

I'm looking for some advice and counsel from people I know
and trust.

Colorado Banking, the firm I worked for the last five years
was sold at year-end and merged with another financial
institution. As a result, my job was eliminated. The
Federal Savings and Loan Insurance Corporation, receiver for
the bank, asked me to remain and assist in managing the real
estate loan/asset portfolio. The position was temporary, as
a relocation would be required to make it permanent. I've
completed that assignment and I'm ready to move forward with
something more long-lasting.

I'd like to continue to be a manager in a financial services
company (bank, savings and loan, credit union, insurance
company, etc.). I'm good at managing people and other
resources to attain corporate profits. I've also managed
data processing installations of all sizes. I like being a
part of a dynamic organization, and I am looking for that
next opportunity.

You're a successful person with friends who are also
successful. Perhaps you, or someone you know, are aware of a
firm that needs someone with my capabilities. If so, I'd
appreciate your giving them a copy of the enclosed resume,
and I'd like their name so that I can contact them
personally.

The past few months have been exciting, but the next few
years hold even more promise. I'm enthused about the
prospect for change and I hope that you can help me make sure
it's a positive change.

I'd appreciate your thoughts and ideas. Please contact me at
(303) 755-6680. Thanks for your help.

Best regards,

John H. Norris

MICHAEL D. BURNS

January 16, 19--

Mr. Richard C. Forest
President
California Oil & Gas
330 Primrose, Suite 310
Burlingame, California 94010

Dear Richard:

The years since Stanford Business School have been varied and
fulfilling for me, and I hope they have been the same for
you. The enclosed excerpt from <u>Fortune</u> magazine and the copy
of my resume will give you a snapshot of what I have been
doing until recently. In late 19--, I left the investment
advisory business to begin marketing myself for re-entry into
the corporate world.

Since leaving Amoco, I have found that I greatly enjoy
working in smaller, more entrepreneurial businesses and
that's what I am looking for now. My job target is a
position with a high management content, either in operations
or in the financial area. Ideally, it would be with a
company that is two to ten years old and has sales of $5-$50
million. Although I am not looking for investment
opportunities, I might consider a limited investment in the
right situation. Geographic location is not a major
consideration.

I have some preference to stay in the oil business, but I am
not limiting my search to this area. A favorite alternate
industry of mine is hazardous waste, however, I am open to
any situation that is challenging and will make adequate use
of my skills.

Should you become aware of any of your business associates,
friends, etc., who might be interested in my abilities, I
would appreciate your sending them a copy of my resume or
letting me have their names so I can contact them personally.

Richard, any assistance or advice you can give me would be
greatly appreciated and I look forward to hearing from you.

Best regards,

Michael D. Burns

Enclosures

*

Douglas P. Arnold, Jr.
295 Treetop Lane N.W.
Ft. Collins, Colorado 80521

December 29, 19--

Dr. Barbara Black
University of Denver
MBA Placement Advisor
Evans at University Boulevard
Denver, Colorado 80112

Dear Dr. Black:

Now that I have successfully completed the financial
turnaround of Robertson Manufacturing, I am seeking a
managerial position in the accounting/finance/MIS field. As
my MBA area of emphasis is Management Information Systems, a
position that utilizes my 17 years' accounting experience in
combination with management of computer systems would be
ideal.

I am particularly interested in a company that has grown
large enough to be professionally managed. Since I prefer
not to relocate, a company headquartered in Ft. Collins is
most desirable.

My resume shows that I enjoy challenge and
responsibility. While I am looking for a steady permanent
position, I am not seeking an unnoticeable niche in a huge
bureaucracy. Since I am willing to travel, extensively if
need be, perhaps the ideal position for me may be as a member
of a consulting firm. I plan to take the CPA examination in
19--, after receiving my MBA from D.U.

Finally, my desired salary minimum is $40,000 per year.
I would consider a lower starting salary for the right
position.

Should you feel a meeting would be productive, please do
not hesitate to telephone. I can be available at your
convenience. Thank you.

Sincerely,

Douglas P. Arnold, Jr.

Enclosure

                    Douglas P. Arnold, Jr.
                      295 Treetop Lane N.W.
                   Ft. Collins, Colorado 80521

                            January 7, 19--

Ms. Roberta Martin
University of Denver, MBA Program
University at Evans Avenue
Denver, Colorado 80210

Dear Ms. Martin:

     You may remember me in connection with SunTek
Industries, last spring. At that time, I was the Controller
of Robertson Manufacturing. I am writing to you as I am
presently seeking a new position and realize you may be able
to help.

     I have enclosed two copies of my current resume, and
would appreciate it very much if you could make me aware of
any interesting situations that come to your attention.
Please note that my skills are not restricted to financial
accounting. Related administrative positions, such as
computer systems management are also of interest, especially
as my MBA degree emphasis is Management Information Systems.

     In addition, I am also looking for temporary and/or
part-time work.

     I was impressed with you as an instructor, and since you
awarded me an "A" in your course, I presume you might not be
uncomfortable recommending me as a first-class accounting
professional.

     Thank you for you attention. I am aware that you must
be very busy, and I appreciate your consideration.

                         Very truly yours,

                         Douglas P. Arnold, Jr.

Enclosures

Douglas P. Arnold, Jr.
295 Treetop Lane N.W.
Ft. Collins, Colorado 80521

January 7, 19--

Dr. Randolph Moore, DDS, MPH
1000 Medical Towers, Suite 3200
Ft. Collins, Colorado 80521

Dear Randy,

I resigned my controllership of Robertson Manufacturing last week. My work there is completed, and I have ridden off into the sunset toward "Happily Ever After Land." However, in order to be happy when I get there, I'll need to find another position.

As a fellow professional, you are no doubt aware that networking is the only way to make the contacts necessary to build a successful practice, or to find a good job in this town. You may be in a position to help me.

I have enclosed a copy of my current resume, and would appreciate it very much if you could make me aware of any interesting situations that come to your attention. Please note that my skills are not limited to finance and accounting. Related administrative positions such as computer systems management are also of interest, especially since my MBA area of emphasis is Management Information Systems. I am also seeking temporary work while conducting this job search--and yes, I do taxes, too.

Thank you for your attention. I am aware that you are busy, and appreciate your consideration. Should you wish to know more about this situation before my next appointment, please feel free to telephone.

Best regards,

Douglas P. Arnold, Jr.

Enclosure

*

Douglas P. Arnold, Jr.
295 Treetop Lane N.W.
Ft. Collins, Colorado 80521

January 8, 19--

Dr. Pamela Swanson
Director, MBA Program
University of Denver
Evans at University Boulevard
Denver, Colorado 80210

Dear Dr. Swanson:

   A few weeks ago, a D.U. seminar entitled "How to Conduct
a Professional Job Search" was cancelled. This was something
of a disappointment since I had just left my position as
Controller of Robertson Manufacturing, and was ready to begin
just such a search. Fortunately, Lee Thomas recommended a
consultant who provides excellent advice, so the search is
underway.

   Networking is the key concept used to locate
opportunities in Denver. I would very much appreciate it if
you would permit me to consider you part of my network. As
Director of the MBA Program, I know you make contact with
many successful business leaders in Denver on a regular
basis. Such contact is invaluable in connection with a
professional job search.

   Will you please take the time to read my resume? I
would appreciate it very much if you could make me aware of
any interesting situations that come to your attention. Any
leads you can provide will be of great assistance to me.
Please keep in mind that my skills are not limited to
financial accounting. Related administrative positions such
as computer systems management are also of interest,
especially since my MBA area of emphasis is Management
Information Systems.

   Thanks for your interest. I regret imposing upon you
for this help--I know you are very busy. Be assured that any
effort you make to help me will be appreciated.

Sincerely,

Douglas P. Arnold, Jr.

DPA/
Enclosure

*

M I C H A E L   D.   B U R N S

January 2, 19--

Mr. Fred Morris
Occidental Petroleum, Inc
9900 West 95th Avenue
Los Angeles, California 92715

Dear Fred:

It's been quite a while since we've been in touch, and I hope
this letter finds things going well for you.

As for me, these years have been filled with change and I've
never been bored. The enclosed resume plus the excerpt from
Fortune magazine will give you a snapshot of what I've been
doing until recently when I left the investment advisory
business to start marketing myself for re-entry into the
corporate world.

Since leaving Amoco, I have found that I really enjoy working
in smaller, more entrepreneurial businesses and that's what
I'm looking for now. My job target is a position with a high
management content, either in operations or financial areas.
It would ideally be with a company that is perhaps two to ten
years old and has sales of $5 to $50 million. Although I am
not looking for investment opportunities, I might consider a
limited investment in the right situation. Geographic
location is not a major consideration.

I am focusing my attention outside oil and hardrock mining,
and although a current favorite industry of mine is hazardous
waste, I am open to any opportunity that has growth
potential.

Should you become aware of any of your business associates,
friends, etc., that might be interested in my abilities, I
would appreciate your sending them a copy of my resume, or
letting me have their names so I can contact them personally.

Fred, any assistance or advice you can give me would be
greatly appreciated, but regardless of whether you are aware
of anything, I'd like to get a note from you to hear how you
are. Or better yet, a phone call.

Best regards,

Michael D. Burns

MDB/
Enclosures

JAMES W. BLACKSTONE
6667 E. Dorado Avenue
Greenwood, Village 80111
(303) 694-6698

March 7, 19--

Mr. Phil Rowley, President
Rowley & Associates
8719 East San Alberto
San Antonio, Texas 78240

Dear Phil,

It's been too long since we've been in touch, and I hope this
letter finds things going well for you. Even when we do get
together, we seldom talk business, so the enclosed resume
will probably fill in some gaps for you on what I've been
doing since law school.

As you can see, I've been primarily involved in building new
businesses. Two of them have been great successes for me,
the other founders, and our investors. I wish I could count
on batting .500 forever!

However, I've made a career decision to look for a long-term
position with a growing but stable small to medium-sized
company. I am totally open to the type of industry since I
have worked with companies in such diverse businesses as
electronics, health care, telecommunications, and consumer
services. Although I am not looking for investment
opportunities, I would consider taking an equity position in
the right situation.

If you know or become aware of any business associates,
friends, or acquaintances who may be in the market for
someone with my abilities, please give them a copy of my
resume or give me their names to contact personally. Any
assistance or advice you can give me would be greatly
appreciated.

Regardless of whether you have any leads, give me a call when
you have a chance and let me know what you've been up to.

Best regards,

James W. Blackstone

Enclosure

BRUCE M. SPENSER
335 Sacramento Street
San Francisco, California 94111
(415) 391-2323

February 10, 19--

William S. Frank
President
CareerLab
7700 East Arapahoe Road, Suite 275
Englewood, Colorado 80112

Dear Bill:

It's been some time since we have talked, and I wanted to
make you aware of my decision to leave my current position as
Vice President of Human Resources for The Health Group (THG).
As you may know, during the past years, THG (like the
industry in general) has undergone severe economic
difficulties resulting in dramatic staff reductions,
budgetary belt-tightening and a general slow down in
activity. These factors have contributed to my decision to
look for another opportunity where the economic climate and
corporate outlook are better positioned to benefit from
strategic business partnership utilizing innovative and
strong Human Resource Management.

I believe my 15 years experience as a Human Resource and
Strategic Business Planning professional and executive has
uniquely prepared me to manage state-of-the-art, integrated
Human Resources systems.

I am interested in talking to executives of companies who are
willing to demonstrate their commitment to expending their
Human Resources management capability. If you are aware of
challenging opportunities within such companies, I would
appreciate the opportunity to share my achievements,
experience and ideas directly with them. I am not restricted
geographically and am anxious to find an opportunity where my
energies and skills in Human Resources Management can be
utilized to achieve bottom line results.

I am anxious to talk with you and will call you in the next
week or so. I would appreciate your help and look forward to
talking with you.

Regards,

Bruce M. Spenser

BMS/br

*

Douglas P. Arnold, Jr.
295 Treetop Lane N.W.
Ft. Collins, Colorado 80521

December 16, 19--

Mr. Matthew Morris
Merill Lynch Pierce Fenner & Smith Inc.
Colorado Building
Ft. Collins, Colorado 80521

Dear Matt,

Seasons Greetings!

I trust things are going well for you and that you are
enjoying settling into your new career. Knowing your
professional style, I have no doubt you will be a very
successful broker within a short time.

My "executive marketing campaign" is coming together
well. It should be in full swing by the new year. I have
not yet contacted Ms. Daniels, but intend to do so soon, now
that my printed resume is ready, and my beard is off once
again.

I have enclosed two copies of my resume, and would
appreciate it very much if you could make me aware of any
interesting situations that come to your attention. Please
note that my skills are not restricted to financial
accounting. Related administrative positions, such as
computer systems management are also of interest to me.

Once again I'd like to thank you for your help and
cooperation in turning around the Robertson situation. While
I have received all the credit, I know that without the
cooperation of the commercial lending officer, the outcome
would have been very different.

Very truly yours,

Douglas P. Arnold, Jr.

Enclosures

Paul H. Gutknecht
11374 Quivas Way
Westminster, Colorado   80234
(303) 465-1236

January 30, 19--

Mr. Paul Robinson
President
Pester Corporation
303 Kensington Way
Des Moines, Iowa   50306

Dear Paul,

    Congratulations! <u>Business Week</u> wrote an interesting
article about you--even the picture was a good likeness.

    Will you have your own financial and accounting group,
or some part thereof? Consulting is a "feast or famine"
profession, and I need to build something for my future.

    Your job at Pester to build a retail organization will
be an exciting one, and I would be glad to be part of it.

    Please think about a way to use my talents, and call me
in the next week or two when you have a moment.

                    Warm regards,

                    Paul H. Gutknecht

Douglas P. Arnold, Jr.
295 Treetop Lane N.W.
Ft. Collins, Colorado 80521

December 15, 19--

Ms. Janet Taylor
MCI Communications
7100 Campus Drive
Ft. Collins, Colorado 80521

Dear Janet:

Thank you for taking the time to speak with me on the telephone two weeks ago regarding the possibility of finding employment with MCI.

During my tenure at Robertson Manufacturing, I had the opportunity to interact with many MCI representatives who were working on our installations. The professional manner in which they dealt with a very difficult situation has shown me that MCI may be the kind of organization where I could find a good "fit" and fully utilize my abilities.

Enclosed are two copies of my current resume. Please feel free to share the information with any employer who may be interested in the skills and experience I can provide.

Please do not hesitate to telephone should you have any questions or require additional information. Once again, thank you for your help.

Sincerely,

Douglas P. Arnold, Jr.

Enclosures

James D. Julius
6148 S. Coventry Lane East
Littleton, Colorado 80123

August 16, 19--

William S. Frank
CareerLab
7700 East Arapahoe Road, Suite 275
Englewood, Colorado 80112

Dear Mr. Frank:

HELP A PERSONNEL SOCIETY COLLEAGUE IF YOU CAN!

Do you know of any upcoming HR openings in the Denver area?

My qualifications:

>   * Ten years Human Resources experience
>
>   * Specialties:
>
>>   Employment
>>   Recruiting - including senior level
>>   Selection testing - assessment
>>   Management development
>>   Manpower planning
>
>   * MBA education

Should you know of a potential opening, please contact me at
(303) 794-2465.

Thanks for your help.

Sincerely,

James D. Julius

Paul H. Gutknecht
11374 Quivas Way
Westminster, CO   80234
(303) 465-1236

March 18, 19--

Mr. Charles F. McCay
Vice President Finance
Bank of America
123 Post Street
San Francisco, California   94104

Dear Mr. McCay:

    I am writing to you as a fellow member of the Financial
Executives Institute and seeking your advice in my job
search. My 30 years of experience includes 3 years of
consulting for the top managements and 20 years in top
management of two different companies, plus 8 years as a bank
director.

    Most of my experience is in the petroleum industry; but
management, financial and accounting skills are valuable in
any industry. Although we enjoy living in Denver, my wife
and I would gladly relocate.

    Please take a few minutes and think about possible needs
among your associates and friends for a man of my talents.
You can either give them the enclosed copy of my resume, or
give me their names so that I can follow through.

    Any assistance or advice that you can give me will be
greatly appreciated. Thank you.

                    Sincerely,

                    Paul H. Gutknecht

PG/jt
Enclosure

Douglas P. Arnold, Jr.
295 Treetop Lane N.W.
Ft. Collins, Colorado 80521

January 8, 19--

Mr. Tom Spaulding, President
Coldwell Banker
4000 North Foothills Road
Ft. Collins, Colorado 80521

Dear Tom,

As a real estate professional in Ft. Collins, I know you're aware that networking is the most effective method of doing business in this town. A case in point is that I chose Coldwell Banker to help me find my home based upon a recommendation from Bill Moore.

Having completed the financial turnaround of Robertson Manufacturing, I am now seeking a permanent position. The Controllership position I held at Robertson has been eliminated as a result of my efforts. Have no misunderstanding--this parting of the ways is by mutual consent. There are no hard feelings between the company and me.

I hesitate to impose upon your good nature, Tom, but unfortunately my network of friends and acquaintances is limited. I believe you may be in a position to help me connect with my next job. I have enclosed a copy of my current resume and would appreciate it very much if you could make me aware of any interesting situations that come to your attention.

Please note that my skills are not limited to financial accounting. Related administrative positions, such as computer systems management are also of interest, especially since my MBA area of emphasis is Management Information Systems.

Thank you for your attention. I know you are very busy and I appreciate your help.

Best regards,

Douglas P. Arnold, Jr.

Enclosure
PS. I still love my house. Thanks for the flowers!

Dick and Laurie Thomas
435 Mountain Way
Colorado Springs, Colorado 80919
(719) 594-3096

September 24, 19--

John and Joan Emerson
300 Nightingale Street
Hatboro, Pennsylvania   19040

Dear John and Joan,

We are looking for some advice and assistance from friends.

As you may know, on July 1st, Electronics, Inc., sold the
Colorado Springs facility to a small company based in
California. As a result, Dick's job was eliminated. In
addition, Electronics, Inc., is currently going through a
major restructuring process which prevents us from continuing
his 22 year career with them by relocating to another
facility. Consequently, we have made a career decision to
enter the job market.

Dick would like to continue his financial management career.
Enclosed is an outline of his job preference characteristics.
As you can see, he is open to a broad range of industries,
and we are willing to relocate to other parts of the country.
Please keep in mind that these characteristics are
preferences, not absolutes, and therefore Dick and I are open
to most opportunities.

If you know or become aware of any <u>business associates,
friends, or acquaintances</u> who may be in the market for
someone with Dick's abilities, please give them a copy of the
enclosed resume, and send us their names so we can contact
them personally.

We are excited about the prospect for change and we hope that
you can help us make it a positive change. In the meantime,
Dick is doing some temporary consulting, Jared has started
kindergarten, and we are getting along just fine.

We would appreciate any assistance that you can provide.
Thanks for your help.

                    Best regards,

                    Laurie

Impress Recruiters and Headhunters

Most middle and upper-level job-seekers work with executive search consultants (also called headhunters or executive recruiters).

Like any letter, a letter to a search consultant should be a work of art. Ken Cole, author of *The Headhunter Strategy,* recommends sending a sales letter and no resume. That's always a good strategy if you have a terrific sales letter.

The more traditional approach is to send a resume and cover letter. Recruiters want to know several basic facts about you, specifically, geographic preferences, salary history, and desired duties and responsibilities.

Look at the letters here. If you still want more, read *The Headhunter Strategy* or *Rites of Passage at $100,000+* by John Lucht.

PAUL L. TURNER

June 29, 19--

Mr. John Whittle
Alexander Grant & Company
Prudential Plaza, 17th Floor
Chicago, Illinois 60601

Dear Mr. Whittle:

I am planning a career move and would appreciate your help to make this transition. The following list of parameters may be helpful in focusing this search:

1.   <u>Desired positions</u>
     -- Controller or Director of Finance

     Note: I am not a "green eye shade" accountant, my strengths are concentrated more in being a "hands-on" advisor to management via financial analysis.

2.   <u>Desired responsibilities</u>
     -- Strategic planning and budgeting
     -- Mergers, acquisitions, and divestitures
     -- Investment analysis (treasury & fixed capital)
     -- Post audits of major capital projects and marketing programs
     -- Development of management-driven reports
     -- Plant and product profitability analysis
     -- Operational responsibilities such as general accounting, formulation of product standard direct costs, and cash flow management

3.   <u>Preferred companies</u>
     -- Manufacturing with sales between $25MM and $400MM

4.   <u>Geography</u>
     I am planning to relocate to Chicago in early September, or sooner, and will be responsible for my own moving expenses.

5.   <u>Compensation</u>
     -- Minimum: $100,000

Please review my background in light of your current assignments and contact me if you would like to talk further.

Sincerely,

Paul L. Turner

Randolph J. Packard

May 27, 19--

Joseph D. Gibson
Executive Search Consultant
Technical Placement
4000 North Belt East
Houston, Texas 77060

Dear Mr. Gibson:

After 20 years with National Laboratories, I have decided to
pursue a new career and would appreciate your help in making
this transition. I have extensive experience in integrated
circuit and computer aided design tool development, and I
have served on a number of technical and professional
committees and organized and managed a number of large
technical conferences. The following profile represents a
list of parameters which may be helpful in focusing this
search:

1. <u>Desired Positions</u>
    Vice President/Director/Manager--Engineering,
    Research & Development, Integrated Circuit Design,
    Computer-Aided Design

2. <u>Desired Responsibilities</u>
    Research and Development, Product definition and
    development, Integrated Circuit Design, Definition
    and development of computer-aided design tools,
    Technical Marketing, Strategic Planning.

3. <u>Preferred Companies</u>
    Profitable Semiconductor Manufacturer, New Start-up
    with defined market niches and business plans, Large
    Research and Development Organization.

4. <u>Geography</u>
    West and Southwest preferred (New Mexico, Arizona,
    Colorado, Southern California, Texas).

5. <u>Compensation</u>
    Salary range: $140K to 200K

Please review my background relative to your current search
assignments and contact me if you need additional
information. I can be reached at (312) 559-1200.

Sincerely,

Randolph J. Packard

Michael Herbert

Ms. Jane Peters
Corporate Search Consultants
324 Wall Street
Princeton, New Jersey 08540

Dear Ms. Peters,

I joined The Worthington Corporation ten years ago when it was a $100 million company and played a major role in its growth to $2 billion.

However, I've progressed as far as possible. (The position above mine, Vice President of Finance, is appointed by the German parent company.) As a result, I've decided to seek a new opportunity. Rather than moving into another large organization, I'd prefer a smaller, more entrepreneurial environment. The following profile may be helpful in focusing this search:

1.   <u>Desired positions</u>

     CFO or Vice President Finance and Administration

2.   <u>Desired responsibilities</u>

     a) corporate finance, including capital markets and bank relations; b) treasury, including cash management and investments; c) tax planning; d) accounting; e) mergers and acquisitions; and f) employee benefits.

3.   <u>Preferred companies</u>

     $10 to $200 million, public or privately held. Almost any industries, <u>except</u>: a) banking, b) real estate, c) non-profit, and d) financial services.

4.   <u>Geography</u>

     Willing to relocate.

5.   <u>Compensation</u>

     $75 to $150K, depending upon equity opportunities.

     Please review my background in light of your current search assignments, and contact me regarding positions that require my skill sets.

                         Sincerely,

                         Michael Herbert

T. CRAIG LINCOLN

April 17, 19--

Mr. Richard Matthews
Georgia Arts Personnel
2584 Peachtree Road
Atlanta, Georgia 30326

Dear Mr. Matthews:

Now and then corporations send out feelers for "just the right type" of creative person. This person must fit very specific criteria. Usually, after all is said and done, the corporation wants a business person who can manage, create and communicate. A seasoned professional who's been around for a while.

If you've been looking for this rare combination of business savvy and design expertise, my background might interest you.

    --Twenty-seven years of national experience.

    --Solid background in the management of creative up-and-comers.

    --Know new technologies that show instant profit, such as computer-aided production via Mergenthaler CRTronic systems augmented with an IBM PC/AT CAD.

    --Consistently bring projects in on budget or below budget.

This is but a brief summary of my abilities. And there is much, much more to share.

Presently, my position is contracted through June of this year. I am beginning my search on a local and national level. I feel I have strong marketable skills in which you would be interested.

At your earliest convenience, please contact me if you would like to hear and see more. During the day you can reach me at (303) 773-1184, extension 4562, or in the evening at (303) 745-0250.

Thank you for your consideration.

Sincerely,

T. Craig Lincoln

MICHAEL D. BURNS

January 18, 19--

Mr. Richard T. Ferguson
Engineer's Search
300 Winter Street, Suite 320
Boston, Massachusetts 02108

Dear Mr. Ferguson:

Your firm has been recommended to me as specializing in the oil and gas industry and I would like you to be aware of my credentials. Enclosed is a resume and an excerpt from _Fortune_ magazine which summarizes my experience and highlights a few of my accomplishments.

Most of my career has been in management and the financial areas. With participation in two turnarounds and one startup, my experience has been varied and I have built a consistently successful track record. I am adaptable and learn fast as evidenced by my level of accomplishment in jobs that varied greatly in content, and in three different industries. I have found that I enjoy working in smaller, more entrepreneurial businesses and that is what I am looking for now.

My job target is a position with a high management content, either in the operations or the financial area. It would ideally be with a company that has an entrepreneurial outlook, perhaps be five to ten years old and has sales of less than $100 million. The position could be in oil or mining, but that is not a requirement. A favorite alternate industry of mine is hazardous waste.

I am flexible on immediate compensation if there is adequate potential for growth. A chance to earn equity would be attractive. Although I am not seeking investment opportunities, I might consider a limited investment in the right situation. Geographic location is not a major consideration.

Mr. Ferguson, this should cover the key points. I will be glad to provide any other information you may need and can provide strong references when appropriate. I look forward to hearing from you.

Sincerely,

Michael D. Burns

Enclosures

Rud Bergfeld

Mr. Richard K. Dean
Richard Dean & Associates
1490 Old Toll Road
Madison, Connecticut 06443

Dear Mr. Dean:

Presently, I am concluding a public acquisition for private investors--I selected the prospect, structured financing and negotiated arrangements with previous management, but have declined the permanent CEO position. Instead, I desire to continue to enjoy the "Thrill of the Hunt" in locating, acquiring and building high technology organizations. Several associates have mentioned your firm often represents technology-driven companies with strong growth/acquisition goals, and I understand you are searching now for a CEO or Executive VP who will make your client money.

My diverse background demonstrates exceptional officer-level sales, marketing, financial and leadership abilities in high tech areas:

-- The technical, management, and executive team I
   identified, recruited and trained boosted corporate
   revenues from $11 to $100 million in only five years,
   increasing ROI by an astounding 300%.

-- Created a worldwide sales organization (affiliates and
   reps) in 40 countries and dominated those markets with new
   technologies in only 1-1/2 years; it took the competition
   over 3 years to respond.

-- Assembled the capital and designed the equity structure at
   extremely favorable terms to the founders, completing the
   project in three quarters of the time called for by the
   strategic plan.

I enjoy the challenge of creating, building and growing a professional organization. Opportunities and potential are of paramount importance. I would be most pleased to discuss with you and your client how I would quickly duplicate these successes and build on them. Could we talk about it in the next week or ten days? My travel schedule picks up substantially late this month and I'll be much more difficult to reach.

Sincerely,

Rud Bergfeld

*

11285 Admiral Road
Albuquerque, New Mexico 87112
(505) 821-5520

February 3, 19--

Ms. Barbara Simms
Director
NYC Executive Search
10 East 21st Street
New York, New York 10010

Dear Ms. Simms:

As a Managing Partner in a $100 million company, as President
of a $15 million company and, as Founder and President of a
$5 million firm, I know how to manage people--projects--
offices--regions--companies--for a profit. My management and
marketing skills have been instrumental in generating profits
in the good times, recessionary periods, and now, as the
economy slowly recovers.

I am interested in a firm that has plans for growth and/or
diversification and which has a executive management position
with both P&L and marketing responsibility and an equity
potential.

I know that it takes enthusiastic, innovative, and decisive
leadership to provide profits in today's marketplace. I have
--and can--provide that leadership.

In addition, I have the financial experience to manage and
analyze accounting information and negotiate with bankers and
other financial groups with respect to long and short-term
borrowings, letters of credit, and payroll arrangements.

I would like to meet or talk with you to see if your clients
need someone with my capabilities. I'll call you next week
to introduce myself.

                    Very truly yours,

                    Steven R. MacDonald

SRM/bt

September 27, 19--

A. J. Hughes
Hughes & Associates
1399 S. Havana, Suite 201
Aurora, Colorado 80012

Dear Mr. Hughes:

I am interested in teaming-up with your recruiting firm in accomplishing an effective search for a middle to upper-level Marketing Management position. I have recently concluded a ten-year career as a Marketing Manager for the Ampex Corporation, where I enjoyed continuous upward mobility in my career.

By way of introduction, let me outline some of my background:

--Developed and implemented comprehensive marketing and public relations plans covering national and local consumer markets.

--Directed over 90 sales promotion events budgeted at $10MM.

--Managed a Marketing Department with a staff of eight and an annual operating budget of $5MM.

--Consistently achieved marketing objectives within budget as measured by sales, publicity and spin-off opportunities.

If I were to characterize myself, I would say that I have strong communication skills with emphasis on creative writing, sensitivity to the corporate environment and an ability to respond to its demands; good organization and budget management skills; and the capacity to motivate professionals to goal achievement.

A minimum compensation package of $50K plus benefits and a relocation allowance is my goal.

An expression of your interest in my background in view of your client requirements would be appreciated. I certainly would be pleased to meet with your representative to conduct an appraisal interview. As you can see, I am not adverse to travel or relocation.

A resume is enclosed for your additional information. Thank you for your assistance.

Sincerely,

Maureen Hubbs

Thomas L. McLean
Five Warren Street
Concord, New Hampshire 03301
(603) 224-3837 (o)
(603) 225-2823 (h)

March 17, 19--

Mr. George R. Reisinger
Managing Partner
Sigma Group, Inc.
717 17th Street, Suite 1440
Denver, Colorado 80202

Dear Mr. Reisinger:

My current position as Executive Vice President of a
Fortune 50 company has been an excellent arena to become
operationally involved in a variety of businesses and
acquisitions from real estate development to image
processing.

As General Manager, Executive Vice President and Chief
Financial Officer, I have played key roles in the execution
of successful turnaround situations, the development and
implementation of acquisitions/divestitures and the design of
marketing and operational strategies. The international
exposure, outlined in the resume, includes foreign operations
and acquisitions in the Far East, Australia and Europe.

Please review my qualifications against your current clients'
needs. Certainly most of your placements come from within
similar industries, however, many of my assignments have
required fast learning curves and I have consistently
produced results beyond what was expected.

Titles are not always an indicator of the responsibilities of
a position. However, my objective will most likely be met by
positions such as President, General Manager, Executive Vice
President or CFO. In recent years my compensation has ranged
from $100,000 to $150,000 annually. Although we love
Concord, my family is ready to move for the right
opportunity. Location, equity or stock options will be
important considerations in my decision.

I would welcome a discussion regarding any possibilities of
which you are aware.

Sincerely,

Thomas L. McLean

                    John W. Van Dyke

October 1, 19--

Mr. A. J. Hughes
Hughes & Associates, Inc.
1399 S. Havana, Suite 201
Aurora, Colorado 80012

Dear Mr. Hughes:

Ten years ago I made a strategic career move to enhance my
commercial, international marketing experience with aerospace
and electronics technologies while continuing my Martin
Marietta education. Today, having earned a 15 year MM "track
record," I am ready to make another strategic career move and
am exploring new career paths.

My objective is the CEO, COO or immediate successor position
in a $50 to $250 million commercial electronics/aerospace
business.

I have prepared for this challenge. MM has given me the
opportunity to develop key leadership skills--strategic issue
resolution, product line restructuring, new business
development and day-to-day operations--and apply them with
P&L responsibilities in businesses ranging from $10 to $215
million. Personal qualifications include a BSEE, a full
complement of MM management training programs and experience
in five MM businesses covering commercial, government, U.S.
and international markets.

Martin is a great place to work; it's an excellent company
and they've invested heavily in my education, relocation and
a $100K compensation package including stock options, but I
am seeking the dynamic environment of an autonomous, market-
driven, engineered products business.

Should you have a current or emerging search for an
aggressive general manager, perhaps it would be worthwhile
for us to talk and investigate how I might be able to
successfully satisfy your client's requirements.

My resume is enclosed for your confidential reference.
Your office may reach me during the business day at
(303) 239-2213.

Sincerely,

John W. Van Dyke

Thomas P. Davis
3200 South Michigan Avenue
Chicago, Illinois 60603

October 12, 19--

Mr. Richard P. Karam
Sigma Group
1350 Seventeenth Street, Suite 350
Denver, Colorado 80202-1596

Dear Mr. Karam:

With the close of my Division earlier this year, I completed
five years as the Division General Counsel of BioTek
Industries. During the final eighteen months of that period,
I also served as Acting General Manager of the Division.

I am enclosing a copy of my resume which I believe reflects a
unique set of qualifications. As counsel to an
internationally-oriented group of high technology businesses,
I have acquired in-depth experience in the numerous legal
areas impacting U.S. corporations today and have demonstrated
my ability to successfully resolve complex business law
problems.

In addition, I have considerable experience in acquisitions,
dispositions and joint ventures, and in international legal
matters. Furthermore, I have a strong background in
litigation and in antitrust. I also have professional and
general management experience, and a proven record of working
effectively as a member of a management team.

My present compensation (salary plus bonus) is $160,000 per
year.

I am interested in a challenging senior legal position with a
dynamic organization which will enable me to utilize my legal
and business skills. I would appreciate the opportunity to
discuss my qualifications, in person if possible, whether or
not you presently have an appropriate search assignment.

I look forward to hearing from you at your earliest
convenience. My office telephone number is (312) 263-2700.

Very truly yours,

Thomas P. Davis

Charles D. Waldron

July 24, 19--

C O N F I D E N T I A L

Mr. George L. Reisinger
Managing Partner
Sigma Group, Inc.
717 17th Street, Suite 1440
Denver, Colorado 80202

Dear Mr. Reisinger:

On February 22nd, following a change in the ownership of the company, I left my position as President/CEO of National Industries. I had served on the Board of Directors of that company for the past six years and had directed its operations for the past four years. During that time the company gained a significant share of market throughout the world as a direct result of improved product quality, improved order fill rates, creative marketing programs and new products.

Also, under my direction, two new assembly operations were successfully established in Mexico and the company has nearly completed a major relocation of much of its operations from Denver and Cheyenne to a brand new facility in Atlanta. My total compensation package at National Industries was approximately $250,000 per annum.

I am interested in finding a challenging CEO or Division President position (or CFO with a $500 million plus organization) commensurate with my skills and background, which would offer an opportunity for a meaningful equity participation and/or performance bonus(es). I am a global-thinking executive who believes both in serving the marketplace and in positive cash flow. I would be very valuable to the right organization.

My preference would be to relocate back to Southern California, although I would be receptive to relocation elsewhere for the proper opportunity.

A copy of my resume is enclosed (solely for your internal use), and I was hoping you might have an open search for which I would qualify as a candidate. Please feel free to call should you have any questions.

Best regards,

Charles D. Waldron

Robert M. Hayes, Jr.

May 23, 19--

<u>PERSONAL AND CONFIDENTIAL</u>

Mr. Hunter T. Randall
Arthur Young & Company
One Post Street
San Francisco, California 94104

Dear Mr. Randall:

I recently learned that you are quite active in the recruitment and placement of executives with general management skills. Therefore, I would like you to know more about my background.

As President/CEO of Mineral Resources, a publicly-traded mining company, I was required to completely restructure and reorganize the company. The enclosed resume highlights my accomplishments and provides my past work experience. I remain very confident of my management skills and believe that I can duplicate this quality of work elsewhere, either as a President/CEO or general manager of a small to mid-size company--or as a vice president of administration, operations, human resources in an important division of a large company.

While I am proud of the many accomplishments and excellent experience I have gained with Mineral Resources over the past three years, three important concerns affect this job:

1.   There is little growth potential in a declining field.
2.   For the first time in my life, my family has come to me and encouraged me to look for another job. They don't like the physical and mental toll the job has taken on me and its concurrent effect upon our relationship.
3.   And I'm not happy with the job. It just isn't fun to go to work anymore. Another first for me.

If you are interested, I would very much like to meet with you in person.

Very truly yours,

Robert M. Hayes, Jr.

P.S.   Please keep my desire to leave Mineral Resources confidential. I do not believe it is a prudent time to advise the Board of Directors of my decision.

Steven L. Hargreaves
3548 Bender Trail
Plano, Texas 75075
(713) 385-5733

January 14, 19--

Ms. Anne A. Dexter
Duggan and Company
City Financial Center
10050 North Wolfe Road, Suite 270
Cupertino, California 95014

Dear Ms. Dexter,

When contacted by you in May 19--, I was not interested in
making a career change. At this time, I feel changing
companies and perhaps an industry change or variation would
benefit the long-term growth of my career.

If you are interested in placing me in an executive position
in another company, please write to me so that we may discuss
the idea further.

Sincerely,

Steven L. Hargreaves

SLH/hb

Enclosure

Paul H. Gutknecht
11374 Quivas Way
Westminster, Colorado 80234
(303) 465-1236

February 25, 19--

Howard Mitchell
Vice President
BankSearch
One Financial Plaza, Suite 1800
Ft. Lauderdale, Florida 33395

Dear Howard:

You heard from me last year, but an updated resume is enclosed to ensure that I am still included in your "active file."

My 30 years of experience includes three years of consulting for top management and 20 years _in_ top management at two different companies, plus 8 years as a bank director. Most of my experience is in the petroleum industry, but management, financial and accounting skills are valuable to any industry.

I want to get back into the corporate world and make another ten-year contribution to a company's success. My wife and I would cheerfully relocate, if the opportunity were not in Denver.

Please call me so that we can talk about your client assignments which could use my experience and talents.

Sincerely,

Paul H. Gutknecht

PHG/lg
enclosure

David K. Palmer

April 28, 19--

Ms. Sandra D. Wright
Healthcare Recruitment, Inc.
7325 North 20th Street, Suite 4500
Phoenix, Arizona 85020

Dear Ms. Wright:

Kansas City Memorial Hospital has undergone an unexpected reduction in force, and my position was one of many that were eliminated. I did not leave because of performance problems or any other difficulties. All of the administrative team has expressed their sympathy and support, and I am leaving on excellent terms with all of them. Just a few weeks before this, I had received my best performance evaluation ever.

I am now very actively in the marketplace seeking an executive position in <u>Hospital Administration, Information Systems Management, Healthcare Consulting, Strategic Planning, or Management Engineering</u>. My resume is enclosed.

Most recently, I have been responsible for the Information Systems departments: Management Engineering, Patient Care Information System (PCIS), Word Processing, and Data Services liaison (our Data Services department is a corporately provided service and reports directly to the headquarters office in Kansas). The three departments reporting directly to me represented over $.5 million to manage and we came in 5% below budget in 19--.

I am interested in expanding my administrative experience. During the last seven years, I have developed my systems and management skills with a focus on cost efficiency. I have learned effective negotiating skills for contracting and which kinds of automation will generate a substantial reduction in costs or increase in revenue (I have included a summary of the automation savings achieved in 19--). I have also co-developed a successful strategic planning methodology for integrating the hospital's corporate goals with its operational and financial goals as well as its employee performance evaluation program to focus the whole organization on achievement and reward for attaining goals.

I would appreciate the opportunity to work with you. Please call me at (816) 842-2376 or return the enclosed postage paid questionnaire. Thank you!

Sincerely,

David K. Palmer

RESPONSE LETTER

David K. Palmer
1102 Grand Avenue
Kansas City, Missouri 64106

Dear David:

_____ Please call me for a telephone interview.
Telephone: (____) _____

_____ We do not recruit at your level.

_____ We do not recruit for Healthcare or related
industries, e.g. State Hospital Associations,
Hospital Information Computer vendors, Healthcare
insurance/consulting/auditing firms.

However, you should talk to the following recruiter
who may be interested in your background.

Name: _____

Street Address: _____

City, State, Zip: _____

Telephone: (____) _____

_____ I have nothing available now. Please contact me
again after _____(date).

Comments: _____

_____

_____

_____

Sincerely,

_____

_____

Company Name

WILLIAM A. STEINHOUR

June 30, 19--

Mr. James D. Wilson
Executive Recruiters, Inc.
6100 Lake Forest Drive, Suite 265
Atlanta, Georgia   30327

Dear Jim:

I hope by now you've had a good long weekend with your family
in Arkansas and find yourself restored and looking forward to
the rest of this short week.

<u>Here are the two documents we talked about</u>:

-- My resume (which touches only briefly on my engineering
   background since my objective is a marketing management
   position), and . . .

-- The professional profile I mentioned, which
   focuses on what I feel are my strongest suits.

As I mentioned, we are now quite open to relocation, having
combed this area pretty thoroughly.

If you have any questions, need references, or want to
discuss a potential opportunity to fill a client's
requirement, please give me a call.

My very best regards,

W. A. Steinhour

Richard A. Petersen
212 Old Lake Road
Worthington, Ohio   43085

August 1, 19--

Ms. Sharon King
Management Recruiters of Cleveland
20950 Center Ridge Road
Cleveland, Ohio 44116

Dear Ms. King:

Thank you very much for taking some time with me in our recent telephone conversation. Your advice has been most useful.

I am seeking a position as an R&D/Technology Manager in a large firm or Director or Vice President of Technology for a small firm with a technology-driven product line. My broad technical background, together with marketing and profit center management experience should make me especially attractive to a smaller firm requiring a strategically-minded technical officer.

I have an excellent track record as a turnaround manager. Most recently, I took over a demoralized, moribund $12 million/year profit center and built its profitability from losses in 19-- to over 10% net on volume at present while restoring morale. This was done without substantial staff reductions.

My geographic preferences are northeast and northern midwest. The Cleveland area is presently quite attractive because of my wife's employment situation. Compensation should range from the mid-70s up and is dependent upon the location and nature of the job and the details of the compensation package.

I appreciate your efforts on my behalf.

Very truly yours,

Richard A. Petersen

RAP/sle
Enclosure

Michael D. Burns
Two Thousand Oak Towers
2000 West Federal Street
Boston, Massachusetts   02110
(617) 765-9898

December 1, 19--

Mr. Tom Garber
Tom Garber & Associates
1106 Second Street, Suite 200
San Leandro, California   92024

Dear Tom:

It was a pleasure talking with you this afternoon. Enclosed
is a resume which summarizes my experience and highlights a
few of my accomplishments. Although I started as a
geologist, most of my career has been in the financial and
management side of business. With two turnarounds and one
startup, my experience has been varied and I have built a
consistently successful track record. I am adaptable and
learn fast as evidenced by my level of accomplishment in jobs
that varied greatly in content, and in three different
industries.

As we discussed, I have been working as an investment advisor
(sales) since leaving InTek. In October, having decided to
re-enter the corporate world, I transferred most of my
clients to other advisors so that I could pursue my job-
search. I was quite successful in investment sales,
designing and implementing a telemarketing approach that
brought about 50 clients in a few months, most with a net
worth of at least six figures. I point this out because I
believe successful sales experience is important for a
general manager.

My job target is a position with a high management content,
either in the operations or financial areas. I would ideally
be with a company that has an entrepreneurial outlook,
perhaps be five to ten years old and have sales of $14 to $50
million.

Regarding compensation, I have a range of $70,000 to $100,000
in mind. Although I have earned more in the past, I expect
some cost to be associated with an industry change, and I
definitely want to get into the hazardous waste industry. At
InTek, my base salary was $135,000 plus bonuses that ranged
from $10,000 to $40,000 per year. Six years ago, at Amoco my
base salary was $85,000 per year.

The potential for growth is as important as immediate
compensation. An opportunity to earn equity would be very
attractive. Although I am not seeking investment
opportunities, I might consider a limited investment in the
right situation. Geographic location is not a major
consideration.

Tom, this seems to cover the items you mentioned on the
phone, and I can provide strong references when appropriate.
I'm looking forward to hearing from you in the near future.

Sincerely,

Michael D. Burns

MDB/fd
Enclosure

Blake C. Campbell, Jr.

February 3, 19--

Ms. Judith Erickson
Manor Oak 3, Suite 611
1910 Cochran Road
Pittsburgh, Pennsylvania 15220

Dear Ms. Erickson:

Thank you for the opportunity to send my resume for the position
you are filling for your Philadelphia client. The position of
vice president in a major agency handing high-tech clients
certainly would provide the challenge I seek to enhance my career.

I was pleased to learn that Diane Roth, with whom I have worked
closely as a fellow officer of the Public Relations Society of
America, passed along my name as a potential candidate.

As I mentioned during our telephone conversation, I am entering
the job market because of major organizational changes at
Ogilvy & Mather.

During my career, I have worked in both agencies and major
corporations, so I know the sensitivities and working
relationships that exist in both arenas.

I am a "quick study" with the ability to apply my communications
and management skills to nearly any industry or discipline. My
several years of experience with high-technology firms are shown
on my resume. These assignments enabled me to work the entire
product spectrum from research and development through
manufacturing and marketing.

Two versions of my resume are attached. The shorter one provides
a quick overview of my career. The more lengthy version--a
dossier, if you will--explains in greater detail exactly what I
have accomplished in each of my professional assignments.

As I mentioned, my present salary is $80,000. The
responsibilities of the position you described and the necessity
to move to the Philadelphia area would place my minimum salary
requirements in the upper $80s.

Thank you for reviewing my credentials. Please contact me should
you need additional information to assess my qualifications.

Sincerely,

Blake C. Campbell, Jr.

M I T C H E L L   B.   S T E V E N S O N

James R. Terry
High Technology Executive Search
1900 Embarcadero
Palo Alto, California   94306

Dear Mr. Terry:

A colleague informed me that you are conducting a search for
Vice President of Development for an emerging high technology
firm.

I am a partner in a law firm where I concentrate on locating
capital for clients starting new business ventures or
expanding existing product lines. My legal experience
enables me to coordinate capital development questions and
manage internal legal matters that increase profitability and
reduce risk.

Prior to private practice, I was Vice President of Investment
Banking for a regional investment banking firm. In a three-
year period my group assembled over $1 billion in new capital
programs. These programs provided uniform cash flow which
saved over $20 million in interest expense, created over
1,000 new jobs and earned our firm $8 1/2 million in
management and underwriting fees.

I also directed the first regional development and new
product innovation center in the United States. I was
selected for this position because of a unique combination of
business and governmental expertise. Our initial funding
came from several Fortune 500 companies and nationally-
recognized private foundations. These efforts resulted in
10,000 new industrial jobs, $300 million in government-
assisted financing, over $100 million in private development
capital and the development of 37 new companies.

I have helped clients cut their approval time by 50 percent
on projects that were affected by environmental and
administrative regulations. I have also coordinated and
successfully guided legislative programs that improved the
business climate in my clients' industry.

I will duplicate these results for your client, and I will
make a change quickly for the right opportunity to play a key
role in a growing technology-driven company.

Please call me next week.

Sincerely,

Mitchell B. Stevenson

R O N A L D   L.   E V A N S

September 16, 19--

Ms. Jan Baxter
Search Alternatives, Inc.
332 Nassau Street
Princeton, New Jersey 08542

Dear Jan:

I want to thank you for all your efforts on my behalf with
regards to the L.L. Bean organization. Needless to say, I
was disappointed to learn that they selected someone else.
I hope it is because they truly felt that the other person
was better able to do the job for them, and not merely for
economic reasons. If the economics were the deciding factor,
I certainly would have entertained a discussion to negotiate
an acceptable salary level.

As I have told you, my family and I would like to return to
the East. Since both my wife and I were raised in Johnstown,
Pennsylvania, we are hoping to relocate somewhere near there.
However, it does not need to be within the state itself. I
would consider any favorable career opportunity in the East,
including states like Indiana, Kentucky, and Virginia.

I'm certain you will be dealing with other new opportunities
in the Eastern states. Please keep me in mind when you are
evaluating those job orders. Anything you can do for me will
be greatly appreciated.

My best regards,

Ronald L. Evans

Michael D. Burns
Two Thousand Oaks Towers
2000 West Federal Street
Boston, Massachusetts   02110
(617) 765-9898

January 28, 19--

Mr. Allen J. Thomas
International Executive Search
2790 Mosside Boulevard
Monroeville, Pennsylvania   15063

Dear Allen:

It was a pleasure talking to you this morning. A short
resume and an excerpt from <u>Fortune</u> magazine are enclosed
which summarize my experience and highlight a few of my
accomplishments.

You stated that Mike Taylor wants to take advantage of
today's strong growth climate and build his company into a
substantial factor. Helping him achieve this sounds like a
challenge I would very much like to meet.

Most of my career has been in management and finance and I
have built a consistently successful track record handling
situations like this. My personal strengths and abilities
have enabled me to work successfully in a variety of
industries, as evidenced by my level of accomplishment in
jobs that ranged from turnarounds to raising large sums of
money for limited partnerships.

With regard to immediate compensation, I am flexible if there
is adequate potential for growth. Equity participation would
greatly influence my salary requirements. Geographic
location is not a major consideration.

Finally, personal chemistry is important for this effort to
be successful. An early meeting between Mike and me would be
a good way to determine if this chemistry is present, as well
as resolve other questions we both may have.

Allen, I very much appreciate your help in all this. After
you have had a chance to review the enclosed materials, I
would like to call to get your reactions and comments.

Best regards,

Michael D. Burns

Enclosures

Michael D. Burns
Two Thousand Oak Towers
2000 West Federal Street
Boston, Massachusetts   02110

February 2, 19--

Mr. Roy W. Laurence
Ward Howell International, Inc.
20 North Wacker Drive
Chicago, Illinois   60606

Dear Mr. Laurence:

Just a brief note to thank you for responding to material I
sent you earlier this month. I am glad to hear that you are
retaining my resume and hope some assignment in the near
future calls for a background and experience that matches
mine.

I have strong and well-balanced experience in general
management and finance encompassing one start-up and two
successful turnarounds. With a track record that was
established in three separate industries, I should not be
categorized as a one-industry specialist. I can offer a lot.

If I can provide you with any more information or be of any
other help, please do not hesitate to call.

Best regards,

Michael D. Burns

Blake C. Campbell, Jr.
2001 Ross Avenue
Dallas, Texas   75201
(214) 345-3548

February 20, 19--

Ms. Judith Erickson
Smith Associates, Inc.
Manor Oak 3, Suite 611
1910 Cochran Road
Pittsburgh, Pennsylvania   15220

Dear Ms. Erickson:

It's been a few weeks since we last talked about the public
relations position you are filling for your Philadelphia
client.

I just wanted to see if you have been in touch with your
client and if there is opportunity for further discussions.
I will call you on Wednesday to determine the status of the
project.

Sincerely,

Blake C. Campbell, Jr.

Answer Want Ads Like A Pro

When you think of want ads, think 5 percent of
your campaign, not 95 percent. Everyone
should answer ads—especially those that are a
perfect fit, but answering want ads should
generally consume no more than thirty minutes
of your day. That's because there are so many
other, better ways to job-hunt.

If you plan to answer ads, I suggest that you
develop a "generic" letter than can be mailed
quickly by simply changing names and dates.
Use this letter to answer most ads. Photocopy
your completed letter and clip the ad to your
copy so you'll have a record if and when
someone calls (they seldom do). Once you mail
the original, forget about it.

Get back to doing more productive things.

If you find an ad that is 100 percent perfect,
your ideal dream job, take the time to tailor a
letter. Find a business directory, look up the
name of the hiring manager—not
personnel—and write that person a sales letter.
That's a letter you can follow up, because you
have a name.

By the way, if you find that you're not ever
getting any response from ads, don't be
discouraged. That's the rule today, not the
exception. Few companies even send rejection
letters anymore. It's too costly. Keep answering
the ones that fit you, and sooner or later, the
phone will ring.

Robert S. Wood
303 North Central Avenue
Phoenix, Arizona 85012
(602) 264-1488

November 28, 19--

Ms. Janet Campbell
Astronautics Corporation
P. O. Box 587
Orchard Park, New York 14127-0587

Dear Mr. Campbell,

> Subject: Stanford Alumni Employment Bulletin -
>   Advertisement for President

Enclosed is my resume in response to your advertisement. I
found the wording of your advertisement with emphasis on
leadership, innovation and change quite intriguing. It is in
response to such challenges that I have excelled during my
career.

Most recently, I was President of a troubled subsidiary of
InTek which I turned around and led to the best performance
in its history. Previous to that, I worked successfully in a
variety of unusual situations, including the startup of a
significant division of Amoco and the turnaround of Collins
Chemical. In each of these situations, the problems (or
opportunities) differed widely. They had in common, though,
a requirement of an ability to size up the situation, assess
the reasonable alternatives and execute a plan of action. My
track record shows that I am able to do this.

With regard to the requirement for manufacturing experience,
I have worked 14 years in mining and milling operations,
where I obtained an in-depth exposure to production problems.
Additionally, of course, I was President of InTek with full
responsibility for all operations and financial activities.

I am free to travel and open to relocation. I would welcome
the opportunity to meet you and to further discuss your
requirements.

Thank you for you interest.

Sincerely,

Robert S. Wood

Robert S. Wood
303 North Central Avenue
Phoenix, Arizona 85012
(602) 264-1488

November 11, 19--

Mr. David O. Ross
Touche Ross Company
1000 Wilshire Boulevard
Los Angeles, California 90017-2472

Dear Mr. Ross:

Subject: Stanford Alumni Employment Bulletin -
Advertisement for Consultant

Enclosed please find my resume in response to your
advertisement. Some of my accomplishments and experience in
your listed functional areas are:

Finance
Set up and managed the accounting, data processing,
acquisitions and planning functions for Amoco's Mineral
Division. Structured and was a principal negotiator in
$40 million customer project financing from
Westinghouse.

Planning
Was member of Amoco's Corporate Planning group and a
major contributor to their efforts, e.g., acquisition of
Bricker Coal Company. Later was manager of planning
activities for Collins Chemical and Amoco's Minerals
Division.

Operations and Organizational Development
As President of InTek Corporation, stabilized and turned
around this troubled company, and then led it to the
best performance in its history.

Systems
Responsible for the design and implementation of new
management information systems for two mining operations
in Amoco's Minerals Division. Later, did the same thing
for the whole accounting system at InTek.

Mr. David O. Ross
November 11, 19--
Page two

    <u>Marketing</u>
    Led efforts in Collins Chemical to analyze marketing
    territories and product lines, which resulted in
    elimination of low margin, low potential products and
    areas. Later, played major role in raising over $20
    million in outside funding for InTek.

My experience, in other words, is extensive and at this point
in my career I am very interested in pursuing a career in
consulting. It should not be possible to be overqualified in
this profession, and I feel I am capable of making a major
contribution.

I am free to travel and open to relocation. I would welcome
the opportunity to further discuss your requirements.

Thank you for your interest.

Sincerely,

Robert S. Wood

Enclosure

Kathleen R. McCormick
7409 Mt. Meeker Road
Omaha, Nebraska 68124

January 25, 19--

Ms. Nancy P. Carson
Employment Manager
Personnel Department
The Alexandria Hospital
4320 Seminary Road
Alexandria, Virginia 22304

Dear Ms. Carson:

The image of Alexandria's stimulating and historic environment caught my imagination when I read about your Director of Planning position in the January career opportunities listing of the <u>Society of Healthcare Planning and Marketing</u>.

I currently hold the position of Director of Marketing at Longmont hospital--a national specialty medical center--which has no planning department, per se. Therefore, institutional planning has, for the most part, been carried out on the basis of market analyses conducted by me and my staff.

This, in addition to my other qualifications, makes me particularly well-suited to your opening. Over the past 16 years I have worked in several progressively more responsible positions within health care. In each position I enjoyed and performed best in the areas of planning and program development.

May I please know more about Alexandria Hospital and its mission? About who the position reports to, and the corporate structure of the hospital? And also the relationship between planning, marketing, and public affairs?

Thank you for you attention.

Sincerely,

Kathleen R. McCormick

Charles D. Wilkerson, Jr.
452 Angeles Crest Highway
Long Beach, California 90807

February 24, 19--

Diane Weatherford
Health Tek Corporation
2356 Horton Street
Emeryville, California 94608

Dear Ms. Weatherford:

Your advertisement for a Director of Corporate Communications
in the February 23rd Wall Street Journal seeks a professional
to communicate your company's successes to investors, clients
and the general public.

My qualifications closely match those you have established
for this demanding new position.

-- An advanced degree in communications plus several
   years of experience at supervisory and staff levels
   in major corporations.

-- Excellent written and verbal communications skills.

-- Experience as a corporate spokesman, a thorough
   knowledge of the news media and the ability to carry
   on effective liaison with the financial media and
   others in the investment community.

-- Familiarity with the operations of a publicly held
   corporation.

-- Ability to monitor budgets, conduct research and
   coordinate other administrative functions that
   support a corporate communications department.

The experience I can offer in both technical and financial
communication would contribute to the continued success of
Health Tek Corporation.

For five years I have been employed by a medical research
center, working directly with doctors, scientists, engineers
and biomedical technicians to communicate the results of
major research. Much of this work has centered on
pharmaceutical studies as applied to respiratory and

immunologic medicine. Other assignments requiring
application of technical knowledge, have been achieved
successfully in the aerospace, computer, and nuclear energy
industries.

In earlier positions I have been responsible for financial
and shareholder communications, investor relations, and
production of annual reports that earned awards from
Financial World magazine. Executive presentations and
financial briefings were included in these assignments.

The many ways in which I could help Health Tek further its
position in the biotechnology industry and in the investor
community could be discussed during a personal interview and
a review of my portfolio of achievements.

A condensed version of my resume is enclosed. A more
detailed version showing specific responsibilities and
accomplishments in each of my positions is available should
you wish to review it.

My salary requirement is competitive based on my background
and experience. A move to Emeryville could be achieved
without major delay.

Please contact me if you would like to hear and see more.

Sincerely,

Charles D. Wilkerson, Jr.

Enclosure

Bruce R. VanDeventer
235 West Maple Avenue
Santa Monica, California 90401
(213) 451-2402

October 22, 19--

Mr. Mike Warner
IDS Financial Services, Inc.
Department 10J
500 IDS Tower
Minneapolis, Minnesota 55402

Dear Mr. Warner:

In response to your recent <u>Wall Street Journal</u> advertisement, I would appreciate your considering me for a career with IDS as a Personal Financial Planner. Your ad listed several prerequisites for favorable consideration, and I feel I meet your requirements, as briefly outlined below:

1. <u>Independent</u>--I have relied on my own work and research to come up with solutions and strategies used in my personal and financial decisions. I look before I leap.

2. <u>Self-motivated</u>--I achieved an M.S. Degree in Geology, and also have the drive to pursue an MBA in the evenings, emphasizing Finance and Management. I feel it is significant to be skilled in one profession, and to actively pursue expertise in another in my spare time.

3. <u>Excellent communication skills</u>--In my career as a petroleum geologist I communicate the advantages and risks in order to make decisions to drill oil exploration wells. This requires skill and finesse to maintain credibility with others.

4. <u>Strong desire for achievement and commitment</u>--I feel these are best exhibited by my recent ongoing job search in the oil profession. In the last few months I have contacted about 110 oil companies on three separate occasions in pursuit of geological professional opportunities. This demonstrates commitment, perseverance, persistence, and strong goal orientation.

5. <u>Listen and Analyze</u>--These skills are essential in my scientific profession and involve sorting out the critically important detailed information, then using it to make decisions sometimes involving millions of dollars.

As you can see from the enclosed resume, my background is based in geology, in the search for new oil and gas deposits. Due to a strong recession in the oil and gas industry at this time, it will likely be difficult for me to continue in my trained profession. Therefore, I have decided to pursue other career opportunities because of the uncertain nature or future for the oil industry.

I have a strong interest in financial matters, and financial planning in particular. My M.B.A. Degree pursuit focuses directly on Finance, particularly emphasizing different types of investments. Also, I have undergone my own personal financial planning through a Financial Planner, and am a definite believer in the overall process.

I am basically familiar with the specific steps of financial planning (the need for adequate insurance, having three to six months cash or liquid reserve, etc.), so I should be able to use my own experiences in helping others.

I also manage my own investments, involving such diverse items as rental real estate, oil and gas limited partnerships, real estate limited partnerships, growth and tax-exempt mutual funds, stocks, and equipment leasing programs. My technical background prepares me for doing detailed investment profit analysis, a requirement for picking successful investments.

I am interested in discussing potential financial planning opportunities with IDS. Thanks for your attention. I'm looking forward to talking soon.

Sincerely,

Bruce R. VanDeventer

CHARLES F. MARTIN

November 12, 19--

Post Office Box 1630
Palmer Lake, CO 80133

Dear Personnel Manager:

I was very excited to find your advertisement for a Director of Video Engineering in last week's <u>Gazette Telegraph</u>. After 23 years in the Government Aerospace communications industry, I am looking for a new challenge with a small, growing company.

<u>I can bring the following assets to your organization</u>:

- BSEE degree and 23 years of hands-on hardware experience with communications equipment and systems. I know how it's designed, manufactured, installed, and fixed. A proven ability to troubleshoot systems in real time.

- Experience with both antenna-radiated and cable-connected equipment from baseband to microwave frequencies; satellite and ground-based segments.

- Project and functional management expertise including project scheduling and cost control.

- Strong customer orientation. My primary responsibility as Program Manager was to keep the customer happy. Satisfied customers bring future business.

- Willingness to meet the world. A good portion of my previous job was traveling to customers' facilities and making "high speed viewgraph" presentations.

- Computer literacy. Auto-CAD was the standard for my projects and my Test Engineering department. I use a similar program, Design-CAD, on my personal computer as well as WordPerfect, Lotus 1-2-3, and telecommunications programs.

The attached resume summarizes my experience and demonstrates my successful advancement. It's time for a change now and I'd like to explore this possibility with you. If, however, you do not see a potential here, I would still like to talk with you about your industry. I'll call next week to set up a convenient meeting.

Yours truly,

Charles F. Martin

William D. Harper
222 Helen Avenue
St. Louis, Missouri 63105

June 10, 19--

Box 025
c/o The Chicago Tribune
Chicago, Illinois 60611

Dear Sir/Madam:

I am writing to you regarding your recent advertisement for a
Plant Engineer.

In my last position, I was very good at "hands on" trouble-
shooting and process development. I am also a "self starter"
and am very mechanically inclined. I strive for simple,
cost-effective, common sense solutions to technical problems,
instead of elaborate schemes to re-invent the wheel. The
position that you describe sounds exactly like the kind of
job I am seeking.

To make myself more competitive with local applicants, I am
willing to pay my own relocation expenses. Because I am
currently renting a home, I can relocate without problems and
I am available immediately.

I started with Dresser Industries in 19-- at $21,500/yr.
After 5-1/2 years and three promotions, my salary was $38,500
plus car. In 19-- I received a superior Performance Award
of $1,350. I was the only engineer out of approximately 15
other candidates to receive this award. I mention my salary
history only to show that I am an achiever and have been
recognized for my accomplishments. My salary requirement is
negotiable.

I would appreciate your time in reviewing my enclosed resume
and I would welcome an opportunity to meet with you for a
personal interview.

Sincerely,

William D. Harper

Home: (314) 241-2999

Daniel J. Goin
6120 South Elm Court
Littleton, Colorado 80121
(303) 773-3417

October 30, 19--

Compensation Merit Systems
P.O. Box 181
Denver, Colorado 80218-0899

Dear Sir or Madam:

Your advertisement for Human Resources Director describes a position that I believe is well suited to my skills, experience and desire to apply my generalist background in a challenging new environment.

I have 14 years of experience in human resource management, including the following key areas:

o Recruitment

o Personnel Policy Development

o Compensation/Performance-Based Pay

o Benefit Program Design and Administration

o Affirmative Action/EEO

o Employee Relations/Supervisory Counsel

o Training and Development

o Personnel Records Management

I would greatly appreciate the opportunity to discuss more specifically how I might apply my background to meet your organization's needs. My current salary is $43,000 per year. My minimum requirement is $40,000. My resume is enclosed for your review.

Thank you for your consideration.

Sincerely,

Daniel J. Goin

DJG/ckr
Enclosure

Carole D. Roberts

April 13, 19--

DAILY CAMERA
P.O. Box 591
Boulder, Colorado 80306

Dear Personnel Manager:

I am responding to your advertisement for a nurse recruiter.

As a results-oriented professional, I have over 14 years' experience in various hospital and HMO environments. I have skills, ability, knowledge and personality to make a contribution to your organization in the minimum amount of time.

These highlights may interest you:

    -- Served as nursing liaison to regional recruitment and
       retention committee for two years.
    -- Presented committee recommendations to top-level
       management for approval.
    -- Conceived and wrote job description, then actively
       recruited an RN for the first Nurse Recruiter
       position in a local major hospital.
    -- Upgraded quality of supervisory staff hired in local
       HMO by revising recruitment and hiring practices.
    -- Actively recruited supervisory and key technical
       staff for 22 patient-care and specialty departments.
    -- Affiliated with National Association of Nurse
       Recruiters.
    -- Successfully recruit volunteers for fundraising,
       social activities, and church functions.

I believe in excellence and have always dedicated my talents and creative abilities to assure the successful accomplishment of company goals.

The ability to work well with people, to have the drive and interest to accomplish the work, and several years of stable work experience make me uniquely qualified for this position.

I look forward to meeting with you personally to discuss the opportunity and how I may contribute to the ongoing success of your organization. Thank you.

Sincerely,

Carole D. Roberts

Richard A. Polson
118 April Waters West
Montgomery, Texas   77356
(409) 588-4269

July 23, 19--

Post Office Box DG-921
National Business Employment Weekly
c/o The Wall Street Journal
1233 Regal Row
Dallas, Texas   75247

Gentlemen:

Your advertisement inviting successful managers to apply for
the position of Vice President of Operations was a challenge
I could not refuse. My qualifications match your stated
preferences.

For the last 22 years I have worked for Dowell Division of
Dow Chemical and for Dowell Schlumberger, Inc. Four of these
years were on assignment in Venezuela, South America, and two
years were on assignment in Dubai, U.A.E. (Middle East).
From a trainee in 19-- I have grown with the company and have
held increasingly more responsible positions in management as
well as in sales.

I am widely traveled, and living and working in several
states and overseas has given me the opportunity to:

-- Manage many different personalities and nationalities,

-- Adapt quickly to different circumstances and
   environments,

-- Be a quick study--show results in a very short time.

Over 20 years of professional experience has allowed me to
gain valuable expertise, as the following summary of my
accomplishments will testify:

-- Reduced sales force 62% while increasing market share from
   14% to 23.5%.

-- As Manager of a new division, opened and organized the
   division with responsibilities covering five states and
   365 employees.

-- Turned Maintenance Shop around from poor performance into
   the top-rated shop in the U.S.

-- Turned an operation from a $100,000 annual loss into the
   third most profitable operation in the region in a 12
   month period.

-- Had the most profitable operation in the central region of
   the U.S.

-- Negotiated a one-year contract with a chemical company in
   Bombay, India, for the purchase of raw hydrochloric acid.
   This was for the Middle East operations out of Dubai,
   U.A.E. The price negotiated was lower than the current
   level and was during a period of rising prices.

I'm 47 years old and in excellent health. I'm married and
have two children (one recently graduated from college, and
the other is a sophomore in college). I hold a BBA degree
from Texas Tech University.

At the present time I am seeking a new challenge--one where
my innovative and management talents can be applied. Your
company seems to offer such a challenge, and my credentials
match your requirements. I look forward to talking with you.

                    Sincerely,

                    Richard A. Polson

RAP:jt

Douglas Gragg

April 25, 19--

Search Committee
Colorado Historical Society
1300 Broadway
Denver, Colorado 80203

Dear Committee Members:

The position of Regional Property Administrator is an
excellent match with my long-term intense interest in
Colorado and Denver history, which culminated last winter in
my receiving a master's degree in history.

At one point, my goals included teaching history, and I
completed over 24 hours of course work in education.

As my resume indicates, I have spent many years in business,
coupled with seven terms of course work at Barnes Business
College, where I focused on business and financial
management.

My extensive political involvement has honed not only my
knowledge of volunteers and their needs, but also my
abilities to organize and manage information. For a number
of years, I have been in charge of our local political
caucus, which includes prominent local politicans and
business people. I have been active in more than fifty
political campaigns, raised funds, and organized and managed
"paper trails" for many elections. In last fall's national
elections, I assisted in recruiting, training, and organizing
more than 3,000 employees.

As a Denver native and third generation Coloradan, I would be
excited and proud to be an employee of the Colorado
Historical Society. The position advertised provides me an
ideal opportunity to use my professional training in history
and my long experience in business management. I look
forward to talking with you.

Very truly yours,

Douglas Gragg

Kenneth W. Grove
1335 Olympian Circle
Lafayett, Colorado 80026
U.S.A.
May 8, 19--

Personnel Manager
International Education Services
Shi Taiso Building
10-7 Dogenzada 2-chome
Shibuya-ku
Tokyo, Japan 150

Dear Sir/Madam:

I am interested in applying for a position as English teacher for Japanese businessmen as described in your recent job announcement bulletin. I am a scientist by training and profession. Enclosed is a copy of my resume listing my academic training and professional experience.

My wife and I have very close ties to Japan and would very much like to live there for a few years. My sister, Linda Grove, is a professor of Asian studies at Sophia University in Tokyo. Her husband, Hideme Kondo, is a Japanese citizen and a curator at an art museum in Tokyo as well. My wife and I spent two weeks in Japan with my sister and her family in May of 19--. In the course of our stay, we thoroughly enjoyed visiting with the various Japanese relatives and felt very comfortable and at ease in the Japanese culture.

I hope that the above information will give you an understanding of our interest in spending more time in Japan and in teaching English to Japanese people.

We do not have a fluent understanding of the Japanese language. However, we have studied the language briefly for preparation for our trip in 19--. We also intend to continue to study Japanese as we have Japanese relatives whom we visit periodically.

I look forward to hearing from you. Thank you for your consideration.

Sincerely,

Kenneth W. Grove

Enclosure

Janet Cummins
255 Omega Way
Colorado Springs, Colorado   80917

August 2, 19--

Continental Airlines
Employment Department
P.O. Box 4330
Houston, TX   77210-4330

Dear Personnel Manager:

As a longtime resident of Colorado Springs, I am well aware
of the outstanding reputation of Continental Airlines, which
leads me to express my interest in this dynamic company.
I am submitting my resume for your review for the position of
Ticket Agent.   I feel I have the necessary qualifications for
your consideration and would appreciate the opportunity to
demonstrate this in a personal meeting.

Although my experience in the airline business is limited,
I am very interested and enthusiastic about learning.   I am
an outgoing, friendly individual who would enjoy developing
personal relationships with customers.   My strong
communication and organizational skills would serve me well
in responding to the needs of your company.   My drive,
determination and leadership ability are evident in my
resume.

I am a hard worker who is noted for accuracy and timeliness.
My performance evaluations have consistently been at the
"above average" and "outstanding" levels, and I can furnish
excellent references should you need them.

A recent staff reduction at KDI Electronics due to lack of
work, has resulted in the elimination of my position as
Senior Manufacturing Controller.   Because of this mass
layoff, I am eligible to participate in an On-The-Job
Training Program which will reimburse you 50% of my wages
during a negotiated training period.   Enclosed is more
information on this subject.

I feel that your airline would benefit from my contribution
as a Ticket Agent.   Should you have a position available on
your staff, you may contact me at (719) 596-6268.

Sincerely,

Janet Cummins

BRUCE D. ROBERTSON, CPA
3182 South Holly Street
Denver, Colorado 80222
(303) 756-7453 (H)
(303) 779-1417 (W)

June 20, 19--

Williams International
P.O. Box 500
F.D.R. Station
New York, New York 10150

Dear Employment Manager:

The overseas position you describe in your recent advertisement in the "National Business Employment Weekly" is exactly the type of position I am seeking! With my diversified international management, finance, treasury, taxes, planning, and consolidations experience, I know I can be an asset to many of your clients. In addition, I speak and read French. In 19-- to 19-- I also studied Business French through classes at Storage Technology Corporation.

Some highlights of my international, finance, and administration experience, which might interest you, are as follows:

-- Number two man in Storage Technology's European operations in which annual subsidiary revenues grew in two years from $5MM to $55MM; in addition, we had OEM revenues of $25MM per year.

-- Prepared worldwide budgets, plans, and consolidations.

-- Established international consulting firm.

-- Seventeen years' experience in management and financial controls.

This is only a brief summary of my abilities--there is more to share. As your Vice President of Finance Assistant, I know I can help your company achieve its worldwide goals and objectives in this fast-paced, high-tech environment.

I am looking forward to meeting with you to discuss this exciting, challenging position in more detail.

Sincerely,

Bruce D. Robertson, CPA
BDR:pr

Arnold C. Stevenson
1200 Midtown Tower
Rochester, New York 14604

Box T-300
The Wall Street Journal
30 Broad Street
New York, New York 10017

Dear Personnel Manager:

I'm responding to your May 19th advertisement in <u>The Wall</u>
<u>Street Journal</u> for a President of your Kitchen and Housewares
Division. The following comments show how my qualifications
match your stated requirements:

<u>YOUR REQUIREMENTS</u>	<u>MY QUALIFICATIONS</u>
1. Dynamic professional with top-level management experience.	1. Former President of $100MM division of corporate giant. Member operations committee of two companies. Board Chairman of two subsidiaries.
2. Proven record.	2. Built sales from $25 to $100MM in three years by internal growth and acquisition. Top profits in corporation.
3. Experience in financial administration.	3. Total P&L responsibility for 4 enterprises comprising the division.
4. Sales Management.	4. Former V.P. Marketing for $400MM Corporation.
5. Consumer hardgoods.	5. Major housewares.
6. Product Development.	6. Brought out new food product for consumer market.
7. MBA.	7. Stanford University.

There are other accomplishments in my background which may be
of interest to you, and I look forward to talking with you
further to discuss this exciting opportunity.

Very truly yours,

Arnold C. Stevenson

T. CRAIG LINCOLN

October 12, 19--

Mr. Richard A. Rathbun
MSF 134
Data General Corporation
4400 Computer Drive
Westboro, Massachusetts 01580

Dear Mr. Rathbun:

This letter is in response to your advertisement in the
<u>Denver Post</u> of February 3, 19--. Your ad outlined
requirements for Graphic Designers within your marketing
department. This position is very appealing to me since your
needs match a great deal of my background. Specifically:

> <u>Project Management</u>--From large collateral print projects
> for Datagraphix, University Computing Company and Dravo
> Corporation, Denver, to corporate identity projects for
> Bank of Oklahoma and Old National Bank of Washington.
> Combined approximate project costs in excess of $500K
> with cost savings to each client.

> <u>Public Relations</u>--As the Communications Director for
> Arapahoe/Douglas Area Vocational Schools, I developed
> new communications tools for 20 individual programs,
> designed a multimedia slide/video production which was
> shown throughout five school districts in the Denver
> area, and thus assisted in a 20% enrollment growth for
> the Area School.

> Additionally, I was able to acquire approximately $300K
> worth of free air time on local radio and television for
> Area School promotion. Both the Executive Director and
> I appeared on two of the programs for a total of 1-1/2
> half hours of air time.

> <u>Print Production</u>--For the past eight years I trained 250
> secondary and post-secondary vocational students in
> graphic print production. In a recent five-year study
> done on my program through the State Board, my placement
> record topped 84%.

From 19-- to the present I've been involved in vocational
education. During this time I successfully took an "arts and
crafts" fine art program into state-of-the-art graphic
communications education. I've proposed and implemented a
program which was originally budgeted at $3K per school year

Mr. Richard A. Rathbun
October 12, 19--
Page Two

to a current $21K per year. With this money, I brought the
computer into the classroom six years ago. Currently, I've
proposed the first CAD system and hope to incorporate this
into the curriculum.

While teaching full time I've also continued to keep my
design talents current with several projects a year through
my private practice. At present, I have had over 27 years of
experience in design. I have attached a resume which will
outline my past employment history. I would be delighted to
review my salary history with you on a more personal basis
when we get together.

In closing, I look forward to meeting you when you come to
Denver so we can discuss your needs in greater detail.

Sincerely,

T. Craig Lincoln

TCL/

Enclosure

Sally W. Larson
2500 East Colorado Boulevard
Pasadena, California 91107

April 1, 19--

Box ME-16
National Business Employment Weekly
c/o The Wall Street Journal
400 Alexis R. Shuman Boulevard
Naperville, Illinois 60566

Re: Real Estate Attorney

Ladies/Gentlemen:

I would like to express my interest in the position of
real estate attorney with your company. I believe my
background in acquisitions and in securities would complement
the goals established by your company.

My experience in land acquisitions and securities is the
result of my tenures with Amoco Petroleum Company, Texaco Oil
Company, and in private practice. The areas, in which I have
had substantial experience and responsibility, include:

* team participation in the acquisition of companies
  valued respectively at $18 million and $40 million

* drafting of purchase and sales agreements for properties
  valued at $500 thousand to $1 million

* title examination and curative

* negotiation and drafting of contracts pertaining to
  lease acquisition, including farmins, options, pooling
  agreements and seismic exchange agreements, many
  involving wells costing between $1 million and $4
  million

* drafting of limited partnerships and compliance with the Blue Sky requirements of numerous states

* team participation in briefing contracts which provided substantial basis for two joint ventures requiring minimum expenditures of $40 million and $100 million each

This list is not inclusive of all areas of authority, but does provide a fair overview of my responsibilities.

I have, for my own account, acquired real estate properties in the Pasadena metropolitan area valued at approximately three hundred thousand dollars. Two of the properties are rental units for which I handled the leasing. These investments are a reflection of my interest in a career in real estate investment.

My resume, detailing my background, is enclosed for your review. I would welcome the opportunity to meet and discuss my experience with you. Correspondence may be directed to me at the letterhead address. However, please feel free to contact me by telephone at (213) 681-3973.

Very truly yours,

Sally W. Larson

SWL/kb
Enclosure

Richard C. Emerson

May 14, 19--

Mr. Michael M. Morrison
Personnel Officer
San Marin County
Personnel Division
27 East Ocean Avenue
San Francisco, California 94105

Dear Mr. Morrison and the Selection Committee:

Your job announcement listed nine requirements for the position of Theater Auditorium Manager and I would like to discuss my experience in light of these requirements:

1. <u>Qualified</u>.

    - Twenty-one years' experience in the meeting and convention management business in such facilities as: The Denver Auditorium Theater, Red Rocks Amphitheater, Currigan Exhibition Hall and the Denver Auditorium Arena.

    - Consultant to Architects and Planning Staff on Major Convention Centers in Calgary, Oklahoma City, Kansas City, Toledo, Colorado and San Francisco.

    - Managed a wide spectrum of events including ballet, opera, symphony, trade and exhibit shows, auto shows, union meetings and other sit-down conventions, banquets, fashion shows, live theater, concerts, medical meetings, church conventions, and associated spin-off meetings.

    - Coordinated meetings involving 10 to 30,000 people.

    - Coordinated banquets involving 10 to 5,500 people.

2. <u>Motivated</u>.

    I have an attitude of excitement and enthusiasm for "show business." During performances I stay on the premises and make myself available. I don't leave problems for subordinates to handle. You will find that I am "right at your elbow if you need me . . ."

3. <u>Thorough Knowledge of Performing Arts Facility Operation</u>.

    I have learned the performing arts business from the ground up. I started in Denver as an usher; then moved to head usher; then to stagehand . . . to assistant manager . . . to manager.

    This has given me expertise in all the different levels of operation.

4. <u>Ability to Manage Small Staff</u>.

    I understand how to choose appropriate personnel and make sure they are well-trained, well-disciplined, and have a <u>professional attitude</u>. I did all the hiring for the Denver Convention Complex for four years (janitorial and ushering personnel) and supervised as many as 150 people at Currigan Hall.

5. <u>Ability to Work with Performers</u>.

    I'm relaxed with performers. They look to me for personal assistance and security. I have always gotten along well with them and have worked with Johnny Mathis, Roger Williams, Al Hirt, Debbie Reynolds . . . Arthur Fiedler . . . Eddie Arnold, Liberace, Leonard Nimoy, and many others.

6. <u>Ability to Work with the General Public</u>.

    I love working with the public, as these comments suggest:

    "We found Mr. Emerson to be the most congenial and helpful building manager we have worked with anywhere in the Nation. <u>As a direct result of his ability and job thoroughness, we have scheduled our 19-- Convention in Denver once again</u>.

        Bill Ackerman, Executive Director
        Western Apparel Manufacturers Association

    "You've undoubtedly been one of the most cooperative men that it has been my pleasure to work with in planning for conventions."

        Michael T. Scott, Financial Planning Secretary
        Southern Baptist Convention

"Your courtesies and kindness were most appreciated, and
I do not think we could have had such a successful kick-
off if it had not been for you and your personal
thoughtfulness and that of the members of your crew."

Robert E. Noonan, Executive Director
Mile-Hi United Fund

"Once again, thank you so much for taking time out of
your busy schedule to review many of the problems
confronting convention and conference bookings."

Robert B. Sullivan, President and General Manager
Pueblo Chamber of Commerce

"Not only does Denver have one of the best designed
facilities in the United States, but also appears to
have one of the most knowledgeable and effective
managers."

Jack C. Thomas, Assistant Executive Director
San Francisco Redevelopment Agency

"I can only hope that our future conferences will have a
Richard Emerson in them. I look forward to working with
you again."

Robert B. Donner, Assistant Director
Public Affairs Section
International Association of Chiefs of Police

7. Knowledge of Fiscal Aspects of Operation.

I originated the annual budget of $400,000 for Currigan
Hall and handled all the ordering and inventory control.

8. Knowledge of Technical Aspects of Operation.

I have complete working knowledge of: (1) heating,
(2) air conditioning, (3) fire and safety regulations,
(4) building codes, (5) crowd control techniques,
(6) first aid, (7) security, (8) catering, (9) lighting,
(10) seating and stage arrangements, (11) sound systems,
(12) lead-in and lead-out time and, (13) union contracts.

9. <u>Strong PR Skills</u>.

I am experienced in sales. I know the way to book
buildings and keep accurate records to prevent double
bookings.

I can coordinate the activities of the performers,
exhibitors, working personnel and management, and I can
keep it all running smoothly.

"Thank you for taking the time to show me some of your
convention center. You're the kind of person we like to
deal with, because you don't try to hand out a lot of
false information--you know what you're talking about."

Jack Barker, C.L.U.
Million Dollar Round Table

The last, and perhaps the most important requirement for this
job is enthusiasm--and I'm excited and enthusiastic about
discussing this unique job opportunity with you in person.

In the meantime, anything I can do to help you would be my
pleasure. Best wishes for a successful venture.

Cordially,

Richard C. Emerson

BRUCE D. ROBERTSON
3182 South Holly Street
Denver, Colorado 80222
(303) 756-7435 (H)
(303) 779-1417 (W)

January 18, 29--

Ms. Jean W. Kingston
Vice President Human Resources
Bank of America
230 California Street
San Francisco, California 94111

Ms. Kingston:

I just received your letter of December 20th, and I am puzzled at not being invited for an interview. My experience and your requirements looked like a perfect "fit."

I understand that you are constantly reviewing resumes and that oversights can occur. Please review the enclosed want ad and my resume and reconsider me for a position in your company.

Sincerely,

Bruce Robertson, CPA

BDR:bl

Guarantee Good References

Few managers trust their own judgment when making hiring decisions—especially at higher levels. Employers want to assess your reputation by learning what others say about you. Then they decide.

That means you need third party endorsements, words of praise from others. Nothing can hurt you worse than a lukewarm reference. Here's how to make sure your references are as good as they can possibly be.

Martin B. Cousins
124 East Bay Street
Miami, Florida 33131
(305) 342-8789

January 14, 19--

Mr. Peter W. Lincoln
334 Houston Tower, Suite 2300
Houston, Texas 77079

Dear Pete,

As a friend, I'd like to enlist your assistance in my search for a new career. I have put together a current resume to begin marketing myself for what should be a new and exciting career.

I'm open to an industry change since the oilfield is depressed. I'm looking for a job in Management or Marketing of technical products and services. I hope to draw on both my management experience and engineering background. Relocation is not a problem as Wendy and I find the prospect of moving exciting.

With your permission, I would like you to be a personal reference for me. I will keep you posted when I have used you as a reference so you will know who might call and won't be caught blind. Please let me know what you think.

If you are aware of any business associates or friends who may be in the market for new, bold and innovative thinking, I'd really appreciate your giving them a copy of my resume or giving me their names to contact personally.

I welcome any assistance or advice you can give me. Thanks for you support now and in the past.

Sincerely,

Martin B. Cousins

MC:ak
Enclosure

*

M E M O R A N D U M

TO: Roger W. Van Dyke
FROM: Jory L. Laine
DATE: June 23, 19--
SUBJECT: Draft of reference statement. Roger, as we
discussed, I've put together an outline for a
letter of reference from you. Please review, and
let's discuss.

Mr. Laine was employed by Amax Environmental Services, Inc.
from August, 19-- through December, 19-- reporting to me. In
January, 19-- he was promoted to a controllership position in
the Exploration Division. In addition he retained the
financial management responsibilities for the Environmental
Division during 19-- and continued his real estate management
responsibilities until his separation in June 19--.

Mr. Laine's position at Amax Environmental Services was
Financial Manager, a position that encompassed a broad range
of financial and administrative responsibilities. He
successfully designed and implemented accounting,
administrative and data processing systems and made a
significant contribution to the management of the division.

His accomplishments include: a) implementation of an
environmental review of capital and operating plans; b)
development of an environmental cost analysis system; and c)
nondisclosure negotiations with government agencies.

In addition, he profitably disposed of assets and played a
significant role in the consolidation of accounting and
administrative services--resulting in reduced costs and
improved service.

Mr. Laine is an effective manager with an open communication
style. He established a good rapport with subordinates,
peers, and superiors at the divisional and corporate level.
I found him to be a good team player and a reliable
professional.

As a result of departmental reorganization and consolidation,
a process in which he took an active and positive role,
Mr. Laine decided, and I agreed, that the organization's
requirements and his career objectives were no longer
parallel and his goals could be better achieved in an
organization that would more fully utilize his expertise.

*

Charles D. White
2121 Eastern Ocean Avenue
San Ramon, California   75944
(415) 363-8630

November 12, 19--

Mr. Timothy Henning
California Home Health Care
24 Sandpiper Road West, Suite 1400
San Ramon, California   75944

Dear Tim:

Thank you for your offer to act as a reference for me. I
believe it is important for me to be able to provide a
reference from my last job. As I mentioned, most prospective
employers prefer to speak personally to the reference rather
than being provided a written document. Should the occasion
arise, I would like to request that you be willing to speak
personally to a prospective employer.

I am following the recommended procedure by contacting
each of my references and sharing with them a brief outline I
have developed for each job. Having such an outline available
serves as a convenient tool to jog the memory and organize
thoughts when a call is received. The outlines cover the
following key factors:

o My strengths as an employee and manager.

o Significant accomplishments achieved during my tenure.

o The reason for leaving the job.

Of course, I want to ensure that the appraisal is honest
and one with which you are in agreement. At the same time
negative comments should normally be avoided.

Please review the attached outline for my job with CHHC.
It parallels what I am communicating in my written materials
(resumes, marketing letters) as well as what I say in
interviews. I'll call in a few days after you've had a chance
to review the material.

Sincerely,

Charles D. White

Charles D. White
General Business Manager
July 19-- - October 19--

Charles was hired through a search conducted by a national retained search firm, interviews with senior company finance and operations personnel and a review by Rohrer, Hibler & Replogle, Inc--a national executive appraisal firm.

SIGNIFICANT ACCOMPLISHMENTS

1. Brought the accounting organization from chaos to a high
    level of professionalism.
    - handled consolidation into new center
    - released poor performers
    - upgraded staff, recruited nine new people
    - coordinated successful implementation of several new
       systems (accounts payable, payroll, fixed assets)
    - set up internal controls and procedures

2. Improved quality of accounting records and reports.
    - accurate and timely closings
    - clean FY19-- audit (per Arthur Andersen)
    - created reports by subunits (board reports,
       statements)

3. Excellent job of handling the yearly budgeting project
    (19-- & 19-- fiscal years).
    - provided historical data and tools for assisting
       managers
    - one of only a few zones to completely fulfill
       requirements for content and timing

4. Significantly improved the yearly physical inventory
    project.
    - wrote detailed instructions for field staff
    - sent accountants into the field to observe and assist
       the count
    - provided instructions and oversight for the
       reconciliation by accounting staff

5. Spearheaded purchase and training of staff on PC's,
    maximized use of PC's for routine or repetitive tasks.

Charles D. White
Page Two

6. Improved human resources support for zone.
    -   hired excellent personnel specialist to support zone
        in hiring and compensation/benefits matters
    -   encouraged improvement in hiring practices to
        reduce turnover
    -   cleaned up personnel records and fulfilled
        corporate data requirements for new retirement plan,
        401K plan, and payroll system

STRENGTHS AS A MANAGER

1. Organizational skills.
    -   thinks through a task
    -   gathers and allocates resources
    -   follows up to ensure completion as planned

2. Recruitment skills.
    -   a good judge of people
    -   careful to do the background and reference checks
    -   trusts his judgement, willing to present people with
        new challenges

3. Innovative.
    -   likes challenges
    -   enjoys bringing order from chaos and improving
        techniques

4. Positive attitude to technology.
    -   tries to maximize use of personal computers and other
        office automation equipment

5. Keeps lines of communication open with subordinates.
    -   highly regarded by his staff

STRENGTHS AS AN EMPLOYEE

1. Good business sense developed through broad experience
    in several industries.

2. An excellent analyst.
    -   researches questions in a logical manner
    -   digs into details, good at manipulating data

3. Does not make hasty or politically-motivated decisions.

4. Good personal work habits.
    -   focuses on organizing the task
    -   meets deadlines

5.   A good communicator.
     - expresses thoughts clearly
     - equally comfortable preparing written or oral material

REASON FOR LEAVING

Charles was hired to be the general business manager of the whole Tustin processing center, supervising accounting, accounts receivable, data processing and personnel. I initially limited his scope to supervision of the accounting group because this was the area where we had the greatest deficiencies which needed attention.

Subsequently, the home office revised the organization model to be used in each of the regional processing centers. The General Business Manager position was eliminated. Supervision of the center was split between an existing manager of receivables and a zone controller. Job specifications for the zone controller -- education, experience and salary grade -- were below those possessed by Charles. Consequently he was released.

PERSONAL CHARACTERISTICS

1.   High level of dedication to his work.

2.   Strong personal values of honesty and integrity.

3.   A stable family life -- a wife with a professional career and two young children.

4.   Excellent education.

5.   Professional appearance and manner.

6.   Even tempered -- handles stress well.

DOWELL SCHLUMBERGER
P.O. Box 3899
2899 E. Villard Avenue
Dickinson, North Dakota   58601

May 27, 19--

To Whom It May Concern:

It is with great pleasure that I recommend Jim Precup to you
in his search for employment. While employed with Dowell
Schlumberger, Jim was a very hard worker. Not only did he
willingly and effectively execute the responsibilities of his
position, but many times performed duties beyond what was
required of him.

Jim's vast technical knowledge has been basically
self-learned; however, I can speak for his technical skills
with a great deal of confidence. Jim has been employed with
DS for eight years, the last five years in sales. He has
performed above our expectations. While employed with our
company, Jim has not let health or personal problems ever
conflict with his job.

Jim has maintained high morale while working in a depressed
market, and while doing so has displayed leadership to his
fellow workers.

I was forced to lay Jim off due to lack of work in our area;
however, I highly recommend Jim for employment with you and
am confident he will be an asset to your business from the
first day he is employed.

Please feel free to call me at (701) 225-4477 if you have
further questions or concerns.

Sincerely,

Robert C. Carpenter
Station Manager

Jane E. Buck
1315 Mountain Street, #A6
Lakewood, Colorado 80215
232-3485

September 29, 19--

Ms. Evelyn Brust
President
Great Western Association Management, Inc.
10200 East Girard, Suite 304C
Denver, Colorado 80237

Dear Evelyn:

Thank you for meeting with me last Thursday. I enjoyed our
visit and lunch very much. I hope your office move went
smoothly and that you are pleased with the change.

I am most interested in a position with your firm and I
believe many facets of my present work and outside activities
are applicable to your business operations, as we discussed.
The administrative work and project coordination are areas I
am most interested in pursuing!

Enclosed are my references which you may contact at any time.
Again, I would like to thank you for your time and interest,
and I will look forward to meeting with you again.

Sincerely,

Jane E. Buck

Enclosure

Sell Yourself to Strangers

Sales letters are letters of self-introduction: they make "cold calls" for you and open doors that appear closed. Use them to scan the market to see who might be interested in talking further. They can save you from being intimidated on the telephone (although you must follow most letters with a call). Calling to follow up on a well-written letter is much easier than calling cold.

```
                  Meet Janet O'Connell
                  FULL CHARGE BOOKKEEPER

Janet is -
     o honest
     o eager to work
     o punctual and organized
     o thorough (she never skips over problems--she asks questions.)

     o qualified . . . strong background in the following areas:
          o accounts payable,
          o accounts receivable,
          o payroll,
          o payroll taxes and reports,
          o cost control,
          o taxes,
          o bank reconciliation,
          o cash dispersements and receipts,
          o profit and loss statements
          o public contact in collections.

Janet is machine-oriented
     She can operate, care for, and service the following machines:
     CRT and IBM computers, typewriters, 10-key by touch adding
     machines, bookkeeping machines like:  L5000 (Mag Card), NCR,
     Burroughs, Olivetti, Underwood and others.

A graduate of Colorado University in 19-- with studies in Business
Administration and English.

Why Bookkeeping?

"I like responsibility . . . I like detail.  I can put things in
order."

                  YOUR COMPANY WILL GAIN

o An employee eager to prove herself.  (I want to get the job done.)
o Someone used to digging in and solving problems.
o A lower turnover rate--I'm career oriented.

One former employer said this:

     "If you are looking for a person who is always on the job,
     reliable, efficient, cheerful and mature, you will be pleased
     with your decision to hire her."

                  Jack Moore, Division Manager
                  Microtek Corporation

          INVEST IN YOUR COMPANY'S FUTURE TODAY!
          Call 893-2541 and ask for Janet O'Connell
```

MEET LINDA!

"A SALESMAN IF I EVER MET ONE!"
(Said by her former employer with over
25 years in sales who now manages a
large insurance company.)

LINDA IS:

    Dynamic
    Creative
    Intelligent
    Resourceful
    Persistent
    Honest
    Direct
    Positive
    Quick to learn
    A risk taker

QUALIFIED . . . STRONG PEOPLE BACKGROUND AND PEOPLE SKILLS IN:

    Handling Complaints
    Problem Solving
    Motivating Others
    Knowing When to Listen
    Knowing When and How to Ask Questions

A graduate of the University of Illinois in 19-- with a bachelor's in
psychology and a minor in math and social work.

    WHY DIRECT SALES?

$--AN OPPORTUNITY AT AN OPEN ENDED INCOME
FREEDOM--TO WORK MORE THAN 40 HOURS A WEEK
CHALLENGE--TO TAKE OPEN ENDED SITUATIONS AND MAKE THEM HAPPEN
ADVENTURE--TAMING THE UNKNOWN

                    YOUR COMPANY WILL GAIN

            A person with a high money drive.
        An enhanced reputation in the business world.
          A lower turnover rate--I'm career oriented.
             Able to travel; excellent health.

The potential is there waiting to be unleashed and molded into one of
your company's top producers! Whatever it takes I can and WILL do--truly
a diamond in the rough!

        INVEST IN YOUR COMPANY'S FUTURE TODAY!

        CALL: 832-3374 and ask for Linda Turnbaugh
        830 Sherman Street, Denver, Colorado   80203

NANCY L. MONTGOMERY

Penthouse Towers
1100-15th Street
Oakland, California 94612

May 17, 19--

Mr. Robert Rawson
Vice President & Controller
1st National Bank of Oakland
P. O. Box 5808
Oakland, California 94612

Dear Mr. Rawson:

Do you need a hardworking, creative and conscientious
individual for your accounting or finance areas?
If so, I can help you.

* Started my career on the audit staff of a "big 8"
  public accounting firm. <u>Have broad industry exposure</u>.

* Became a <u>CPA</u> in 19--

* Deal well with people. Good communication skills.

* <u>Heavy exposure</u> in development of cash management
  programs and accounting systems development and
  automation.

* Have <u>good supervisory experience.</u>

* <u>Special interest</u> in financial accounting, cash
  management and finance and systems development.

I would like to meet with you to discuss the contribution
that I could make to 1st National Bank of Oakland.

<u>If you need someone who is highly motivated, eager to learn,
and willing to work hard/smart to succeed, please contact me
at 839-5600 before 8:00 a.m. or after 5:00 p.m.</u>

Sincerely,

Nancy L. Montgomery

NLM/

Mr. Brandon Broga
7555 Tanbark Drive, NE
Bremerton, Washington 98310
(206) 692-2626

March 14, 19--

Mr. John Steele,
Owner
Architectural Drafting Services
2123 South Broadway
Seattle, Washington 98133

Dear Mr. Steele:

Do you need help with . . .

        -- cleanup
        -- running errands
        -- filing
        -- bookkeeping
        -- drafting
        -- typing
        -- small jobs

If you need help, I think we should talk. I'm a high school
senior. I learn easily and am capable of doing any kind of
entry-level work.

                    Qualifications

        -- 4 years Drafting
        -- 1-1/2 years Computer Drafting
        -- 2 years Commercial Art
        -- Business Math
        -- Typing 60 wpm

If you need reliable part-time or full-time help, call me now
at 692-2626.

Sincerely,

Brandon Broga

<u>LOOKING FOR A HEALTH CARE MARKETER</u> ?

<u>ONE WITH A HIGHLY SUCCESSFUL TRACK RECORD</u> ?

If you are, please take a look at me . . .

o   Sixteen years experience . . .
    from clinical care in rehabilitation . . .
    to director of marketing for a national medical center.

o   A proven track record in getting patient referrals. . .
    in just five years achieved 42 percent increase in
    inpatients, and a 386 percent increase in outpatients.

o   Innovative and creative . . . developed and managed
    LUNG LINE, the first professionally answered, Q&A
    national telephone service . . . it has answered more
    than 130,000 calls at an average rate of 250 calls per
    day.

o   A skilled manager . . . managed a 24-person marketing
    department with a budget of $800,000+ (excluding
    advertising).

o   Ideas that work . . . with documented results to show
    that successful marketing is more than advertising.

o   An accomplished diplomat . . . highly effective with
    both administrative and medical personnel.

o   An established reputation . . . known for being a
    highly motivated achiever of even the most difficult
    marketing and management tasks.

I'm looking for a position at the level of vice-president or
national director of marketing and planning in a medical
setting committed to market-driven, consumer-focused treatment.

For a resume please call or write:

CHRISTINE R. KLOTZ

7409 Mt. Meeker Road / Longmont, Colorado 80501 / 303-530-5426

Judy K. Ramirez
2828 North Mobile
Chicago, Illinois 60634

January 29, 19--

Eric Erickson
Plant Manager
Baxter Pharmaseal
11060 Irma Drive
Chicago, Illinois 60630

Dear Mr. Erickson:

GOING, GOING, GONE!!

The last time I went to bat, I hit a home run! Let me have
the opportunity to join your successful team, and I can hit
a home run for you.

Here are just a few batting statistics for you to consider:

--   Developed, packaged, documented, advertised, and
      spearheaded marketing and sales effort for new
      computer software product that attained "premier"
      status in the Cardiology Marketplace.

--   Developed advertising and promotional pieces that
      led to 175 sales leads in a 12-month period.

--   Conducted field sales presentations/seminars to an
      audience of physicians, nurses, clinicians, and
      hospital administrative personnel. Achieved 100%
      close ratio.

Want to hear more? I would appreciate the opportunity to
further discuss not only my portfolio, but also how I can be
a successful member of your team.

Let's go to the World Series! Please call me at 232-9087.
Thanks for your time and consideration.

Sincerely,

Judy K. Ramirez

NEED HELP?

I love to repair, remodel, restore and
renovate. Freelance craftsman does
quality work at an excellent price. If
you need help from someone who's hard
working, dependable and who <u>cares</u>, call
me. (Will consider barter or swapping
for services.) For free estimate or
advice, call Scott at 771-4343.

Brad C. Bawmann
203 East Exposition Avenue
Denver, Colorado 80209
(303) 342-4638

3 August 19--

Mr. Marv Rockford
News Director
KCNC TV, Channel 4
1044 Lincoln Street
Denver, Colorado 80203

Dear Mr. Rockford,

First, fast and accurate are a sharp reporter's trademark.
Like your own staff, I can promise those qualities, and MORE,
to KCNC.

Over 25 times, my scoops have been replayed by a host of
Denver media. A more tenacious, ambitious and enthusiastic
reporter you won't find. And I'm ready to put my assets to
work for you.

Let's talk. I've enclosed a few clips for your inspection.
I'll call in a few days to arrange a time to meet.

Sincerely yours,

Brad C. Bawmann

BCB/s
Enclosures

Susan J. Ottinger
7242 South Tamarac Street
Englewood, Colorado 80112
(303) 771-8108

July 14, 19--

Mr. Robert Davidson
Regional Sales Manager
Medical Pharmaceuticals
2000 E. Marketplace Road
Denver, Colorado 80210

Dear Mr. Davidson:

Are you searching for a salesperson in the Denver area who is outgoing . . . confident . . . loyal to a company and product she believes in?

If so, then I am the person you are looking for.

I am presently employed--with five years as Retail Sales Manager for a home oxygen and medical equipment company--but now plan to intensify my sales career.

My background as a Registered Nurse fits beautifully with pharmaceuticals. Because of my teaching background, talking to your customers or to large groups is easy.

I want to meet you to learn more about Medical Pharmaceuticals. Please contact me at your earliest convenience.

Enthusiastically,

Susan J. Ottinger

SJO/ao

Robert L. Kaufmann
7020 Mountain Peak Drive
Littleton, Colorado 80127
(303) 979-3589

June 1, 19--

Mr. Frank P. Jones, President
HiTek Manufacturing Company
325 West Prospect Avenue
Mt. Prospect, Illinois 60056

Dear Mr. Jones:

1. Do you have trouble keeping track of your sales force?

2. Are you leaving markets untapped?

3. Are your salespeople spending enough time on your products?

4. Does your sales force need reinforcement or extra training from the main office?

If you have any of these problems, I would appreciate the opportunity to discuss working with you in a sales liaison capacity. I have broad sales supervisory experience. My background includes work with manufacturer's representatives and direct sales personnel.

I would propose to manage your field staff by means of good communications and frequent sales calls with them. This close support and involvement would free your time and ensure that your sales goals are met.

I will call you in the next week or so to determine your level of interest.

Very truly yours,

Robert L. Kaufmann

RLK:s

```
                    E. J. Carr
              17741 East Berry Place
             Aurora, Colorado  80015
                 (303) 693-7436

                September 27, 19--


Michael J. Levy
Vice President Operations
Sears
189 Wells Avenue
Newton, Massachusetts  02159

Dear Mr. Levy,

LOOKING FOR A SALESMAN OR GENERAL MANAGER?
      --ONE WITH A HIGHLY SUCCESSFUL TRACK RECORD?

      If you are, please take a look at me . . .

I've spent the last 19 years selling and servicing clients
with outstanding results for both the customer and my
company.

                 For example:

-- Sold company services exceeding $900,000 in 19-- (134% of
   quota) and $1,950,000 in 19-- (110% of yearly quota in
   only nine months).

-- Managed laboratories providing services to 15 states with
   80 employees generating in excess of $300,000 in monthly
   revenue.

I know I can bring the same positive results to your company
--or to some other growing company.

I will contact you in the next 10 to 14 days.  I would like
to hear your thoughts about where you think someone with my
skills and abilities might be needed.

                 Sincerely,



                 E. J. Carr

P.S.  I will not be asking you for a position in your firm,
      but would like five minutes of your time . . . and
      the benefit of your experience.
```

Marsha B. Winston
400 South Fourth Street
Clear Lake, Iowa 50428
(515) 420-7271 (w)
(515) 307-2977 (h)

August 30, 19--

Mr. Melvin G. Birky
Vice President, Human Resources
    Lutheran Medical Center
8300 West 38th Avenue
Wheat Ridge, CO 80033

Dear Mr. Birky:

-- Do you face increasing demands for training?

-- Do you want more efficient, cost-effective ways to
develop your staff?

-- Would you like to increase revenue by offering
continuing education for healthcare professionals?

<u>If so, I could be the "new blood" you need to put
innovative projects into operation.</u>

I am currently implementing a Regional Health Education
Center--the first of its kind in Iowa.

Last year I planned and directed the design of a
mandatory Nurses' Education Day which increased attendance
from 60% to 90%.

Because of my efforts, Saint Mary's Hospital is
recognized as "the" resource for health education in north
Iowa.

I would like the opportunity to talk with you. I will
call in the next week or so to talk briefly about your ideas
regarding education and training in healthcare today.

Sincerely yours,

Marsha B. Winston

I KNOW OF NO BETTER
TYPIST THAN
ME

<u>HOW CAN I HELP YOU</u>?

- I type 90 WORDS PER MINUTE.

- I believe a typewritten page should be a WORK OF ART.

- I'm a painstaking PROOFREADER.

- I finish all work ON TIME.

- I don't miss any DETAILS.

- I charge very REASONABLE RATES.

                         SO,

- If you have a manuscript (any length) or an article that
  needs to be typed,

                    CALL ME.

- If you have a term paper to be typed,

                    CALL ME.

- If you have anything to be typed,

                    CALL ME.

               Bobbi Winston
        <u>MY NUMBER IS: 232-5999</u>

        MONDAY THROUGH FRIDAY

Break Into New Companies

Even if you have an extensive personal network, you may eventually need to introduce yourself to strangers. There are literally hundreds of approaches to take, and you have to decide which fit you best.

If you write a good letter—and all these qualify—most businesspeople will be courteous enough to talk to you on the phone, if only briefly. Usually, a short conversation is enough.

Try several different kinds of letters. Don't get stuck doing only one thing. Too much repetition can kill you. You'll get bored with your campaign, and so will your readers!

R O N A L D   L.   E V A N S

June 29, 19--

Mr. R.L. Blackburn
Technical Sales, Inc.
1212 Woodland Place
Arlington Heights, IL   60004

Dear Mr. Blackburn:

I am writing to you because your company may be in need of
someone with my financial and business experience. Here are
some of the things I've recently accomplished:

-- As Chief Financial Officer of a major, regional wholesale
   distribution company, I reduced excess inventory by $2.5M.
   However, customer service was improved to 96% and turnover
   to 8.0 turns for stock goods. This inventory disposition
   reduced interest expense by $350K over a five-year period.

-- Implemented freight cost analysis to identify negative
   impact of absorbed costs on profitability. The company is
   now realizing annual savings of $240K.

-- Solicited, negotiated and managed insurance risk programs
   to reduce annual expense by $40K. Loss control programs
   improved worker's compensation experience ratio from 1.61
   to 1.00 in five years.

-- Reduced personnel within my areas of responsibility while
   expanding both capabilities and productivity. Absorbed
   functions from other departments during this period.

-- Improved quality of receivables, decreased bad debt
   expense and added new techniques for collection and
   protecting monies owed. Restaffed department. Reduced
   DSO by nine days, stabilized monthly collection percentage
   at 67%-68% level, and improved past due balances to less
   than 10% of receivables.

If you feel that your company is in need of someone with my
background, I would enjoy talking with you about any
opportunities. Please call me.

Very truly yours,

Ronald L. Evans

Robert K. Venture

May 22, 19--

Diane B. Holmes
Financial Search Group
7825 Washington Avenue, Suite 550
Minneapolis, Minnesota 55435

Dear Ms. Holmes:

I am currently seeking an executive position in the Thrift/Mortgage Banking industry and have taken this opportunity to enclose a brief synopsis of my experience for your review and consideration.

I am a thoroughly seasoned executive with extensive experience/expertise in all areas of mortgage banking. Specific areas of expertise include:

1. Turnaround situations where my management experience can be used to identify and then effect necessary operating efficiencies.

2. Establishing a complete turnkey operation to include organizational setup, getting all required approvals, developing and training a staff, establishing credit lines, setting up all departments including the design, development and automation of all key functions, creating necessary forms and manuals, and installing necessary operating procedures and controls.

3. Well-developed oral and written communication skills including the ability to reduce complex issues to basic understandable action plans.

4. Sharply developed negotiating skills.

5. Common sense approach to problematic situations.

Finally, I have taken pride over the last 15 years in the fact that during each year of employment I have generated substantiated income to my employer many times the amount of my annual compensation.

Please contact me at your earliest convenience so that we may discuss the possibilities in detail.

Sincerely,

Robert K. Venture

Richard R. Estes
6372 South Birch Court
Littleton, Colorado 80121
Office (303) 635-0987
Home (303) 635-0785

November 8, 19--

Mr. Robert Dillon
Dillon Laboratories
2111 Northwest Maple Street
Denver, Colorado 80215

Dear Mr. Dillon:

My accomplishments and experience in eight years of
corporate finance and ten years of public accounting should
be of interest to you if you need a seasoned financial
executive to help guide your organization.

I am a CPA with extensive experience in finance,
management, accounting, and tax. I am Vice-President and
Controller of a subsidiary of Allegis Corporation, the
Fortune 500 Company. I have also been controller of other
companies and have broad expertise gained through experience
with a wide range of clients and industries in public
accounting.

At Allegis I participate in policy-making with senior
executives and make and implement financial policy. I direct
all accounting, consolidations, budgeting and profit planning
for the subsidiary and its profit centers and work closely
with the company's tax, treasury, and legal staffs on related
matters. I participate in negotiations with outside
contractors, financiers, and customers and provide liaison
for internal and independent auditors. I report to the
subsidiary president and its board of directors and am
directly responsible for the quality and timeliness of work
of a finance staff of approximately 25 people.

In public accounting, I was an audit supervisor with
Mills & Company, the national CPA firm. I successfully
managed several of the largest engagements of the Colorado
Springs and Tucson offices, including construction,
hospitals, auto dealers, direct mail sales, and manufacturing
clients, among others. Coupled with experience in a large
local CPA firm, my audit and tax work at Mills provided a
broad base of expertise in finance and accounting.

My accomplishments include:

- Successfully operated multi-million dollar distressed income property pending its sale, enforcing stringent cash expenditure restrictions which saved $25,000. Negotiated increased sale price and terms at closing table to save $5.6 million sale.

- Confronted contractor operating in conflict of interest. Took control of records, negotiated release of files and recovered $12 million of the subsidiary's notes receivable.

- Prepared, evaluated and negotiated financing proposals for construction and permanent loans, working capital and equipment loans, and bond issues.

- Reorganized several headquarters and division finance staffs, including personnel decisions, which enhanced expertise, upgraded performance, and eliminated unnecessary work.

- As an audit supervisor in public accounting, discovered a major error by client in use of LIFO inventory. Recommended change in accounting method which allowed 50% increase in client's income.

I'm seeking a Vice-President, Finance or Chief Financial Officer position which is responsible for treasury, accounting, budgeting, profit planning, and tax, in which there is significant opportunity to contribute to achieving company goals.

I'd appreciate the opportunity to discuss how my qualifications and accomplishments may meet the needs of your company. Please phone me at my office (303) 241-7868 to schedule a meeting.

Sincerely,

Richard R. Estes

William R. Davidson
334 Ocean Front Boulevard
Panama City Beach, Florida   32407
(904) 343-4876

November 22, 19--

William S. Frank
CareerLab
7700 East Arapahoe Road, Suite 275
Englewood, Colorado 80112

Dear Mr. Frank:

I recently joined CSPA and perused your article entitled
"ASPA Is The Winning Edge." I liked what you said regarding
professional activities giving candidates an edge in the job
market. I also read your article in the "National Business
Employment Weekly" entitled "Get to Know Your Product."

I like your aggressive business style and would like to have
lunch with you to discuss business philosophies. When I plan
my next trip through Denver, I will call you several days in
advance to schedule a luncheon meeting.

I look forward to meeting you.

Respectfully,

William R. Davidson

WRD/jd

♥

Timothy P. Wood

November 20, 19--

Mr. William Frank
CareerLab
7700 East Arapahoe Road, Suite 275
Englewood, Colorado 80112

Dear Mr. Frank:

CareerLab's reputation has reached Scottsdale. Several
associates have mentioned your firm, and you specifically.
I understand you are well-connected with senior corporate
executives and do quality work. We should certainly talk
soon--It's very likely we can help each other. Here's a bit
of my background:

> After becoming President and CEO of Realty Corporation, led
> our 52 person, entrepreneurial, full-service, commercial
> real estate development team into 2 new markets--Phoenix and
> Denver--much to the dismay of our competition. Land sales
> volume set new records topping $40 million in one year. I
> understand the relationship between leadership and
> profitability.

> Our major joint ventures and key lender relationships have
> been more than a little surprised at our ability to make
> them money even in a tough market. I have streamlined the
> administrative staff, refocused the marketing efforts and
> fashioned various new and significant debt and equity
> financial structures. Overhead has been reduced 50% and
> building sales have doubled.

My multi-disciplined expansion of the company's businesses no
longer fits Realty's long-term strategy; our chairman and owner
recently announced his return from statewide political
involvement and desire to actively liquidate the company's
present inventory to accomplish his personal estate planning
goals. I have been offered opportunities to acquire portions of
the company's operations, but declined because of my desire to
work in a more substantial organization which optimizes my
contributions.

The timing is perfect to consider new opportunities. We should
talk soon. Please call me at your convenience next week (week of
11/27). I have alerted my secretary that you will be calling--
she'll put your call right through.

Sincerely,

Timothy P. Wood

Kenneth M. Evans
2133 Kipling Street
Wheat Ridge, Colorado 80033

August 26, 19--

Mr. Bill Frank
7700 East Arapahoe Road, Suite 275
Englewood, Colorado 80112

Dear Mr. Frank:

     I would like to thank you for your informative and
helpful column which appeared in The Rocky Mountain News on
Tuesday, August 24. If it is not too much trouble I would
appreciate hearing your thoughts on a problem I have been
having in implementing one of your suggestions.
Specifically, suggestion number 30 is difficult for me in
that no particularly helpful answer presents itself to the
most predictable and relevant question that presents itself
in interviews.

     To briefly fill you in on my situation: I have been
admitted to the Bar in Colorado for approximately one year.
I also have a Bachelor of Science in accounting. This is a
double threat which should make me very employable given the
conventional wisdom. The problem is that in today's tight
job market I find myself competing for entry-level positions
against attorneys and accountants who have three to five
years experience. The question which is always present,
spoken or unspoken is: "Why should we hire a person with
limited experience whom we will have to train, when for the
same money, we can hire a fully-trained experienced
professional?"

     Being a rational-economic man I can see their point.
It is difficult to justify not hiring an experienced person,
especially if they are to be paid an entry-level salary.
Many of my friends are facing the same sort of problem. We
are very interested in how to run the race when the starting
gate won't open.

     I fully realize that there may not be any adequate
answer to the experience gap question. In any case I would
be interested to hear your thoughts on this issue. If you
don't have time to write, please feel free to call me at
889-0098.

Very truly yours,

Kenneth M. Evans

KATHY THOMAS

September 20, 19--

Mr. Bill Frank
CareerLab
7700 East Arapahoe Road, Suite 275
Englewood, Colorado 80112

Dear Mr. Frank:

On Tuesday, August 24, I read your article in the Rocky Mountain News, "Fear Checklist Calms Job-Hunting Nerves." At the time, I was not looking for a job, but had plans to do so soon. So, I decided to clip your article and post it on my refrigerator.

Now that I am actively seeking employment, I have many times referred to your list of helpful hints in overcoming job-hunting fears. And, sure enough, they work! Thank you for sharing your valuable ideas with me and the countless others in my situation.

As you may have guessed, your article made quite an impression on me. Not only were your suggestions helpful, your writing revealed admirable qualities about your organization. After reading your work, I determined that you probably must run a company that recognizes the needs of its employees.

Anyone who can suggest:
      "Don't withdraw. Don't hide. Stay active."
      "Laugh more often. Cry more often. Get angry."
      "Share your feelings."
                                and
      "Develop an emotional support group."

must surely have keen discernment of human nature and needs. And, this is the type of organization I want to work for!

For this reason, I am enclosing my personal data "flyer" and my resume. I would appreciate your perusing these two items, in hopes you would consider me for employment.

In the meantime, I shall try to heed your suggestion, "Don't put all your eggs in one basket."

I would be delighted to hear from you soon!

Respectfully submitted,

Kathy Thomas

Michael Treasure, Jr.

January 3, 19--

Mr. Roger W. Davis
Boyden International
400 North Michigan Avenue
Chicago, IL 60614

Dear Mr. Davis:

You are recognized to be a proven expert in the Illinois career market. Perhaps we can combine forces to our mutual benefit.

At 40, I am a seasoned business professional with a rich and varied management background. My 12-year career at NyTek Oil Corporation has encompassed accounting, finance, budgeting and planning, financial analysis, project management, corporate communications, and policies/procedures.

My education includes an MBA and many years of experience working closely with senior management at NyTek, a 70 year-old, $500 million (assets) public corporation headquartered in Denver. I am a proven team leader and team player.

I have successfully planned and directed multi-million dollar, multi-departmental projects. I managed the dissolution and liquidation of $60 million of public limited partnerships and have directed asset sales in excess of $40 million. I completed the selection and installation of a corporate local area network of personal computers.

As Vice President of Investor Relations and Administration for NyTek Exploration, Inc., 10,000 limited partners have looked to me as their primary information link with the corporation. I provide investment status, drilling results, financial statements, tax projections, ownership and estate questions, and general hand-holding. An ongoing reduction in partnership activity by NyTek, however, leaves me underutilized and unchallenged.

I value my oil and gas experience, but being a business generalist, am not tied to a single industry. An updated resume is available at your request. Feel free to call me at home or at my direct office number, 697-5743. I would very much like a chance to chat with you about today's job market and, of course, my prospects in particular.

Very truly yours,

Michael Treasure, Jr.

Phillip T. Wright
1931 S. Cherry Street
Green Bay, Wisconsin 54301
(414) 432-2357

June 12, 19--

Mr. William S. Frank
President
CareerLab
7700 East Arapahoe Road, Suite 275
Englewood, Colorado 80112

Dear Mr. Frank:

Could CareerLab, or one of your divisions, benefit from a
strong financial officer?

Having been repeatedly recognized for my financial and
management contributions, I have a succession of rapid
promotions from Plant Controller to Division Controller to
Vice President Finance/Administration and Treasurer,
including operational experience and responsibility, in
companies whose sales ranged from $40 million to $700
million. On one occasion, I was considered for the
presidency of the company.

Although nonquantitative in nature, I am proudest of my
proficiency in managerial and leadership skills to build a
highly-respected and credible financial organization whose
resources were sought by members of the management team at
all levels of the corporate organization.

Opportunity and challenge in a growing company are my prime
considerations, but you should know that in recent years my
total compensation has been in the range of $75,000 to
$90,000.

If you have a need, I could make a valuable management
contribution. Thank you.

Sincerely,

Phillip T. Wright

Katherine M. Arnold
2324 Van Buren Street
El Cerrito, California 94530
(415) 473-3729

March 2, 19--

Mr. Lawrence K. Hill
Dean of Faculty
University of California
601 University Avenue
Sacramento, California 95814

Dear Mr. Hill:

This is perhaps the most unlikely letter seeking employment
that you have ever received. Why? Because I am very happy
in my present position. It offers the responsibility and
challenges I need. I have discretion and authority, plus an
opportunity to travel, to take on new projects and to be
innovative.

Why, then, am I sending you the attached resume? Simply
because the qualities that make me an effective employee
require continuing opportunity to grow and develop. I have
gone as far as I can developing the office that I head. I
realistically acknowledge the fact of future budget cutbacks
for local government in general and non-violent activities by
law enforcement agencies. Good sense and an awareness of
what motivates me tell me to explore the possibilities of a
new work experience.

I hope you will take time to glance through my resume. My
background and experience are varied and lend themselves to a
wide range of possible applications.

I will call to see if we may discuss how I can be of value to
your organization.

Sincerely,

Katherine M. Arnold

Enclosure

Brad C. Bawmann
203 East Exposition Avenue
Denver, Colorado 80209

June 15, 19--

Mr. Lawrence Paddock
Managing Editor
The Boulder Daily Camera
1048 Pearl Street
Boulder, Colorado 80302

Dear Mr. Paddock,

I'm not going to pretend I've learned it all as a reporter
for a Denver weekly newspaper. But I've learned an awful lot
and I'm ready to help The Camera become the paper it aspires
to be.

A more tenacious, aggressive reporter you won't find. Your
own Entertainment Editor can attest to my drive, energy and
enthusiasm--which are more than any three people might enjoy.
I'm a go-getter, never satisfied with mediocrity.

Mr. Paddock, let's talk. I'm anxious to put my assets to
work for you. I've enclosed a few clips. You may notice
that many of the stories are scoops, which triggered other
attention by Denver's electronic and print media.

I'll call in a few days to arrange a time to get together.

Looking forward to meeting you soon.

Sincerely yours,

Brad C. Bawmann

Enclosures

Patrick Kellogg
1420 Tenth Avenue
Portland, Maine 04110
(207) 385-4758

December 2, 19--

Ms. Kimberly Clark
Division Supervisor
Neenah Paper
Neenah, Wisconsin 54956

Dear Ms. Clark:

Can you use a person who has:

* An imaginative way of handling problems?

* Verbal skills, and the ability to deliver messages
  with impact?

* Personal confidence, especially in face-to-face
  contact?

* An extraordinary sensitivity to others?

* Organizing and planning ability?

I have these talents as illustrated in the enclosed resume.
I would like to put them to work for Neenah Paper as a
financial public relations specialist.

Although it may seem unlikely that Neenah Paper has a need
for an individual with these skills, I would like to share a
few ideas I have that could benefit Neenah Paper and your
investors.

I will call Monday or Tuesday of next week to determine when
a brief meeting would be appropriate.

Sincerely,

Patrick Kellogg

Enclosure

T. CRAIG LINCOLN

April 16, 19--

Mr. William T. Randolph
Executive Vice President Sales
Caterpillar Tractor Company
100 Northeast Adams
Peoria, Illinois 61629

Dear Mr. Randolph:

I've always been fascinated with the "Big Yellow" Caterpillar image. As a child, I received a toy Caterpillar tractor, and the gift has lasted as long as my fascination with Caterpillar.

> In 1972 in Fresno, California, a Caterpillar representative brought your corporate story alive. The movie which told your story was incredible. It showed your approach to industrial education, international marketing (with special interest being given to the up-and-coming Third World Nations) and an overview of Caterpillar philosophies.

At a basic level, I was sold. If I hadn't been working on contract, I would have approached you the next day.

<u>I could very well imagine myself working in corporate design somewhere within the Caterpillar Organization.</u>

My background is sufficiently varied to lend you many avenues of expertise through good sound communications design at all levels within Caterpillar.

> --From corporate image to international education.

> --From advertising to product marketing.

> --From film to video design.

Caterpillar still maintains the strongest image in design, engineering and manufacturing of heavy equipment in the world. Your name is synonymous with building. And I want to be a part of your team.

In the next few weeks I will be in touch with you to see if you want to discuss this further.

Sincerely,

T. Craig Lincoln

Norman L. Steele
339 South Broadway
Redondo Beach, California   90277
(213) 540-2545 (o)
(213) 454-8383 (h)

May 22, 19--

Mr. Thomas K. Allison
MTK Incorporated
33015 Paramount Boulevard
Downey, California 90241

Dear Mr. Allison:

I am searching for a young, aggressive company that has the desire to become a national and then international leader in their field. If your objective is to increase your stock price and sell to a large conglomerate, then our goals are not compatible.

I have followed your fine company for the last three years and invested in it as a result. Now that the financial community has recognized your potential, as evidenced by the $18 share price, I hope you view this as the beginning and not the end. Our country needs entrepreneurs with vision and dreams who are willing to invest in the future.

I am a very knowledgeable individual, but more importantly, I am creative, imaginative, and wish to share in someone's dream. As you can see from my resume, I have been responsible for the accounting, finance, and leasing areas, as well as substantial involvement in the tax, employee benefits, and corporate secretary functions. You may not yet realize you need a person like me, but I believe you have reached a stage where my experience can be of great value as you continue to grow.

Please contact me at your earliest convenience.

Sincerely,

Norman L. Steele

Wesley T. Cornell
123 Moss Hill Lane
Laguna Hills, California 92653
(714) 586-2998

January 6, 19--

William S. Frank
President
CareerLab
7700 East Arapahoe Road, Suite 275
Englewood, Colorado 80112

Dear Mr. Frank:

In light of the phenomenal 600% growth in outplacement since
19--, there is a strong probability that your plans for
CareerLab call for continued growth and expansion for 19--
and beyond.

If so, then perhaps my enclosed resume will be of interest.
In it, you will find the highlights of a progressive career
in outplacement services. My background encompasses all
aspects of building and managing an outplacement firm from
start-up through national expansion.

As a follow up to this letter, I hope to contact you directly
by phone to learn your reaction to my background and
determine whether setting up an exploratory meeting is
indicated.

I have enjoyed bringing my background to your attention and
look forward to speaking with you soon.

Sincerely,

Wesley T. Cornell

WTC:bh
Enclosure

Mr. William Robertson
Executive Vice President
Ogilvy & Mather, Inc.
Two West 45th Street
New York, New York 10036

November 18, 19--

Dear Mr. Robertson,

Advertising agencies are different in New York than here
in Denver. Much bigger. More professional. Better people
who are paid better. That's why I'm coming to New York to
look for work.

I'm intending to send this note to the executive who
does the hiring for the Creative Department. From your title
I think that's you. But I'm not sure. So if I'm talking to
the wrong person please send this in the right direction.

I was thinking about the difference between advertising
and public relations the other day. One difference, it seems
to me, is that in advertising there is an emphasis on ads as
products. More so than in public relations where the concern
seems to be more on a total image.

The emphasis on ads as things which perform a function
explains in part my love for advertising. Craftsmanship
becomes very important. Making better and better ads
provides a satisfaction and sense of accomplishment.

I've always liked making things, but ever since I
started making ads I haven't enjoyed making anything as much.
My goal is to see if I can find a job doing the thing I enjoy
most.

My interests are primarily in the area of copywriting,
but I also do layouts. I've put together a portfolio of my
best work. I'd like to show it to you.

I'll be in New York Monday, Tuesday, Wednesday and
Thursday. November 27, 28, 29, and 30.

I'd really like to meet with you sometime during those
four days. I'll call you as soon as I arrive to see if we
can arrange to meet at a time that is convenient for you.

Sincerely,

Jim Brodie

1225 College Avenue / Boulder, Colorado 80302/ (303)449-5048

J I M   B R O D I E

August 26, 19--

Red Gates, Creative Director
Tallant-Yates Advertising
502 Fifth Avenue
New York, New York 10036

Dear Mr. Gates:

When I got my first ad agency copywriting job I thought all copywriters were pretty much the same.

I soon found I was very mistaken. Some writers were specialists. Others, generalists. Some used humor whenever they could. Others did the same with music.

For myself, I discovered I had a preference for technical products. I like the challenge of having to find out how a complex product worked before I could write about it. I much preferred working on industrial accounts to writing about candy bars or ice cream. And I discovered I was good at it.

Over the years I've written copy for agricultural chemicals, oil drilling equipment, building materials, dairy farming equipment, electronic sensing devices, mining equipment and cable-stringing trucks.

A year ago I came back to school to complete a master's in journalism, a project I had been working on and off for several years. Freelance jobs helped carry me through the year. Now I'm starting to shake the bushes for another full-time copywriting job.

I thought I'd contact you first because your client list looks pretty technical. And that excites me.

I'd like to meet with you, at your convenience, and show you my book.

I'll call in a few days to see if we can arrange a time to meet.

Sincerely,

Jim Brodie

1050 14th Street / Boulder, Colorado 80302 / (303) 440-8477

Jim Brodie / 2258 Fairmount Avenue
Cincinnati, Ohio 45238/ 513-651-3892

February 16, 19--

Mr. Rick Olson
Creative Director
Campbell-Mithun Inc.
210 Park Avenue
New York, New York 10021

Dear Mr. Olson,

As a Creative Director you know how difficult it is to get a first job as a copywriter.

Agencies hire copywriters when they get new business. They need experienced writers who can handle the new business. Not beginners.

Training programs have been trimmed or cut entirely in an effort to streamline agency costs.

So there's a gap in the skill level of graduating students and the level required on the job.

I've been studying advertising for some time. As I'm approaching the time when I'll be seeking a full-time copywriting job I've become aware of the gap between school and work.

I feel an internship is a possible way to bridge this gap.

I'm in the process now of arranging an internship with an agency in the Twin Cities. Ed Richardson at Martin-Williams gave me your name as a person to contact at Campbell-Mithun.

I wonder if you'd have some time to meet with me and discuss the possibility of arranging an internship at your agency?

I'll call in a few days to see if we can arrange a time to meet.

Sincerely,

Jim Brodie

Jack P. Fallon
783 Whister Drive
Houston, Texas 77027
(713) 617-3893

Mr. William D. Cooke
Regional Manager
Amoco Production Company
1717 East 71st Street
Tulsa, Oklahoma 74136

Dear Mr. Cooke:

I am writing to you regarding employment opportunities that
you may have for a Drilling Engineer or Cementing Specialist.

Due to current economic conditions, Halliburton has found it
necessary to terminate my employment. For the past few years
I have enjoyed a very good working relationship with Amoco
and I would like you to consider me for employment. I think
my background in cementing [oil wells] would be an asset to
Amoco, especially in today's market.

Let me give you a brief summary of my qualifications:

- Five years field experience in cement slurry design
  and placement procedures for deep wells in
  Utah/Wyoming Overthrust Belt.
- Four years experience in supervision and operation
  of cement test equipment (high pressure consistometer,
  fluid loss, autoclave, etc.).
- Made major contributions to development of
  Halliburton's Slurry Placement Analysis program
  (cement job simulator).
- Contributed to development of annulus return rate
  monitoring system to measure U-tube effect during
  cement placement.

I would appreciate your taking the time to review my resume.
(I have also included a list of personal references whom I
think would give me a favorable recommendation.)

Thanks for considering me. After you've had a chance to
review my background, I'll call to hear your reactions.

Sincerely,

Jack P. Fallon

Brad C. Bawmann
203 East Exposition Avenue
Denver, Colorado 80209
(303) 980-5643

June 15, 19--

Mr. Bill Baxter
Program Manager Scoopline Services
Mountain Bell
1005 Seventeenth Street
Denver, Colorado 80202

Dear Mr. Baxter:

If there's one thing I've learned in doing several stories
involving Mountain Bell, it's that your company is a vibrant
and growing force in our community.

The limits of Mountain Bell are only determined by the limits
of its employees. And I'd like to help [Mountain] Bell set
its limits even higher.

Mr. Baxter, as you know I am an aggressive, tenacious
reporter with an eye for detail. My drive, energy, and
enthusiasm are enough for any three people. I'm not easily
satisfied with mediocrity--nor is Mountain Bell.

Let's talk. I'd like to put my assets to work for your
company. I've enclosed some clips and a resume for your
inspection.

I'll call soon to arrange an appointment to get together.

Thanks for your time and consideration.

Sincerely yours,

Brad C. Bawmann

Enclosures

August 8, 19--

Mr. William S. Frank
Principal
CareerLab
7700 East Arapahoe Road, Suite 275
Englewood, Colorado 80112

Dear Mr. Frank:

I am writing you because of my interest in joining your firm
in the outplacement industry.

My strengths include a broad knowledge of industries,
organizations and jobs, an intense curiosity about people and
careers, and a desire to help displaced employees find career
satisfaction.

During my business career of 22 years, I have held various
positions including my current position as a Human Resources
Consultant for a New York-based financial services firm of
20,000 employees.

<u>As Regional Marketing Manager:</u>

> Marketed employee communication services and had profit
> and loss responsibility for eight offices in the
> Southwest.

<u>As Corporate Personnel Director:</u>

> Installed a company-wide performance evaluation system
> and developed corporate human resources policies.

<u>As a Senior Benefit Consultant:</u>

> Sold, designed, and implemented employee welfare
> programs and trained employees for Southwest clients.

My consulting clients have included Motorola, Crown
Zellerbach, Arizona Public Service, Alcan Aluminum, San
Francisco State University, and Reliance Insurance Company.

If your firm has any expansion plans in the Southwest, I
would welcome the opportunity to discuss them in a brief
meeting.

Very truly yours,

Charles D. Bridgeport

Charles D. Bridgeport
2493 Central Avenue
Woodland Hills, California 91367
(818) 788-3873

August 18, 19--

William S. Frank
Principal
CareerLab
7700 East Arapahoe Road, Suite 275
Englewood, Colorado 80112

Dear Mr. Frank:

This is a follow-up to my letter of August 8, 19-- regarding
my interest in joining your firm in the outplacement
industry.

Attached is my resume outlining more details on my work and
education background.

As I mentioned in my previous letter, I empathize with
displaced managers and believe in career guidance to assist
individuals to find career satisfaction.

If your organization plans to expand in the Southwest, I
would like to discuss my background in more detail with you.

Very truly yours,

Charles D. Bridgeport

CDB:bh
Enclosure

Charles D. Bridgeport
2493 Central Avenue
Woodland Hills, California   91367
(818) 788-3873

November 28, 19--

William S. Frank
Principal
CareerLab
7700 East Arapahoe Road, Suite 275
Englewood, Colorado   80112

Dear Mr Frank:

This is a second letter to my initial inquiry in August about entering the outplacement field.

I have attached a resume summarizing my human resources experience and indicating my desire to enter the outplacement business on a full-time basis.

I solicit your comments and suggestions on how I can effectively make this transition into the outplacement industry in 19--.

Very truly yours,

Charles D. Bridgeport

CDB:ml
Enclosure

Increase Response to Your Letters

There is nothing more frustrating than mailing dozens of letters and not hearing from anyone. Response forms included with letters help guarantee answers when you send mailings.

Here's how it works. You enclose a response card or letter and a self-addressed stamped envelope (SASE) with your mailing, so the recipient can reply by checking a few boxes or by answering one or two questions. It's quick, it's easy, and it gets a fast response. Best of all, it works.

You can use response forms with virtually anyone: friends, recruiters, employers, venture capitalists—you name it. Be as creative as you can.

Jon B. Bartoshek
593 South Cole Street
Morrison, Colorado 80465
(303) 463-8326

March 15, 19--

Mr. Lawrence A. Wilson
President
HCB Contractors
4600 National Bank Building
Dallas, Texas 75202

Dear Mr. Wilson:

I am moving my family to Houston in the very near future and
am seeking an entry-level construction management job.

The enclosed material helps to explain <u>what I can do for you</u>
and shows <u>why you might want to hire me</u>.

To answer, please return the enclosed response letter
(postage is paid) or call me in the evenings at the above
number.

Sincerely,

Jon B. Bartoshek

Enclosures

FROM:
Jon B. Bartoshek
593 South Cole Street
Morrison, Colorado 80465

TO:
Mr. Lawrence A. Wilson
President
HCB Contractors
4600 National Bank Building
Dallas, Texas 75202

REPLY LETTER

_____ Please call me for an appointment.

Our telephone number is:_____

_____ Please call I'd be willing to give advice.

_____ We're not hiring right now, but expect to be
hiring on _____ (Date).

_____ You're talking to the wrong person.
You should contact:

Name: _____

Title: _____

Company: _____

Address: _____

City, State, zip: _____

Comments:_____

_____

_____

_____

M I C H A E L   D.   B U R N S

January 26, 19--

Mr. Leslie S. Carey
President
Wendy's
5000 Medco Road
Birmingham, Alabama   35217

Dear Mr. Allen:

Are you unable to take advantage of attractive market opportunities because of lack of senior management people?

o   Do you have plenty of good ideas--but too few managers to put them into play?

o   Does your rapid pace leave insufficient time to develop good managers?

o   Are you concerned about missing the window of opportunity as the stronger companies position themselves for the long term?

If so, perhaps I can help. I recently took a fast growth company that was having serious performance, cash control and internal coordination problems--turned it around, and then added $42 million to reserves. My business career is extensive and includes one start-up, two turnarounds and substantial merger and acquisition experience. I can hit the ground running.

My depth of experience in management means I can offer you a lot. Please take the time to give me a call or fill out the enclosed reply letter. I look forward to hearing from you.

Best regards,

Michael D. Burns

Enclosure

FROM:
Mr. Leslie S. Carey
President
Wendy's
5000 Medco Road
Birmingham, Alabama   35217

TO:
Michael D. Burns
Two Thousand Oak Towers
2000 West Federal Street
Boston, Massachusetts   02110

Dear Michael:

_____   Please give me a call, so I can get to know more
about you.

_____
          Telephone Number

_____   I suggest you talk to the following people:

_____ Name

_____ Address

_____ Telephone

_____ Name

_____ Address

_____ Telephone

_____   I don't have any ideas for you right now, but

contact me again after _____ (date).

Comments: _____

_____

_____

                    Sincerely,

                    Mr. Leslie S. Carey

Kenneth L. Hargrove
2475 S. Oakland Circle
Aurora, Colorado 80014
(303) 696-6754

September 24, 19--

Mr. Clifford Allen
Control Software, Inc.
777 S. 6th Street
Louisville, CO 80027

Dear Mr. Allen:

I am interested in joining your firm in the development of
its exploration workstation.

My strengths include a broad knowledge of petroleum
exploration techniques, a strong interest in exploration
workstation development, and a demonstrated ability to manage
a profitable business.

During my ten years in the petroleum industry, I have held
both geological and geophysical positions, have conducted
research in the use of geophysical workstations, and have
been a principal in a geophysical services firm.

As Senior Geologist
Researched seismostratigraphic exploration needs and assisted
the development of a geophysical computer-aided workstation
for a major oil company.

As Geophysicist
Developed seismostratigraphic expression of subtle traps and
managed a $4.4 million program to exploit the results with a
large integrated petroleum firm.

As Principal
Guided start-up geophysical services firm to $5 million in
annual sales while managing its geophysical research and data
processing efforts.

I am interested in integrating my knowledge and interest in
seismic stratigraphy with your computer-aided workstation. I
have several concepts that integrate seismic attributes with
the expression of stratigraphy that would be ideal on a
workstation.

As your firm may be developing such capabilities, I would
welcome the opportunity to discuss them with you.

Sincerely,

Kenneth L. Hargrove

From:

Mr. Clifford Allen
Control Software, Inc.
777 S. 6th Street
Louisville, CO 80027

Dear Ken,

I'm returning the questionnaire that was included in you
letter of September 24, 19--.

_____ Please call me to discuss your concepts and
abilities

_____ Please call to set up a meeting

_____ This letter reached the wrong person. You should
contact:

Name _____

Title _____

Phone _____

_____ We have no plans to develop such capabilities at
this time. However you might contact:

Name _____

Title _____

Company _____

Comments:

_____

_____

_____

_____

Bill Frank & Associates

February 3, 19--

Dr. Charles D. Crane
American Geriatric Society
1503 Downing Street
Denver, Colorado 80218

Dear Dr. Crane:

<u>Are you a good candidate for PR?</u>

-- On the cutting edge of your profession?

-- Doing something new and different that the public
   needs to know?

-- Enthusiastic about what you're doing?

-- Already successful, desiring more success?

<u>Are you concerned about increased competition in your field?</u>

** In 1970 there were 310,000 doctors; in the year 2000
   there are likely to be 643,000.

** <u>Private Practice</u> magazine says that "doctors must
   realize that no matter where they went to medical
   school or how 'board certifiable' they are, they are
   not guaranteed a successful practice." (July 19--).

** "Physicians feel they are under siege," says
   Dr. Richard Wilbur, Executive Vice President of the
   Council of Medical Specialty Societies.

<u>Public relations (PR) can help you specialize or increase the
size of your practice without advertising</u>.

(Last year one of our clients received free radio, television
and newspaper interviews worth $28,824.50. Another doctor
added 250 patients to his practice.)

If the topic of "practice-building" interests you, I'd like
to visit your office to show you what we do and explain the
results others have gotten.

Please return the enclosed response letter, or call
(303) 771-4357.

Warm personal regards,

William S. Frank

BUSINESS REPLY LETTER

FROM:
Dr. Charles D. Crane
American Geriatric Society
1503 Downing Street
Denver, Colorado 80218

TO:
Mr. Bill Frank
Bill Frank & Associates
Denver Corporate Center
7800 East Union Avenue, Suite 420
Denver, Colorado 80237

Dear Bill:

1. _____ Please call me for an appointment.

2. _____ Send your brochure and written materials.

3. _____ I don't need your services right now, but I would
like to find out more about what you do.

4. _____ Send articles on marketing for physicians.

5. _____ Let's discuss a marketing seminar for our group.

6. _____ Please keep me on your mailing list.

_____
Signature

JAMES J. PRECUP
1969 East 116th Avenue
Northglenn, Colorado 80233
(303) 450-9587

September 25, 19--

Mrs. Beverly Richard, President
Intrawest Bank of Northglenn
10701 Melody Drive
Northglenn, Colorado 80234

Dear Ms. Richard:

Most people can't sell!

They're doing a job they don't wish to do.

It isn't natural for them.

For me, sales is natural.

> I'm a trained professional.
> I'll hit the ground running.
> No downtime.
> Quick start-up!

I'll start producing sales for you immediately--tomorrow.

If you'd like to learn how you can improve sales TOMORROW,
please telephone me at your earliest convenience, or return
the enclosed postage-paid questionnaire.

Cordially,

Jim Precup

JJP:pr
Enclosure

From: _____

_____

Dear Jim:

_____ I'd like to meet you. Please call (number)_____
for an appointment.

_____ I'd be willing to talk with you on the telephone to
trade ideas. Call me at (number)_____

_____ You're talking to the wrong person. You should
contact:

_____
Name   Title   Phone

_____ We're not hiring now. Re-contact me after_____

_____ We're not hiring now. Try this company:

_____
Name   Title

_____
Company

_____
Street Address

_____
Telephone

_____ You have my name and title wrong. It should read:

_____   _____
Name   Title

_____
Comments

_____

_____

_____

_____

BRUCE D. ROBERTSON
3182 South Holly Street
Denver, Colorado 80222
(303) 756-7453 (H)
(303) 779-1417 (W)

October 15, 19--

Robert B. Wood
Vice President and Treasurer
Sears Roebuck & Co.
10 Riverside Plaza
Chicago, Illinois 60606

Dear Mr. Wood:

As a fellow member of the Financial Executive's Institute, I
want you to know that I am seeking a permanent position in
International Business as a Manager of Administration and
Finance. This decision is based upon a careful, in-depth
analysis of my abilities and experiences. Consequently, I
have put together a current resume in order to market myself
for what I believe will be the most productive and exciting
years of my life.

A friend of mine from my STC days in London, John Dexter,
works for Burroughs in London. If you see him, give him my
regards.

I am totally open to any industry with positions located
almost anywhere in the world.

Should you become aware of any of your friends, or business
associates, who may be in the market for new blood and
innovative thinking, I would appreciate your listing their
names and phone number on the enclosed, postage-paid
questionnaire and returning it to me.

Also, any advice or assistance that you can give me would
be greatly appreciated.

Sincerely,

Bruce D. Robertson

BDR:pr
Enclosures

April, 19--

FROM:
Robert B. Wood
Vice President and Treasurer
Sears Roebuck & Co.
10 Riverside Plaza
Chicago, IL   60606

Dear Bruce:

I'm returning your questionnaire. I have the following
information for you.

_____I'd be willing to talk with you to trade information and
ideas.

     Please call me at (number)_____

You could contact the following people:

     Name_____

     Title_____

     Company_____

     Telephone_____

     Name_____

     Title_____

     Company_____

     Telephone_____

Comments:_____

_____

_____

MICHAEL D. BURNS

January 18, 19--

Mr. William B. Nolan
Partner
Advanced Technology Ventures
1000 El Camino Real, Suite 210
Menlo Park, California 94025

Dear Bill:

Is your firm capitalizing companies in need of experienced managers? If so, I would like you to be aware of my credentials. Enclosed is a resume and an excerpt from <u>Fortune</u> magazine which summarizes my experience and highlights a few of my accomplishments.

Most of my career has been in management and the financial areas. With participation in two turnarounds and one startup, my experience has been varied and I have built a consistently successful track record. I am adaptable and learn fast as evidenced by my level of accomplishment in jobs that varied greatly in content, and in three different industries. I have found that I greatly enjoy working in smaller, more entrepreneurial businesses and that is what I am looking for now.

My job target is a position with a high management content, either in the operations or the financial area. It would ideally be with a company that has an entrepreneurial outlook, perhaps be five to ten years old and has sales of less than $100 million. I have no particular industry preference, having worked in several, and am open to any situation that is challenging and will make good use of my skills.

I am flexible on immediate compensation if there is adequate potential for growth. An opportunity to earn equity would be attractive. Although I am not seeking investment opportunities, I might consider a limited investment in the right situation. Geographic location is not a major consideration.

Bill, this should cover the key points. I will be glad to provide any other information you may need and can provide strong references when appropriate. I'll call you next week.

Sincerely,

Michael D. Burns

RESPONSE LETTER

FROM:
Mr. William B. Nolan
Partner
Advanced Technology Ventures
1000 El Camino Real, Suite 210
Menlo Park, California 94025

TO:
Michael D. Burns

Dear Michael:

_____ Please give me a call for a telephone interview.

_____
     Telephone Number

_____ I need more information. Please send _____

_____

_____ We do not invest in areas appropriate for your skills.

_____ I suggest you talk to the following people:

_____ Name

_____ Address

_____ Telephone

_____ Name

_____ Address

_____ Telephone

_____ I don't have any ideas for you right now, but contact me again after _____ (date).

Comments: _____

_____

Sincerely,

Mr. William B. Nolan

Uncover Hidden Job Markets

When asked why Sony Corporation has been so successful, Chairman Akio Morita said, "We never follow. We do what others don't." To me, that's the essence of marketing: going where others aren't.

Most job-hunters confine themselves to traditional job- search approaches, like answering want ads and working with recruiters. Anyone who tries something else will have a big advantage. Few people write to career consultants, conference attendees, media people, and venture capitalists.

That's why you should try it.

The letters here will give you some good ideas, or you could modify your recruiter letter for this audience.

Phillip T. Wright
1931 S. Cherry Street
Green Bay, Wisconsin 54301
(414) 432-2357

March 17, 19--

William S. Frank
President
CareerLab
7700 East Arapahoe Road, Suite 275
Englewood, Colorado 80112

Dear Bill:

As a career consultant, you must from time-to-time come
across companies that are in need of a strong financial
management team. I am a Chief Financial Officer in search of
a challenging corporate position where my financial skills
can be utilized in the development and growth of an
organization.

I am a highly-motivated individual with excellent people and
leadership skills, high business ethics, good management and
business acumen, and a verifiable track record of many
successful financial and business achievements. I am also
willing to work long and arduous hours to accomplish the
desired results.

My experience includes multi-location manufacturing and
retail, real estate, IPOs, public stock and debt offerings,
cash management, banking relations, loan negotiations, tax
planning, budgeting and long-range planning, acquisitions and
divestitures, SEC reporting, data processing, shareholder
relations, and general office administration.

I have taken the liberty of enclosing a resume for your
review. Any assistance or advice that you can give me will
be greatly appreciated. If you have any questions, please do
not hesitate to contact me at (414) 432-2357.

Very truly yours,

Phillip T. Wright

PTW/rj
Enclosure

*

March 18, 19--

I am seeking employment at the executive
level of a small company. In particular,
I am requiring a position with high
visibility that has a significant impact
on both the operating and strategic
decisions of the company.

Specific management positions in which I
have experience and for which I am
qualified include Vice President of
Finance, Vice President of Manufacturing,
and Chief Operating Officer. In addition
to Fortune 100 companies, I have
experience with a start-up company that
successfully acquired venture funding,
bank financing, and a merger partner.

My education includes a BSEE and MBA.

I am only interested in opportunities in
Boulder County.

If you have referrals that will help
expand my job search network, please
contact me at either number below.

Keith B. Kellogg

Home: 424-1300
Office: 449-2208

James B. Garrington
343 East Randolph Avenue
Chicago, IL   60601
(312) 782-6930

February 10, 19--

Bruce J. Howard
Director of Pilot Operations
United Airlines
O'Hare International Airport
Chicago, Illinois 60601

Dear Mr. Howard:

Your company's projected growth was highlighted in this month's <u>Professional Pilot</u> magazine. I enjoyed reading the article and am hopeful for the growth it projected.

As a professional pilot with six years experience, I thought my background might interest you, since you appear to have future jobs opening up.

My most recent experience was with Regional Carrier operations, and I have listed some of my experience:

- Flew single-pilot IFR for Air Taxi/Air Cargo in the mountain states region.

- Maintained terminal operation for Air Cargo away from home base using C-210/C-310 equipment.

- Maintained consistent record of on-schedule operations in flying jobs.

At 26 years and unattached, I have a degree from Mesa College. Relocation and travel present no problem.

I will call you in a few days to introduce myself and learn more about your operation.

Very truly yours,

Dick Baldwin

Richard H. Greene
891 West 23rd Avenue
Burlington, Vermont 05402
(802) 862-4277

December 2, 19--

Mr. Marshall Austin
President
Neenah Paper
Neenah, Wisconsin 54956

Dear Mr. Austin,

I recently noticed Neenah Paper's first quarter earnings.
But despite this significant improvement, I also noted
Neenah's common stock is selling far below book value on the
NASD-OTC market.

I would like to share a few ideas I developed while working
for Hill and Knowlton in financial relations. Many of our
clients had a problem apparently similar to Neenah's. I
think a brief meeting could benefit Neenah Paper and its
investors.

I will call Monday or Tuesday of next week to determine when
a brief meeting would be appropriate.

Sincerely,

Richard H. Greene

Kenneth K. Phillips
1800 One Dallas Centre
Dallas, Texas 75201
(214) 979-1200 (w)
(214) 979-4653 (h)

March 31, 19--

Mr. Steven A. Baldwin
The Dallas Venture Group
4500 LBJ Freeway
Dallas, Texas 75240

Dear Mr. Baldwin:

I have recently left Texas Instruments as Vice President
of Operations and am looking to join a small to medium sized
manufacturing company in a chief executive or senior
management role. My intentions would also include obtaining
an equity position in the company.

I have been very successful and have been acknowledged
for my accomplishments in startup operations in both domestic
U.S. and international locations.

Most recently, I have been consulting with Toy
Manufacturing, Inc. managing a major new product introduction. I have been coordinating the engineering pilot
runs, sourcing, and manufacturing startup for TWI's main-line
new product being introduced this fall. This product is now
being shipped to customers per the original plan.

My annual salary and bonus compensation at TI totaled
$140,000 annually. While I prefer remaining in the Dallas
area, I will definitely consider relocation for the right
opportunity.

I have enclosed a copy of my resume which details the record
of my accomplishments over the past several years. I would
appreciate your taking a few moments to look it over for a
possible match with one of your start-up companies.

I will call you within the next week to discuss any possible
opportunities of which you may be aware.

Thank you very much for your consideration.

Sincerely,

Kenneth K. Phillips

13

Say "Thank You"

The best marketing letter in the world is one that simply says "Thank you, I appreciate you." There's no more powerful appeal. No one I know gets tired of hearing it.

Use a handwritten note when you want to say thank you quickly and effectively. Use plain stationery, nothing fancy. Keep it businesslike. Make sure your handwriting is easy to read. My note cards are 3 1/2 x 5″ folded, which is an ideal size.

Use a letter to say thank you at greater length. Letters must be professionally typewritten—no exceptions. Since a thank-you letter is often a sales letter in disguise, put some "sell" into it. Send one to everyone who gives you any kind of help, no exceptions, no excuses.

Nancy L. Green
49 Locust Street
Denver, Colorado 80222

June 22, 19--

Karen Bewley
Manager of Compensation and Benefits
National Jewish Hospital
1400 Jackson Street
Denver, Colorado 80206

Dear Karen:

Just a quick note to thank you for my interview on June 21.
I find your interviewing style very refreshing, and I
appreciate your openness and honesty.

I am very excited about the compensation and benefits
assistant position and the chance to work with such a great
team. This position is exactly what I have been looking for,
and I sincerely hope I am the person you are looking for as
well. If you have any questions or concerns, please feel
free to contact me at 736-7374. Thank you once again,
and I hope to hear from you soon.

Sincerely,

Nancy L. Green

D A V I D   K.   S A W Y E R

July 21, 19--

Dr. William W. Anderson
Vice President, Technical Affairs
Motor Vehicle Manufacturers
   Association
300 New Center Building
Detroit, Michigan 48202

Dear Dr. Anderson:

Thank you very much for considering me for a position with
MVMA. I enjoyed talking to you and the senior staff. In
your position, you enjoy a unique view of the automotive
industry. From my resume and our discussions, you have a
pretty good idea of what I am interested in and can do for
the industry. I would appreciate it if you would pass on
any opportunities you see in the areas of program management
or technology planning and management.

Thanks again for your help.

Sincerely,

David K. Sawyer, Director
Industrial Business Development

DKS/jlg

STEVEN D. JORGENSEN
4482 South Argonne Court
Aurora, Colorado 80015
303/690-4459

February 13, 19--

Mr. Paul Gardner
Texas Oil Company
P.O. Box 269
Houston, Texas 77056

Dear Paul:

I wish to thank you and the other staff members at Texas Oil
Company for taking the time out of your busy schedules to
interview me last Thursday. I feel the day went extremely
well and I appreciate the opportunity to talk to each of you.

During our conversations I gained an understanding of how
your petrophysics group interacts with the geological and
geophysical staff. I feel that with my geology background
and open hole log interpretation skills, particularly with
the Dipmeter, I could quickly make a significant and positive
contribution to your company. I have developed a tentative
plan to reach the goals that we had discussed.

If you decide to make this position available to me, I
predict that Texas Oil Company and Steve Jorgensen could have
a long and mutually rewarding association.

I look forward to talking again soon.

                          With kindest regards,

                          Steve Jorgensen

SDJ:bl
Attachment

Michael D. Burns
Two Thousand Oaks Towers
2000 West Federal Street
Boston, MA   02110
(617) 765-9898

October 27, 19--

Mr. Cole McClure
Bechtel
P. O. Box 3965
San Francisco, California   94119

Dear Cole:

Just a brief note to thank you for taking the time to meet
with me last week--especially on such short notice.

As you know, I spent the week talking with people in the
hazardous materials industry and these interviews confirmed
my initial positive impression about its potential. I want
to become part of it and I appreciate your concrete
suggestions. As you suggested, I am writing letters to
Edward S. Hall and Hugo Edwards. Please thank Suzanne for
sending me Mr. Hall's business address.

Once again, thank you for your help, and tell Art I also
appreciated his comments. I hope our paths will cross again
soon.

Best regards,

Michael D. Burns

MB/fl

Tim,
It was nice to see you
so happy at lunch. You're a
very special person — don't ever
forget that. Thanks to you
I made contact with Mike
Raud. We're off and running.

Bri

April 29, 19--

Judith E. Martin
Senior Vice President
Merrill Lynch
1800 112th Avenue Northeast
Bellevue, Washington 98004

Dear Judy,

Thanks for taking the time to have lunch today. It was great seeing you again, and I admire you for the big challenge you have accepted.

I know you will do well in your new job, and I think you'll also love Bellevue once you finally get settled here.

Wishing you all the very best.

Sincerely,

Audrey Lake

AL/mf

BRUCE D. ROBERTSON, CPA
3182 South Holly Street
(303) 756-7435 (H)
(303) 779-1417 (W)

October 14, 19--

Dr. Peter A. Firmin
M+A International, Inc.
600 South Cherry Street, Suite 1125
Denver, Colorado 80222-1712

Dear Peter:

Thank you for the time you spend with me at lunch October 13.
I am working on the many suggestions and ideas you raised
during lunch. I will keep you posted on my progress in this
job search.

I have put together the enclosed recap of my Administrative
and Finance Capabilities in order to market myself for what I
believe will be the most productive and exciting years of my
life. Should you become aware of any of your business
associates or friends who may be in the market for new blood
and innovative thinking, I would appreciate your sending them
a copy of my resume or capabilities recap.

Any additional advice that you can give me at this exciting
time in my life would be greatly appreciated.

Also, I thought you might enjoy a couple newspaper articles
about M+A International, Inc. from the October 13, <u>Denver
Post</u>.

Sincerely,

Bruce D. Robertson, CPA

BDR:bl
Enclosures

Mark D. Espinoza
18 West Princeton Place
Lakewood, Colorado 80227

October 6, 19--

William S. Frank
President
CareerLab
7700 East Arapahoe Road, Suite 275
Englewood, Colorado 80112

Dear Bill:

Just a note of appreciation for the time you spent with
me yesterday. Your insights into the Human Resources job
market in Denver were helpful--not particularly encouraging,
but certainly realistic and helpful. Per your suggestion, I
have included three resumes--let me know if you need more!

I'll give you a follow-up call next week. Thanks again
for your interest.

Sincerely,

Mark D. Espinoza

Enclosures

Richard E. Hart
2700 Valley Drive
Hermosa Beach, California   09254
(213) 376-3897

November 18, 19--

Robert Owens
Legal Department
Levi Strauss & Company
1222 Seventh Street
Santa Monica, California   90401

Dear Bob,

    I am very grateful for our meeting last Friday. I
appreciate the information and your assistance in my career
search. I also appreciated the information about Levi
Strauss, and I especially want you to know that I am very
impressed with, and interested in, Levi Strauss. Your
company has successfully made a transition into a very
competitive business environment. I believe that I could
offer a combination of experiences to you from my involvement
with my own firm.

    Even if you do not currently have a position into which
I could fit, I thank you for your advice and help. I was
particularly interested in the similarities in our legal
backgrounds and was very glad to have the opportunity to talk
to someone who seemed to be able to relate to what I was
saying.

    Thank you very much.

                          Very truly yours,

                          Richard E. Hart

RH: jd

JOHN HAAG
2533 East 11th Avenue, #9
Denver, Colorado 80206
(303) 321-4688

February 22, 19--

Mr. William S. Frank
CareerLab
7700 East Arapahoe Road, Suite 275
Englewood, Colorado 80112

Dear Bill:

I've just accepted a position with Jewish Family Services as
a Career Counselor/Job Developer. The position offers an
opportunity to refine my skills in doing workshops,
individual and group counseling, job development and job
placement.

I'd like to share some thoughts with you about these past two
years, the completion of my career change, and the beginning
of the next stage of the journey. You played a part in
making my career change a success. You're part of an
important network of people who provided the advice,
suggestions, referrals and support that helped bring to life
my career change.

To use the garden metaphor, you helped provide the necessary
sunlight, temperature, moisture, soil and nurturing. I
provided the seed. Together we did it! My new career has
sprouted and, along with it, an amazing feeling of
satisfaction and fulfillment.

Thank you.

                        Sincerely yours,

                        John Haag

Nancy M. Connors
820 South Madison Street
Kansas City, Missouri 64106

July 29, 19--

Ms. Janet Nelson
2001 Central Park Avenue
Kansas City, Missouri 64107

Dear Janet,

On August 8, I will start working as a research
associate in the laboratory of Dr. Edward Bell. He is
Chairman of the Department of Microbiology at the University
of Missouri Medical School. His research interest is Herpes
Simplex Virus, primarily Type 1 which causes fever blisters.
Thirteen years ago, I was a postdoctoral fellow in that
department and that probably helped. Also, the fact that I
have a Ph.D. made me hireable as a research associate, a
position outside the State Civil Service system.

Dr. Bell is a consultant for American Genetics
International, whose president I interviewed in May. That
interview was arranged by an employment agent who had called
Forty Plus of Missouri. One of the members had given the
agent my name and a summary of my background.

So, association with Forty Plus, a self-help group of
unemployed executive, administrative and professional people,
ultimately resulted in finding a job.

I am looking forward to the challenges of working and to
learning about glycoprotein isolations, recombinant DNA
techniques, and immunology as related to Herpes simplex.

Karen will be in the fifth grade in September. She and
Todd are not really looking forward to the adjustments which
will have to be made in our lives, but all of us will do just
fine, eventually.

Thanks for your encouragement, advice and help during
the past ten months while I was looking for a job.

Your employed friend,

Nancy M. Connors

♥

Richard E. Hart
2700 Valley Drive
Hermosa Beach, California   09254
(213) 376-3897

November 18, 19--

Mr. Frank Holland
Vice President Marketing
Bank of America
3939 South Broadway
Redondo Beach, California   90277

Dear Frank,

Thank you for taking time out of your busy day to
discuss some ideas regarding my job search. Your input and
information has been of tremendous help.

You were the first person I talked to on this journey,
and I think I was both fortunate and lucky to have contacted
you first. I felt a tremendous amount of support from you
and I cannot begin to tell you how important that has been.
I have talked to Sandy, who put me in touch with Bill
Ralston, the head legal counsel for United Banks of
California. I had lunch with Bill, who also turned out to be
very helpful. U.B.C. did not have any openings, but Bill
gave me the name of another person. I will be meeting with
that person in the next few days.

I have been involved in this process long enough that I
am beginning to be able to determine who the key players are
in this city with respect to corporate practice. I have also
met numerous persons, and have been astounded at how helpful
almost everyone has been.

At this time, I have not really been in touch with many
people who are in a position to offer me a job; however, I am
narrowing in on some of them. This is a time-consuming
process, but I believe I am beginning to see how it all
works. Since you were the first person I talked to, I am
particularly grateful for your encouragement. I will let you
know when something more definite develops.

Thank you very much.

Very truly yours,

Richard E. Hart

John H. Norris
2694 S. Lima Street
Aurora, Colorado 80014
(303) 755-6680

June 13, 19--

Mr. Peter K. Reiter
720 South 33rd Street
Federal Way, Washington   98003

Dear Peter,

I sincerely appreciate the assistance and support you
provided me during my search for new employment. I'm pleased
to let you know that I've accepted a position with Fireman's
Fund Insurances in California. While leaving so many old
friends here in Colorado will be difficult, we are looking
forward to new friends, an excellent career opportunity, and
the fabled California lifestyle. I find in Fireman's Fund
many of the same positive qualities of young, progressive
business leadership that I found at Silverado Banking.

Bill Frank, the outplacement consultant who guided my search
efforts, told me that the process would be illuminating in
terms of who my friends really are. He was right--it's been
a powerful and positive experience. Bill also told me it was
highly likely that my next job would come via a friend. My
entre to Fireman's Fund was Virgil Pittman, a friend of
eighteen years. Virgil is a very strong businessman who
lives his beliefs every day. While I won't be working
directly for him, I am looking forward to working with him
and to renewing the relationship between my family and his.

Thanks again for your help and support. Please, let's make a
mutual effort to stay in touch despite the miles between us.

Best regards,

John H. Norris

Jory L. Laine
2700 Julian Street
Denver, Colorado 80211
(303) 455-9370

October 29, 19--

Mr. George Ochs
Urban Investment and Development Co.
1801 California Street, Suite 4600
Denver, Colorado 80202

Dear George:

I appreciate our meeting this morning and your insight
into the real estate development and property management
industries.

Property management is of particular interest as it
provides the opportunity to manage assets as well as people.
From your description, it's apparent that a large component
of the job is client relations, an aspect which is most
challenging and rewarding.

George, I am a resource manager with excellent
interpersonal skills and a participatory management style.
I thrive in an environment which is challenging and dynamic.

I look forward to speaking with you on Wednesday
afternoon. Again, thank you for your time and consideration.

Sincerely,

Jory L. Laine

JLL/lac
cc: Mr. William Frank

Jory L. Laine
2700 Julian Street
Denver, Colorado 80211

November 1, 19--

Mr. George Ochs
Urban Investment and Development Co.
1801 California Street Suite 4600
Denver, Colorado 80202

Dear George:

Many thanks for taking the time to provide the contact names. I plan on calling Mr. Becker and Mr. Hansen within the next week or so.

If I may ever be of assistance to you, please do not hesitate to contact me.

Very truly yours,

Jory L. Laine

JLL/lac
cc: Bill Frank

Herman Doering
2911 S. Downing Street
Englewood, Colorado 80110

September 5, 19--

Brad Frank, M.D.
Chief of Medicine
Deputy Chief of Professional Services
Greater Bridgeport Community Mental Health Center
1635 Central Avenue
Bridgeport, Connecticut 06610

Dear Dr. Frank:

Thank you for the referral to the job opportunity at the Department of Mental Health in Hartford, Connecticut. I immediately followed up with a cover letter and resume to Ken Nicholson, the Director of the Information Systems Division. I hope to be hearing back from him in the near future thanks to your thoughtfulness.

Sincerely,

Herman Doering

❤

Richard E. Hart
2700 Valley Drive
Hermosa Beach, California   09254
(213) 376-3897

November 14, 19--

Mr. Thomas Rollins
666 East 17th Street
Santa Ana, California   92701

Dear Tom,

Thank you for taking time out of your day to discuss some ideas regarding my job search. Your input and information have been of tremendous help. I have been gratified and deeply touched by all of the help and support that I have received. The information, leads and support which you gave me are truly appreciated.

I have tried to call both John and Sherry Bradbury, but have not yet spoken to them. I am sure I will talk to them in the near future. I have had a couple of meetings since our luncheon, and I incorporated some of your suggestions into my discussions with the persons I met with. Your comments were very helpful, and seemed to make a favorable impression.

Again, thank you very much. If ever there is anything I can do for you, please let me know.

Very truly yours,

Richard E. Hart

RH: jd

BRUCE ROBERTSON, CPA
3182 South Holly Street
Denver, Colorado 80222
(303) 756-7435 (H)
(303) 779-1411 (W)

October 14, 19--

Ms. Gail Adler
1444 Kingswood Court
Willowbrook, Illinois 60521

Dear Gail:

Thank you for agreeing to help me out in my job search by
sending me the classified ads weekly from the Tuesday <u>Wall
Street Journal</u>, Southern Edition. I hope it wasn't too much
trouble. If for any reason you are unable to continue
sending these ads, please feel free to stop.

I will keep you posted as to the progress of my job search
and its forthcoming successful conclusion.

Your friend,

Bruce Robertson

BDR/bl

Bruce K. Ward
188 West Randolph Avenue
Oak Brook, Illinois 60521

January 30, 19--

Mr. Allen S. Sutton
President
TransCon, Inc.
5000 Medco Road
Birmingham, Alabama 35217

Dear Mr. Sutton:

Just a brief note to thank you for returning the response
form I sent you earlier this month. Also, thank you for the
Mike Bergmann suggestion. That is not exactly the type of
work I am looking for, but I may contact him later after I
see how this effort works out.

In my search I'm focusing on the management area rather than
sales. I would not be adverse to combining the two in the
appropriate position, and this might be possible in the
financial services area. Please keep me in mind if you hear
of any other situations that might be appropriate.

Thanks again for the note and interest.

Best regards,

Bruce K. Ward

BKW/dk

Follow Up

Sooner or later, every job-search becomes mostly follow-up. You reach the point at which initiating new contacts ceases to be productive—you spread yourself too thin. It's better and quicker to follow up two or three opportunities aggressively, and bring your job-hunt to an end. There are literally hundreds of creative ways to follow up without pestering.

RICHARD P. RUBY
1128 2nd Avenue South
Edmonds, Washington 98020

October 25, 19--

Mr. Michael B. Dixon
Holland and Hart
P. O. Box 2147
Denver, Colorado 80302

Dear Mike,

I was interested to hear that your firm is considering
ways to acquire more capability regarding international
business transactions.

As you know, I have worked as an independent consultant
these past two years dealing with the business, financial and
governmental problems that accompany overseas investments. I
have found, however, that companies large enough to have
significant international exposure are bombarded by major
league players such as:

a) the large investment banking houses,

b) major law firms,

c) consulting firms such as McKinsey and
    Arthur D. Little,

d) and, increasingly, by the consulting units operating
    within the major accounting firms.

It has become pretty clear that marketing my "Lone
Ranger Act" in the face of this kind of competition is, at
best, a difficult job. For the past few months I've been
investigating ways to merge my talents into a better known
and more broadly based entity. If you are looking for
additional arrows to round out Holland and Hart's quiver of
talent, then perhaps we should do some talking.

The many hi-tech firms in the Front Range area are
beginning to push into the international arena, and you
mentioned that you have already taken steps to strengthen
your intellectual property team. These hi-tech groups often
face significant trade issues in Washington as well as
complex government and financial negotiations abroad.

There are many other exporters in this area--such as the U.S. Meat Exporter Federation (composed of entities such as Monfort)--that are large enough to have real international needs as well.

Some of your "competition" has already mounted a campaign to try to serve these needs--see the attached flyer on "Going International."

The clipping from the Wall Street Journal of October 16, 19--, shows what firms such as Stearns Roger and Morrison-Knudsen are up against internationally. I've marked the clipping to show how the things we did for Cuajone parallel what Bechtel is doing now.

The resume information attached after the clippings just mentioned is probably a bit on the over-kill side, but lawyers love to read and it does demonstrate the extent and depth of my international experience.

I expect to travel back east the 6th and 7th of November to talk to Price Waterhouse's new affiliate partnership that deals in "International Financing Consultancy Services," but will be here Monday, November 5.

Best regards,

Richard P. Ruby

RR:cr

*

BRUCE D. ROBERTSON
3182 South Holly Street
Denver, Colorado 80222
(303) 756-7435 (H)

October 8, 19--

Mr. Robert C. Kingston
Corporate Controller
232 Main Street
Tiburon, California 94920
(415) 435-2000

Dear Bob:

It was great to meet you at the Financial Executive
Institute's 55th International Conference here in Denver. I
thought it was a stimulating meeting and found the sessions
most interesting. One of the things I really enjoyed was the
opportunity to meet you. I look forward to visiting with you
at future conferences and meetings. I trust you enjoyed your
stay in Colorado.

I am seeking a permanent position in finance or international
business. To help market myself, I have put together the
enclosed resume. I am open to any industry with positions
located almost anywhere in the world.

Should you be aware of any openings, which might be
appropriate for me, I would appreciate your informing me so
that I may follow up. Thank you very much for your
assistance.

Sincerely,

Bruce D. Robertson, C.P.A.

BDR/bl
Enclosure

Douglas P. Arnold, Jr.
295 Treetop Lane N.W.
Ft. Collins, Colorado 80521

December 22, 19--

Mr Scott A. McLean
Vice President
The First National Bank of Columbus
5000 Royal Atlantic Avenue
Columbus, Ohio 43201

Dear Mr. McLean:

When I mentioned to Mr. Charles Hill that I would be leaving my position as Controller of Robertson Manufacturing at the end of this month, he suggested I contact you with regard to locating a new position.

During my tenure at Robertson, I had the opportunity to work closely with Mr. Hill and some of the financial analysts at the bank. The professional manner in which they dealt with a very difficult situation has shown me that The First National Bank of Columbus may be the kind of organization where I could find a good "fit," and fully utilize my abilities.

While I understand that there may not be a suitable position open at the bank at this time, you or the commercial lending officers may be aware of a bank customer who may be in need of my skills.

Enclosed are two copies of my current resume. Please feel free to share the information provided with any employer who may be interested in the skills and experience I can provide.

After the New Year, I will call you to arrange a time, at your convenience, when we could meet should you decide a meeting would be appropriate.

Thank you for your consideration.

Seasons Greetings!

Douglas P. Arnold, Jr.

DPA/
Enclosures

William T. Kyle
7800 South High Street
Littleton, Colorado 80122
(303) 770-4344

April 15, 19--

Mr. Larry Forest
Health Care Centers of America
3570 Keith Street N.W.
P.O. Box 3480
Dallas, Texas 75237

Dear Mr. Forest

    My interest in pursuing a position with Health Care
Centers of America has increased following my interviews in
Cleveland and follow up visits to several of your centers in
Denver. I'm concerned that I have not had the opportunity to
discuss this with you personally. I am aware that the
resignation of Tom Patrick has put additional demands on your
time, but please know that I would make myself available to
meet with you whenever it is convenient.

    My contact and conversations with your staff in Dallas
and in Denver have really excited me about the challenges and
opportunities that your organization offers.

    I am sincerely interested in exploring how I can be a
part of the continued success of Health Care Centers of
America, given my interests and financial management
background.

    I'll look forward to your call.

                    Sincerely,

                    William T. Kyle

Samir Y. Naguib
7704 West Coal Mine Place
Littleton, Colorado 80123
(303) 973-3456

July 21, 19--

Jeffery D. Emerson
Arthur Andersen
501 Second Street
Sixth Floor
Rockford, Illinois 61110

Dear Jeff,

It was great meeting with you the last two days. I would like to take this opportunity to let you know I enjoyed my visit to the office and Rockford very much. I feel that things went beautifully and that I got along well with everyone I met.

I especially liked the total client service attitude and the professionalism the partners displayed. I also enjoyed my tour of Rockford in the afternoon. I was even tempted to extend my visit an extra day to get a chance to see more of the community.

Jeff, I feel that there is a good match between my background and expertise and your needs. The office, and the firm in general, seem to have many learning and professional growth opportunities for me. I also feel that I have talents and expertise I can contribute to you--especially in the area of research and consulting and the area of advancing the automation of the tax and accounting functions.

I am very interested in pursuing a career with Arthur Andersen and I am looking forward to talking to you again in the near future.

Very truly yours,

Samir Y. Naguib

T. Craig Lincoln

April 28, 19--

Mr. Norman S. Powers
Executive Vice President
Ogilvy & Mather
520 Fifth Avenue
New York, New York 10017

Dear Norm,

I don't know if our lunch last Friday could be considered a
"power lunch," but if it was I did feel a definite boost in
horsepower. And it wasn't the jambalaya.

Your ideas and your philosophies on the business of advertising
are impressive. I'm sure that when your concepts are
implemented, Ogilvy & Mather will not only be the oldest ad
agency in New York . . . it will be the best!

Where and if I fit into your plan at present is still an
unknown. But I do know this. On many levels, I totally agree
with the way you do business. And I strongly identify with your
frustrations regarding the creative profession.

Simply stated, I believe that advertising is really marketing
and that creative design means as much to the "bottom line" as
it does on the layout pad. I would very much enjoy learning
from your business and marketing expertise. In return, I would
bring to your organization . . . creative accountability.
Together, we would be a formidable account team.

Let's meet again. Let's talk again. Let's see how I could help
you keep your organization out in front of the competition.

Till then, thanks for a most enjoyable Friday.

Sincerely,

T. Craig Lincoln
Lincoln & Associates

*

J O R Y   L.   L A I N E

December 14, 19--

Mr. Norman B. Ferris
Certified Financial Planner
Ferris & Associates, Ltd.
2414 South York Street, Suite 2700
Denver, Colorado 80222

Dear Norm:

I thoroughly enjoyed our discussion yesterday. I had almost forgotten how stimulating business luncheons are. I sincerely appreciated your time and interest.

Even though I had the opportunity to tell you a little about my background, the enclosed resume will provide further detail. Briefly stated, I have 18 years' experience in financial management including controllership, treasury, planning and administrative responsibilities. I have worked with large and small organizations in automated and manual financial systems environments. My management responsibilities ranged from 2 to 20 people and I am equally effective in "hands on" or staff management roles.

I am looking to the "smaller" organizations which employ between 300 and 500 people. I believe these organizations offer the opportunity to make significant contributions and reward hard work with increased responsibility.

Norm, I would appreciate your reviewing the resume and mentioning my qualifications to your business associates. You could also assist me by providing the names of two or three people to contact and discuss my career plans and objectives. I will call you within the next week to discuss this.

Again, thank you for your time and consideration. Best wishes for a Happy Holiday Season and Prosperous New Year.

Sincerely,

Jory L. Laine

JLL/Lac
Enclosure

Brad C. Bawmann
203 East Exposition Avenue
Denver, Colorado 80209
(303) 985-3425

9 July 19--

Mr. Randy R. Hanson
Manager of Public Information
St. Anthony Hospital Systems
4231 W. 16th Avenue
Denver, Colorado 80204

Dear Randy,

You're fantastic!

I can't tell you how much I enjoyed meeting you this morning
and learning more about your hospital system. I was most
impressed by your enthusiasm and attention to detail.

I know we could work well together. Like yourself, I am
versatile, accepting of constructive criticism and deeply
committed to doing a good job.

Let's get together again, soon. Perhaps we could meet for
lunch--that's the least I could do to thank you for taking
the time this morning.

Have a great today!

Warmest regards,

Brad C. Bawmann

Brad Bawmann
203 East Exposition Avenue
Denver, Colorado 80209
(303) 735-0345

15 September 19--

Mr. Dan Richards
Vice President Account Services
New York Advertising, Inc.
300 Cherry Creek North Drive
Suite 3000
Denver, Colorado 80209-3852

Dear Dan,

You're super!

Thanks so much for taking time to meet with me today.

Per our discussion I've enclosed a few clips of my stories
for your inspection. I'd appreciate any feedback you might
have. Otherwise, I'm taking your suggestions to heart and
contacting other agencies.

I thank you again for your time.

Sincerely yours,

Brad C. Bawmann

Enclosure

Richard A. Petersen
212 Old Lake Road
Worthington, Ohio 43085

July 25, 19--

Dr. Milton Bennett
Vice President, Technical Resources
  Service and Technology Department
TRW, Inc.
19 Bridgestone Road
Cleveland, Ohio 44124

Dear Dr. Bennett:

Ron Price discussed my interest in TRW with you recently. My nearly 20 years in contract research has involved the development of close working relationships with various levels of industrial management in the United States and Japan. From this experience, I bring certain strengths that I believe could be effectively utilized by TRW:

*   Very broad technical interests and understanding;

*   The ability to understand technology in strategic business terms; and,

*   Excellent people management skills.

I am seeking a position in line management, program management or technology planning that allows me to use these strengths in a creative environment. An acceptable salary level would be contingent upon the nature of the job and the location. The Cleveland area is especially attractive right now because of my wife's employment situation. I will call you in a week or so and answer any questions that you might have.

I appreciate your efforts on my behalf.

Very truly yours,

Richard A. Petersen

RAP/sl

James T. Evergreen
117 N. Jefferson Street
Chicago, Illinois 60606

December 29, 19--

Mr. Raymond K. Martin
Personnel Manager
Digital Equipment Corporation
290 Shasta Boulevard
Rockford, Illinois 61107

Dear Mr. Martin:

Kathy Quinn told me you were looking for someone to fill the position of Finance and Information Systems Manager. She suggested that the position description matched my qualifications very closely, and that I should look into it.

She also gave you a draft copy of my resume. Enclosed is a finalized version. I do understand that the particular position mentioned above may not be a possibility at this time. Nevertheless, I would appreciate the opportunity to meet with you. Condensing a 17-year career into a two-page resume necessarily omits many significant achievements that may be of interest to you.

Everything I know about Digital leads me to believe that "DEC" is the kind of organization where I could fully utilize my skills, experience and education, and make a valuable contribution.

Please note that I am presently an MBA student, majoring in Management Information Systems. I will be awarded the degree in June, 19--, and will take the CPA exam soon thereafter.

Thank you for looking this over. I want to meet at your convenience, and I will call you in the next week or two.

Sincerely,

James T. Evergreen

Enclosure

John F. Conway
6122 Snow Mountain Road
Bakersfield, California 93309
(805) 424-7111

February 24, 19--

Mr. Bob Stevenson
EDS International
Devonshire House-4th Floor
London, WI, England

Dear Mr. Stevenson:

You were referred to me by Mike Sherman. He and I talked
about your European Division when I was in Lansing last
summer doing some EDS-related telephone work for Butler
Telecommunications.

I am deeply interested in working for EDS and further,
expressly interested in working for EDS in Europe.

I know that EDS has entered, and continues to aggressively
penetrate, telephone markets worldwide. And since I have an
extensive telephone design and engineering background, as
well as some solid experience in other related areas, I
believe I could be a genuine asset to your organization.

Enclosed is a recent resume for your perusal. I believe two
of my greatest strengths--which do not appear on my resume--
are a strong work ethic and an ability to learn rapidly.
I will provide references, both business and personal, at
your request.

Please let me hear from you.

Sincerely,

John F. Conway

Enclosure

David K. Swanson
6704 Stanford Street
Washington, Ohio 43085

July 23, 19--

Mr. Philip J. Robins, President
Research International, Inc.
Post Office Box 3253
Gorham, Maine 04038

Dear Mr. Robins:

Richard Thomas recently introduced me to your company
and I have learned something of your activities from Richard
and from your promotional literature.

After over 14 years of contract research and management
at Battelle, I have decided to seek career opportunities in a
smaller, more innovative company where I can have an impact.
Research International is involved in many areas in which I
have actively worked in my nearly 20 years in contract
research and I would like you to consider me as a candidate
for your senior staff.

My technical background is in the materials area--
specifically tribology. In this area I functioned in both
the principal investigator and program manager roles. In
addition to laboratory-oriented R&D and hardware development,
I also have engaged in techno-economic studies related to
synthetic lubricants and led two classified trade impact
studies in the areas of ball bearings and synthetic
lubricants.

For the past several years, I have managed profit
centers engaged in R&D and commercialization in the
transportation (air and automotive), structures and energy
areas for both industry and government. My organizations
have been active in the conception and execution of
multiclient programs and cooperative research programs.
I am experienced and knowledgeable in intellectual property
exploitation and innovation management.

Since I took over as Director of Industrial Business
Development, our industrial sales have grown 20% and our
profitability in industrial business has increased from
losses in 19-- to nearly 10% return on volume. This is due
in large part to a focused marketing strategy that I was
instrumental in planning and implementing. For the past year

Mr. Philip J. Robins, President
July 23, 19--
Page Two

I have been actively involved in the Japanese marketplace. I have a good understanding of Japanese business practices and and the transfer of technology both to and from Japan.

I understand the business from the lab bench to the marketplace, and I believe that I have a great deal to offer to Research International. I would like the opportunity to discuss my qualifications in greater detail and I will call you next week to see if we can meet.

Very truly yours,

David K. Swanson

DKS/sle

Richard P. Ruby
1128 2nd Avenue South
Edmonds, Washington 98020

October 23, 19--

Mr. John D. Macomber
Presidential Search Committee
The Americas Society, Inc.
1280 Park Avenue
New York, New York 10021

Dear Mr. Macomber:

Please include my name on your list of persons
interested in succeeding Russell Martin.

Last week in New York, Edward Page--who knows me well
from my years with ASARCO--indicated that you hope to attract
a major figure from the U.S. corporate world or a significant
and highly-respected public official.

If you ultimately determine that the person you seek
should function basically as:

o   a staff leader, and as

o   a facilitator/arranger of quiet dialogue between the
     heads of U.S. companies and top officials of both Latin
     and U.S. governments, rather than speaking in his own
     name,

then you should find my records interesting.

Having dedicated most of my working life to Latin
America, including 15 years of residence in four countries,
the strengths I would bring to the Society are:

* Substantial experience and significant personal
   accomplishments in the development of U.S. investments
   in Latin America and the conduct of day-to-day
   business operations.

* An understanding of the economic development of Latin
   America over the last two decades--its strengths of
   success, and its many failures.

* Years of successful negotiations at the ministerial
  level and contact work at the presidential level.

* Thorough familiarity with the structure and
  functioning of the expatriate communities in Latin
  countries, and considerable accomplishment and
  recognition within same.

* The ability to understand, develop rapport with, and
  be meaningfully accepted by Latin businessmen and
  government officials.

* A consistently clean and honest record as the
  spokesman/defender of U.S. interests--both corporate
  and public.

* A love of the arts and a lifetime of participation
  (mostly amateur) in musical activities both here and
  in Latin America.

My participation in the activities of the Americas
Society goes back to the early 70's, and I am well known to
some of your senior staff. Also:

* I have become acquainted, through the good offices of
  his former general counsel, with Mr. William Davidson.

* Steve Baker is a friend of many years.

* Hans Steiner is a friend and working colleague.

* I am well known to St. Joe's people in Lima, Hal and
  Lisa Wright--especially Lisa because of our years of
  work together on the board of the American school in
  Peru.

Thank you for considering me. I expect to be in New
York in early November if you wish to schedule a meeting.

                    Yours sincerely,

                    Richard P. Ruby

RPR:djs

Bruce K. Ward
188 West Randolph Avenue
Oak Brook, Illinois 60521

February 1, 19--

Norman B. Simpson
Management Advisory Services
5919 East Jean Avenue
Phoenix, Arizona 85018

Dear Norm:

Just a brief note to thank you for returning the response
form I recently sent you.

You might find it interesting that the exercise of looking
for a new position has one real positive side. It has
brought me in contact with people that I wouldn't have known
otherwise, such as yourself. I've enjoyed meeting you.

With regard to the search itself, I'm still actively looking
and hope you will keep me in mind if you hear of a situation
that might be appropriate.

I appreciate the help and encouragement.

Best regards,

Bruce K. Ward

BDW/dk

Stuart T. Jackson
27 Northeast 105th Street
Miami Shores, Florida 33138
(704) 342-9093

January 29, 19--

L. Robert Williams
CRS Sirrene Engineering Group
216 South Pleasantburg Drive
Greenville, South Carolina 29607

Dear Mr. Williams,

Thank you for returning the response form I sent you. I
realize business conditions limit the opportunities to bring
new people on board at this time. However, I am still
interested in learning more about your company.

I would like to call you next week to talk about your
organization. I won't take more than ten minutes of your
time.

So that you know more about me, I have attached a resume
outlining my professional career.

Sincerely,

Stuart T. Jackson

STJ/ha

Attachment

*

Susan J. Ottinger
7242 S. Tamarac St.
Englewood, Colorado 80112
(303) 761-8229

August 3, 19--

Ms. Nancy K. Rawlins
Research Pharmaceuticals, Inc.
Department 578
211 Carnegie Center
Princeton, New Jersey 08540-6213

Dear Ms. Rawlins:

Thank you for acknowledging receipt of my resume. I am anxious to hear from you concerning a time we can get together and discuss my background and objectives further.

I am most impressed with the Research commitment and quality of its products for the consumer. I have been marketing and retailing the ostomy and urological products from your HealthTek Division for the past five years. This is the kind of corporation I want to be associated with and especially to represent in this area.

In my present management position, I have just completed developing a mail order catalog system, the first of its kind in our corporation, which is expected to generate an additional $1,800,000 annually to our present revenue locally. This has created a great deal of excitement with our regional office and is expected to be spread to our other 400 stores across the country.

The recent completion of my Certificate in Management from the graduate school at the University of Denver gives me added confidence to broaden my business administration responsibilities and become a top-notch representative for Research Pharmaceuticals in the Denver area.

I am certainly looking forward to hearing from you again soon!

Enthusiastically,

Susan J. Ottinger

Douglas P. Arnold, Jr.
295 Treetop Lane N.W.
Ft. Collins, Colorado 80521

January 20, 19--

Mr. Glenn T. Gordon
Xerox Equipment Corporation
Human Resources Department
3000 Southern Boulevard
Ft. Collins, Colorado 80521

Dear Mr. Gordon:

Thank you for taking the time to speak with me on the telephone last week, regarding the status of the Finance and Information Systems Manager position at Xerox. I appreciate your candor and encouragement.

Since you indicated I would be considered for the position should the decision to "look outside" be made, I have enclosed a summary of my recent career accomplishments. This summary should indicate the range of my abilities, and the kinds of results I have achieved.

Please do not hesitate to telephone should you have any questions or wish additional information.

Best regards,

Douglas P. Arnold, Jr.

Enclosure

Brad C. Bawmann
203 East Exposition Avenue
Denver, Colorado 80209

10 June 19--

Mr. Timothy Wilson
News Anchor
KUSA Channel 9
1089 Bannock Street
Denver, Colorado 80204

Dear Mr. Wilson,

The last time I spoke with you on the telephone you mentioned
positions at your station are created. "Openings," you said,
"don't just <u>happen</u>--they have to be made."

I'm intrigued by that notion. And I'd like to sit down with
you to discuss it. Perhaps we could meet for coffee.

As you know, I'm anxious to learn more about the field of
television journalism. I think you could provide some key
insight into the industry.

I'll call in a few days to set up a time to meet.

Thanks for your time Mr. Wilson. I'm looking forward to
meeting you soon.

Sincerely yours,

Brad C. Bawmann

Kenneth K. Phillips
1800 One Dallas Centre
Dallas, Texas 75201
(214) 979-1200 (w)
(214) 979-4653 (h)

October 19, 19--

Mr. William Gill
Vice President, International Division
Medical Products, Inc.
5020 Technology Drive
Dallas, Texas 75202

Dear Bill:

Thank you for taking time to talk with me over the phone this past week. I have enclosed a copy of my resume which details my accomplishments over the past several years.

While Vice President of Operations for Texas Instruments, I was responsible for the development and implementation of Just-in-Time (JIT) throughout the entire manufacturing and distribution operations. The approach taken with JIT was to eliminate waste, whether it was wasted effort, time, space, inventories, machine setup, materials handling, or financial accounting practices.

The hard results produced through implementation of the various programs allowed TI to consolidate Denver manufacturing operations from three facilities to one with over 200,000 square feet of floor space savings. Inventories were reduced substantially, scrap was reduced, product quality was improved and materials were pulled through the manufacturing process in much less time.

JIT is an ongoing program as there are always opportunities to reduce waste in every area. I found that JIT was an attitude and was especially successful because of the commitment developed throughout the total organization.

Bill, I will call you early next week after you have had a chance to review my resume. I would like to meet with you personally to discuss my capabilities.

Thanks you for your interest.

Sincerely,

Kenneth K. Phillips

Michael D. Burns
Two Thousand Oak Towers
2000 West Federal Street
Boston, Massachusetts 02110
(617) 765-9898

January 25, 19--

Mr. George W. Blake
Fortress Enterprises
7399 South Tuscon Way
Englewood, Colorado 80112

Dear George:

It was a pleasure talking to you this afternoon. I am
enclosing a resume and an excerpt from <u>Fortune</u> magazine which
summarizes my experience and highlights a few of my
accomplishments.

My career has been in management with a strong finance
background. During the last year I worked as a personal
investment advisor. I was successful in this profession,
designing and implementing a telemarketing approach that
brought over 45 six to seven figure net-worth clients in less
than five months. Prior to joining Intek, I was offered the
position of Vice-President for Marketing at Canadian Coal,
but the excitement of the oil business at that time was just
too strong.

My ideal job target is with a company that has an
entrepreneurial outlook, perhaps be five to ten years old and
has sales of less than $100 million. I am flexible on
immediate compensation if there is adequate potential for
growth. An opportunity to earn equity would be attractive.
Although I am not seeking investment opportunities, I might
consider a limited investment. Geographic location is not a
major consideration. I am open to any situation that is
challenging and will make good use of my abilities.

George, this should cover the key points. I will be glad to
provide any other information you may need and can supply
strong references when appropriate. I look forward to our
next conversation.

Sincerely,

Michael D. Burns

Enclosures

R O N A L D   L.   E V A N S

September 17, 19--

Mr. Michael Williams, President
L.L. Bean
2805 Liberty Boulevard
Dubois, Pennsylvania 15801

Dear Mike:

Needless to say, I was disappointed to learn that you have
chosen someone else to fill your Controller's position.
I felt that your company's needs and my background very
closely paralleled, and that I possess the management
experience to work with you in building the organization.

If something changes, please do not hesitate to call me.
I know that I can meet the high standards which you are
striving to achieve. I was very excited, and hopeful, that
I would have the chance to work with you and your staff as a
member of the team.

Please thank your managers for their time and consideration
on my behalf. I know how difficult it is to make a decision
such as you were all faced with.

Your organization is producing a high quality product. That
was obvious from my observations during my tour of the
facilities. I was very impressed with the company and its
personnel. I truly enjoyed my visit in August.

My best regards,

Ronald L. Evans

R O N A L D   L.   E V A N S

August 7, 19--

Mr. Norman Dean, Vice President
National Electric Industries, Inc.
750 North Taylor Street
Philadelphia, Pennsylvania 19130

Dear Norm,

Needless to say, I was disappointed to learn that you have
chosen someone else to fill your Controller's position. I
felt that your company's needs and my background very closely
paralleled, and that I have the management experience to work
with you and Mike in building the company. The fact that I
have worked in a variety of industries, including engineering
and construction, would have provided the opportunity to use
techniques from many different disciplines.

If something changes, please do not hesitate to call me.
I know I can meet the high standards you are striving to
achieve. I was very excited with the prospect of helping
develop a growing organization.

Now, however, I would like to ask for your assistance.
Should you be aware, or become aware of any business
associates, friends, or others who may be looking for someone
with my talents, please provide them with a copy of the
attached resume, or give me their names to contact
personally. Positions involved with general or financial
management in the industries of manufacturing, distribution,
engineering and construction, or equipment sales and service,
are my primary targets. I am willing to relocate to further
my career.

Any further advice or counsel that you can provide will be
greatly appreciated. For instance, it would be very helpful
for me to know your thoughts on my qualifications and whether
I related well to your company needs. If possible, I would
like to meet with you once more to obtain any counsel
regarding my search. If lunch or breakfast would suit you,
I would be happy to meet.

I want to wish you and the company much success in the
future. I really enjoyed meeting you and Mike. Thank you
for your time and effort during your consideration of my
candidacy.

My best regards,

Ronald L. Evans

W I L L I A M   A.   K A U F M A N

April 8, 19--

Dr. Robert Bond
The Cardiology Corporation
1960 Main Street
Belleview, Washington 98004

Dear Dr. Bond:

Our talk last Thursday left me with the impression you felt
my experience in getting clinical cardiovascular devices to a
successful product launch was exactly what you need. Hence,
my difficulty understanding the note I received yesterday
from Cindy Black, indicating my application is not under
current consideration.

I do understand the potential difficulty you mentioned
regarding the new person who will be assuming control soon
and his possible desire to select his own people for the
function. That may be a risk, as you suggested, and it is a
calculated one.

Unless you have new information since we talked, my judgment
is that the risk is counterbalanced by the opportunity to
demonstrate my unusual combination of technical, clinical,
and marketing skills. They are precisely those skills your
group now needs during clinical trials, to assure the excimer
angioplasty laser is the successful product it should be when
you receive commercial approval.

If you've already selected the person you want in that slot,
I'd still like to talk to you about your alternate
suggestion--working with you on a temporary or consulting
basis. As you said, the highlighted points in my cover
letter corresponded exactly with what you feel the company
needs.

Right now, The Cardiology Corporation is a small company with
a few people and a big job to do. You need good people with
as many of the right talents as possible, who understand what
is needed to develop the products and the company to its
potential, and who will do the job to make sure it happens.
I have that diverse background and a drive to make those
contributions. Let's get together and discuss what we could
do and how to do it. Please give me a call--days or evenings
are fine.

My best regards,

William A. Kaufman

Brad C. Bawmann
203 E. Exposition Avenue
Denver, Colorado 80209
(303) 897-9086

29 June 19--

Ms. Penny Harcourt
Vice President Public Affairs and Education
Colorado Hospital Association
2140 South Holly
Denver, Colorado 80222

Dear Ms. Harcourt:

You're fantastic!

Thank you for your time on the telephone last week. Enclosed
is a sampling of my work at <u>The Creek</u>.

As a reporter for a weekly newspaper, I've been fortunate to
sink my teeth into a wide range of subjects. However, none
are ever more enjoyable than a story about the medical
profession.

My contacts in the industry are numerous, and they can speak
to the credibility of my work. A more tenacious, aggressive
reporter you won't find.

Some say my energy and enthusiasm are enough for any three
people. And my drive, desire and determination make me an
ideal candidate for a top-notch organization in the medical
field.

Moreover, my educational background drew heavily on the
natural and social sciences, as I once contemplated attending
medical school.

Ms. Harcourt, if there is anything more I can share with you
please let me know.

I will be in touch to make sure you have received my
materials.

Once again, thanks for your time and consideration. Any
suggestions or referrals you could make would be most
appreciated.

Sincerely yours,

Brad C. Bawmann

Brad C. Bawmann
203 East Exposition Avenue
Denver, Colorado 80209
(303) 897-5443

8 July 19--

Ms. Barbara Barrow
Public Relations Director
University of Colorado Health Sciences Center
Box A092
4200 East 9th Avenue
Denver, Colorado 80262

Dear Ms. Barrow,

Per our phone conversation earlier in the week I've enclosed
a few clips of pertinent stories.

Being a journalist I watch the medical profession intensely
for new developments whether good or bad. But my reporting
style is always unbiased and sensitive to the needs of the
public.

When Florida's trauma network fell on hard times I
investigated Denver's trauma system, only to find it doing
quite well. And when the Taiwan flu threatened the area I
was the first to alert both the public and the rest of
Denver's media to the potential hazards.

A more tenacious, aggressive reporter you won't find. And my
communication skills--both oral and written--are honed razor
sharp. In addition, my energy is limitless; my enthusiasm
unequaled; my attention to detail unparalleled.

Let's at least talk. I know I can help the Health Sciences
Center become the hospital it aspires to be.

I'll call in a few days to arrange a time to meet.

Sincerely yours,

Brad C. Bawmann

Michael J. Treasure, Jr.
6220 South Pinion Way
Littleton, Colorado 80121

                                    October 13, 19--

William S. Frank
President
CareerLab
7700 East Arapahoe Road, Suite 275
Englewood, Colorado 80112

Dear Bill:

     I enjoyed our phone conversation today and look forward
to meeting you for breakfast on the 27th. I will see you at
the Harvest restaurant at 7:00 a.m. By the way, so you have
no trouble finding me, I am 6'4" with a brown mustache.

     My resume is enclosed.

                                    Very truly yours,

                                    Michael J. Treasure, Jr.

MJT/s

Enclosure: resume

Douglas P. Arnold, Jr.
295 Treetop Lane N.W.
Ft. Collins, Colorado 80521

January 15, 19--

Ms. Deanna Randall
Chief Financial Officer
Metropolitan Systems Incorporated
1600 West Center Street
Salt Lake City, Utah 84047

Dear Ms. Randall,

Thank you for selecting me as a candidate for a position
at Metropolitan Systems. I appreciate the opportunity to
meet with you, and look forward to learning more about your
Company.

So that our meeting can be most productive, I have
enclosed a list of my significant career accomplishments for
your examination. I believe this summary shows the way in
which I approach my work and the kind of results I have
achieved.

I will be pleased to provide any additional information
you require when we meet on Tuesday the 19th.

Enthusiastically,

Douglas P. Arnold, Jr.

DPA/

Enclosures

Michael D. Burns
Two Thousand Oaks Towers
2000 West Federal Street
Boston, Massachusetts   02110
(617) 765-9898

October 23, 19--

Mr. Larry L. Johnston
President
Petroleum Waste, Inc
2701 Patton Way
Bakersfield, California   93308

Dear Larry:

The following, plus the attachment, sets out a brief summary of my experience and qualifications:

1. Worked over 20 years with Amoco and Exxon before joining InTek in 19--. Have a BS in Geology from Colorado University and an MBA from Stanford.

2. At Exxon, as a geologist, discovered the South Eola field in Garvin County, Oklahoma (30-40 million barrels).

3. At Amoco, progressed through a series of jobs in operations and in headquarters where I was associated with, or a member of the management groups directing the exploration, production and financial activities of Amoco's various natural resources activities, both in the U.S. and overseas.

4. As President of InTek, turned the company around and then led it to the most successful exploration program in its history, participating in the drilling of 125 prospects in midcontinent, Gulf Coast and Rockies, with a success ratio of 44%. Success ratio for follow-up drilling was 85% and InTek's reserves were nearly doubled.

I look forward to talking with you next week and will be glad to provide any additional information.

Best regards,

Michael D. Burns

Attachment

*

THOMAS K. JACOB
8118 South Garfield Way
Littleton, Colorado 80122
(303) 694-2412

April 6, 19--

Mr. Frank Murphy
N L Baroid
P.O. Box 60070
Houston, Texas 77205

Dear Frank:

I really enjoyed our phone conversation concerning your plans
to market Ml79 soil sealant. Your comments reminded me of
many similarities between my past experiences with Dowell and
what you are looking for in your new venture.

     -- Selling to industry and government
     -- Developing new markets for existing products
     -- Solving client technical problems
     -- Designing solutions with the aid of laboratory data
     -- Melding various groups to achieve the desired goal

I've included an example of a problem I faced with Dowell
that is very similar to problems you might face. In fact,
this project used a crosslinked, dry powder form of
polyacrylamide; similar to the Ml79 system.

After you've had a chance to look this over, I'll give you a
call to get your reactions. Or you call me.

Sincerely,

Tom Jacob

TJ/bl

Attachment

PROBLEM

I had the opportunity to perform the first enhanced oil
recovery project on the North Slope of Alaska. Dowell's
normal products and equipment would not do the job due to the
severe weather and environmental concerns of the client. In
addition, the client's technical and operation people
disliked each other.

STRATEGY

I arranged for our chemical specialist and our equipment
specialist to meet with me and the customer's engineers and
operation personnel, then led an eight-hour meeting to design
a new system (chemistry and equipment) to perform to the
customer's requirements.

RESULTS

I moved men, materials and equipment to the North Slope, then
assembled the equipment and began operations on time with
outstanding technical results. This pilot project generated
additional revenue of $300,000 for Alaska operations in a
two-month period.

*

Thomas K. Jacob

Mr. Craig D. Sutton
1343 Wilshire Boulevard
Beverly Hills, California 90212

April 22, 19--

Dear Craig,

I'm writing to remind you that I am still in the job market.

I'm seeking a job that involves modifying technical products
and equipment in the field to meet customer specifications.

This job could be called something like:

      -- Field Engineer
      -- Sales Engineer
      -- Service Sales Engineer
      -- Field Applications Engineer, or
      -- Product Troubleshooter

The chemical, industrial controls and instrumentation, water
treatment, hazardous waste, machinery and manufacturing,
sales/marketing, construction and materials handling
industries would appeal to me.

I have created a non-oilfield resume that focuses on sales
and marketing. Please review it and pass it along to anyone
who might be looking for someone with my talents.

Any help you can give me will be greatly appreciated.

Sincerely,

Tom Jacob

TKJ/bl
Enclosure

Jack Mooney
5711 E. Crestline Ave.
Englewood, Colorado 80111
(303) 771-0987 (W)
(303) 987-8654 (H)

February 27, 19--

Mr. Conrad W. Andersen
Transportation Engineering, Inc.
1250 Broadway
New York, New York 10001

Dear Conrad,

I have taken a temporary job in financial research but I am
still very interested in working with your firm.

I have recently updated my resume to include some important
accomplishments missing in the earlier version. I think it
represents me more accurately.

Please review it and I'll call you in a couple days for your
comments.

Sincerely,

Jack Mooney

JM:kar
Enclosure

Samir Y. Naguib
7704 West Coal Mine Place
Littleton, Colorado 80123
(303) 973-3456

July 21, 19--

Kent Sullivan
U S West Financial Services
8200 South Quebec Street, Suite 330
Englewood, Colorado 80111

Dear Kent,

In our last conversation you asked me to call you on or about
July 7th. I am not having much luck calling you while you
are available. Therefore, I thought I'd drop this note in
the mail to let you know that I am still interested in
pursuing a position with U S West.

Kent, I recently revised my resume and I am enclosing a copy
for your review.

I am looking forward to hearing from you in the near future.
I may be reached at 897-0987.

                              Very truly yours,

                              Samir Y. Naguib

Enclosure

Brad Bawmann
203 East Exposition Avenue
Denver, Colorado 80209
765-8967

September 16, 19--

Mr. Butch Montoya
News Director
KUSA-Channel 9
1089 Bannock Sreet
Denver, Colorado 80204

Dear Mr. Montoya,

Thank you for your letter dated August 28, 19--.

Even though there are no openings currently at KUSA, I want
you to know I'm still interested.

I'm a "content" man, able to squeeze every drop out of a
story. And my drive, enthusiasm and energy, most agree, are
astounding.

My tenacity in getting the most out of a story is made
manifest by my recent revelation that actress Shirley
MacLaine plans to open the first of her spiritual centers
here in Colorado. I fought long and hard for that story and
I broke it first.

Let's at least meet for a cup of coffee. I want to show you
how my assets are too valuable to forego.

I'll call in a few days to arrange a time to meet.

Sincerely yours,

Brad C. Bawmann

Brad C. Bawmann
203 East Exposition Avenue
Denver, Colorado 80209
(303) 987-6754

June 17, 19--

Mr. Scott Wade
Editor
The Denver Post
650 - 15th Street
Denver, Colorado 80201

Dear Mr. Wade,

A no simply won't do. I can help make <u>The Denver Post</u> the
newspaper it aspires to be.

My news sense is made manifest by your paper frequently
replaying my scoops. A more tenacious, aggressive reporter
you won't find.

My drive, energy and enthusiasm are enough for three people.
I will work for you like no other.

Let's talk.

Some say times are tough at <u>The Post</u>. I prefer to think
you're rebuilding for the future.

I'm ready to be with the best. Are you ready to have the
best?

I'll call in a few days to set up a time to meet.

Sincerely yours,

Brad C. Bawmann

Enclosure

R O N A L D   L.   E V A N S

July 27, 19--

Mr. John Hill, Vice President
Materials Equipment Company
2 Pennsylvania Plaza
New York, New York   10001

Dear Mr. Hill

I want to thank you for the assistance you have so kindly
provided me. As I told you yesterday, I have contacted Mr.
Morris and forwarded him my resume. I appreciate your
suggesting that Mr. Sloan and Mr. Rice be contacted since
they have good business contacts and can probably offer
suggestions.

I was disappointed that you decided not to add a financial
management position for the company, because I'm certain I
could make a significant contribution with service work order
controls, parts inventory management, computer system
opportunities, reliable financial reporting, personnel
productivity measurements, and assisting with your efforts
for enhanced service to customers. As you know from our
conversation, I am a proponent of the importance of excellent
customer service.

I was very impressed with you as a concerned manager and with
the pleasant environment I observed in your facility. That
atmosphere, friendly and yet productive, represents the kind
of situation I am seeking.

I hope you will reconsider your decision. I would be glad to
meet with you and the owners further to explore the benefits
of adding a financial management position.

I don't want to belabor the subject; however, because I
believe there is very good potential, agree with your stated
ideals and goals, and like the attitude of the organization,
I know I would enjoy being a member of your management team.

Again, I want to express my appreciation for the help that
you are providing. I will keep you informed about any
developments or changes in status.

Sincerely yours,

Ronald L. Evans

RICHARD P. RUBY
1128 2nd Avenue South
Edmonds, Washington 98020

January 24, 19--

Dr. Richard C. Taylor
Scientific Software, Inc.
1801 California
Denver, Colorado 80202-2799

Dear Dr. Taylor:

Some months ago Jim Stovall suggested that I make a second effort to see you.

Recently Mike Hildebrand of Federal Express indicated that early February might be a good time.

Most of my life has been spent working through or around the many obstacles that third world governments love to put in the way of the continuing relationship that SSI must want to have with the overseas oil agencies. I've also participated in the development and day-to-day functioning of several significant international partnerships--which is an option that SSI might want to begin exploring.

Could we schedule a meeting to see if SSI is encountering enough third world roadblocks to warrant making use of my experience? We could consider employee status or an outside attorney relationship, as I'm well into conversations regarding joining one of Seattle's major law firms, and could serve SSI equally well from that base.

Yours truly,

Richard P. Ruby

cc: Jim Stovall
     Price Waterhouse

Michael D. Burns
Two Thousand Oak Towers
2000 West Federal Street
Boston, Massachusetts   02110

March 22, 19--

Mr. Allen E. Tufts
President
Tufts Technical Services
660 Kirkville Road
East Syracuse, New York   13057

Dear Allen:

It was good to talk with you last week, but I am disappointed
to see that our discussions are proceeding so slowly.

From my side, I am eager to get to work and, as you might
suspect, I have been pursuing a very active search. This
search has developed several possibilities, but I keep
thinking about your situation, which is such a good fit with
what I do best, and I am reluctant to see it possibly closed
off by a coincidence of timing rather than actual decision.

It is my understanding that you are looking for someone who
could provide strong assistance with day-to-day management
responsibilities so that you could concentrate more on the
longer-term issues. You feel you have assembled a strong
group of people, whose only deficiency is a lack of broad
management experience. This will come with time, but you
need someone to help you right now.

If this understanding is correct, I think I can provide you
some real help. As you know, my management experience has
been quite broad and varied, and at InTek I had a similar
situation. Most of the department heads there were also in
their early 30s and quite bright. It was a situation in
which I served as both leader and teacher. I very much
enjoyed doing this and along the way, we also built a very
strong and aggressive organization.

Please give these comments some serious thought, and
I will phone you in early April when you are back from your
trip.

Best regards,

Michael D. Burns

*

RICHARD P. RUBY

Mr. Kenneth D. Blackman
Corporate Counsel
Storage Technology Corporation
2270 South 88th Street
Louisville, Colorado 80027

Dear Kenneth,

You will recall that I visited you a few months ago at Bill Henry's arranging. Our discussion started with copper--which has been a large part of my life--and then moved to the role and responsibilities of a corporate counsel for a smaller hi-tech firm.

Since our talk, I have been interviewing in the east, and expect to be back there in the next week or so--but, as I mentioned to you, I would much prefer to stay in this area.

Your current state of work overload may well last for much longer than anyone suspects. I wonder if you might be feeling the need for some additional, battle-scarred strength in your office, to help you keep track of and deal with the many outside big-league players now buffeting STC.

A press release describing the financing we put together for the Peruvian copper mine in the '70s is enclosed--simply to give you an idea of the complexity of the undertaking. I had a lot to do with the entire effort, and would be glad to explain my work and accomplishments in detail if you should ever wish.

Chase Manhattan was the lead commercial bank on the financing. The Millbank Tweed lawyer who carried their load is now the senior outside legal counsel to Chase. He knows me well from that period, and he or his assistant (also a Millbank partner) could give you a reading on my contribution. ASARCO'S outside legal counsel was Covington and Burling, specifically Phil Rathbun and Dick West both of whom knew amd valued my work highly. Phil, after it was all over, commented that my ability to master a complex tangle of financial and commercial relationships, and to keep all the pieces lined up and moving in the desired direction, was crucial to the success of the legal side of the endeavor.

Please call me if you think there might be something to talk about in this suggestion.

Yours truly,

Richard P. Ruby

William B. Campbell
1302 West 22nd Street
Willmington, Deleware 19810
(302) 475-4829

May 27, 19--

William S. Frank
President
CareerLab
7700 East Arapahoe Road, Suite 275
Englewood, Colorado 80112

Dear Mr. Frank:

A few months ago I wrote to you regarding the possibility of doing some work with you. I am a consulting psychologist with 25 years background in a variety of different roles, and have had experience in career testing and counseling.

I am writing to you again to see what opportunities might presently exist to do some part-time consulting work with you.

Since writing to you before, I have been doing some career management consultation work, part-time, with two other firms in the Denver area. However, they use a marketing approach to career development exclusively, which I do not prefer and feel is not fully appropriate for clients.

I think that a solid understanding of an individual's preferences and capabilities, together with a keen awareness of his or her emotional motivations, are needed to help a person implement their career goals. I prefer more of a counseling approach to career development, and as I explained in my previous letter, use a directive approach in my counseling and work with clients.

If your firm has a need, I feel that I can provide assistance to you in such ways as the following:

* Career counseling in helping clients learn to manage their own career development and job search campaign.

* Career testing and assessment of a person's preferences, attitudes, and values.

* Consultation with more difficult clients who are experiencing motivational problems, or are even resisting the efforts of your program.

* Assisting with the difficulties encountered when a client is going through a outplacement process.

I also understand that there appears to be somewhat of a declining market for career services with certain firms in the Denver area. If this has not affected your business, and there is a continuing call for your services, then you might have need for some additional assistance.

If I can be of help to you, and my qualifications are of interest, please contact me so that we might arrange a meeting.

Sincerely,

William B. Campbell

*

Michael D. Burns
Two Thousand Oaks Towers
2000 West Federal Street
Boston, Massachusetts   02110
(617) 765-9898

November 9, 19--

Mr. Larry Anderson
President
Petroleum Waste, Inc.
2701 Patton Way
Bakersfield, California 93308

Dear Larry:

Just a brief note to thank you and your group for the time
you spent with me last Thursday and Friday. I appreciate the
detail that was provided and candor that was evident. You
have an excellent group of people in your operation and it
would be a pleasure to work with you and them.

<u>Expanding a few points that we discussed</u>:

Yes, I am interested in the job of Site Manager. You are
apparently concerned that this job does not have the scope of
some of my previous positions, but I know that it has plenty
of challenge and problems and it will give me a great deal of
satisfaction to be allowed to handle them. You can see from
my resume that once I take a job I stick with it. I have
only worked for three companies; my shortest time with any
one was more than four years, and I worked nearly 20 years
for Amoco.

Another concern seemed to be whether I feel I can handle a
job that requires "hands-on" management, and also an ability
to cope with a frustrating corporate environment. My time
spent managing start-up and turnaround situations has given
me considerable OJT in both these areas. I enjoy "hands-on,"
and I have always been able to achieve efficiency regardless
of the environment.

Larry, I would appreciate a shot at the job.

Best regards,

Michael D. Burns

MB/mb

Jonathan B. Field

February 13, 19--

Mr. Jerry D. Speer
Senior Vice President
International Environmental Services, Inc.
P.O. Box 609
Deer Park, Texas 77536-0609

Dear Mr. Speer,

This is in response to your request for additional
information about me. I have enclosed a resume as well as
completing your application.

I would like to point out what I feel are my areas of
expertise.

o   Solid management experience in the operations of an
     organization.

o   Success in sales/marketing of technical products and
     services.

o   Consistent financial results through market penetration
     and cost control.

o   Firm dealings with personnel issues of discipline,
     compensation and employee development.

As I indicated in my original letter to you, the similarities
between my background and your business would allow me to use
my experience effectively.

I worked with Halliburton following graduation from Illinois
Technological University in 19-- until the end of 19--. My
ending salary was $6,700 per month. I have been the
recipient of several incentive stock options since 19--.

I will provide you with references, including the Vice
President and General Manager I last reported to, assuming
our discussions develop further.

I will call you next week after you have had an opportunity
to review my resume.

Thank you for your interest.

Sincerely,

Jonathan B. Field

BRUCE D. ROBERTSON, C.P.A.
3182 South Holly Street
Denver, Colorado 80222
(303) 756-7435 (H)
(303) 779-1417 (W)

June 3, 19--

Michael J. Browning, Ph.D.
Vice President and Academic Dean
Roberts Wesleyan College
2301 Westside Drive
Rochester, New York 14624-1997

Dear Dr. Browning:

I am very interested in applying for your vacant faculty
position in Accounting at Roberts Wesleyan College. Thank
you for sending me the application forms, which I have
completed and enclosed. I am looking forward to visiting you
to discuss this exciting teaching opportunity in more detail.

Since your letter of May 20, I had an informative telephone
conversation with Dr. Jim Baker. Dr. Baker filled me in
concerning your school, new accounting programs, and teaching
philosophy. This position is exactly the type of teaching
opportunity that I am seeking--one in which I immerse myself.

Last night, I was talking with my choir partner, Bill
Griffith, at our Colorado Chorale Concert. He mentioned that
you two worked together at NCHEMS in Boulder.

If you have any questions, or need any additional
information, please feel free to call me at 303-779-1417 (W)
or 303-756-7435 (H).

Sincerely,

Bruce D. Robertson, CPA

BDR:pr
Attachments

cc: Dr. Jim Baker

Michael D. Burns
Two Thousand Oaks Towers
2000 West Federal Street
Boston, Massachusetts   02110
(617) 765-9898

November 24, 19--

Mr. Robert T. Wagner
Ecology and Environment, Inc.
P. O. Box D
195 Holtz Road
Buffalo, New York   14225

Dear Mr. Wagner:

First of all, I want to thank you for the time you took to talk with me on the phone last week. Your comments make sense and your enthusiasm about the future of Ecology and Environment, Inc. is contagious. The company sounds like a very dynamic and progressive place to work.

As we discussed, I am looking for a position in general management, and I do have those "well balanced, multi-discipline skills" necessary to make one effective in such a job. I began my career in a technical area as a geologist, and then broadened it through both education and job experience. I have worked in three different industries, in situations that have included both startups and difficult turnarounds. I am a true management professional and feel I have a lot to offer your company.

A summary of my credentials is enclosed and I will be glad to provide any additional information you might need. As we discussed, I am free to travel and open to relocation.

Once again, thank you for your help and I look forward to talking again in the near future.

Sincerely,

Michael D. Burns

Enclosure

BRUCE D. ROBERTSON, CPA
3182 South Holly Street
Denver, Colorado 80222
(303) 756-7435 (H)
(303) 779-1417 (W)

October 14, 19--

Mr. Donald B. Martin
Pendleton Resources
1899 Logan, Suite 250
Denver, Colorado 80203

Dear Donald:

Hope you have a great vacation! As you suggested I will call
you after your return the week of October 20th.

Just to jog your memory, I am the individual referred by Bill
Black for the international position which is on hold until
late October while the new President is traveling the world
to see the company.

In addition, I have put together the enclosed recap of my
Administrative and Finance capabilities in order to market
myself for what will be the most productive years of my life.
This is the same information as in my resume I gave you, but
in a different format that you may find useful.

I am looking forward to meeting with you to discuss the
exciting, challenging international position in more detail.

Sincerely,

Bruce Robertson

BDR/bl
Enclosure

Bruce D. Robertson, CPA

Consulting Capabilities, Specialties and Experience

I. International Operations

    A. Was Managing Director of IMEC, Ltd. (International Management and Engineering Consultants, Ltd.).

    B. Lived and worked in Europe.
        Was number two man in European operation which grew in two years from $5 million to $55 million in sales.

    C. Planning and control
        Developed international strategic plan and budgets.

    D. Communicate in French in business matters.

    E. Administrative, finance, organizational, and operational experience.

II. Strategic Planning and Budgeting

    A. Develop and implement plans.

    B. Feasibility studies.

    C. Cash flow planning.

    D. Budgets and forecasts.

    E. Develop budget control systems based on business flow.

III. Business Management

    A. Problem Solver.

    B. Operations management.
        Chief Operating Officer for 300-person operation.

    C. Management assessment and auditing.

IV. Management Development

    A. Strategic planning, international business, finance, and accounting systems.

    B. Motivate enthusiastic employees.

    C. Develop management personnel.

    D. Develop successful Management by Objective (MBO) systems.

    E. Help managers to use MBO as their own key personal management tool.

V. Accounting and Finance

    A. Accounting systems and operations.
        Design and solve operational problems.

    B. Establish foreign bank lines.

    C. Venture capital.

Brad Bawmann
203 East Exposition Avenue
Denver, Colorado 80209
(303) 385-8574

August 10, 19--

Mr. Jeff Rundles
Managing Editor
The Denver Business Journal
2401 - 15th Street, Suite 350
Denver, Colorado 80202

Dear Jeff,

Lunch was fabulous!

Your suggestions and insight concerning the media industry
were most relevant and quite welcome.

I've enclosed samples of my work from both The Creek a weekly
newspaper and UPI, where I interned in London.

I'll call in a few days. I'm anxious for your feedback.

Warmest regards,

Brad C. Bawmann

Enclosures

Brad Bawmann
203 East Exposition Avenue
Denver, Colorado 80209
(303) 798-4357

August 10, 19--

Ms. Janet Case
Publications Manager
The Children's Hospital
1800 Emerson Street
Denver, Colorado 80204

Dear Ms. Case,

It was great speaking with you over the telephone Friday. As promised, I've enclosed a few work samples.

Let me emphasize, however, I am much more than an aggressive reporter/writer. Versatility, enthusiasm, and ceaseless energy are but a few of the assets I can promise you.

In addition, as my letters of recommendation indicate, I'm willing to go the extra five miles it sometimes takes to make a project sparkle and shine.

If there is more I can do in your decision-making process please feel free to call.

I'm anxious to show you how I am the best candidate for the position.

Thanks for your time.

Sincerely yours,

Brad C. Bawmann

Enclosure

Get Help from Consultants
—or Become One

Most consultants know a lot of successful, influential people. (They must to stay in business.) If you know consultants, call them. If not, meet some through friends. Ask for their advice and ideas. If they like you—and why shouldn't they?—they will offer to share their contacts.

It's not uncommon for job-seekers to pursue consulting and a "real job" at the same time. Typically, what happens is that one direction emerges as the winner. Don't be afraid to let people know you could either consult or work full time.

*

G R E G O R Y   A .   H A T F I E L D

July 25, 19--

William S. Frank
President
CareerLab
7700 East Arapahoe Road, Suite 275
Englewood, Colorado 80112

Dear Mr. Frank:

I saw your listing in the Boulder County Manufacturers
Directory. My fiance will be entering the University of
Colorado in September, so I am seeking placement with firms
in the Boulder area. I hope you can assist me.

I am currently living with my parents in Indiana. Their
failing health required me to move there temporarily while
attending to family business. Now that things are under
control, I am beginning my job search.

I have enclosed a copy of my current resume. I would
summarize my strengths as follows:

- Ten years' management consulting experience during
  which I developed superior business communication and
  presentation skills.

- A detailed, results-oriented consulting approach.
  Many consultants' primary product is a report with
  recommendations for action. My experience and
  inclination is to take the next step and assist
  clients in implementing necessary change to
  organizations, policies, procedures and systems.

- Strong functional experience in the areas of
  Strategic Planning, Accounting, MIS, and
  Manufacturing Operations.

- Extensive project management experience--in some
  cases managing projects entailing multi-million
  dollar budgets and employing scores of personnel.

- A solid business education focused on marketing.

I am interested in pursuing one of the following positions:

o   A product marketing or staff marketing position with
    a growth-oriented manufacturing concern.

o   A consulting position with opportunity for attaining
    partnership within one or two years.

o   A product marketing or sales support position with a
    software development concern.

I worked slightly less than nine months in 19-- and my income
was just over $75,000. I need your advice on salaries in the
Boulder area. My gut feeling at this time is that $40,000
per year would be a minimum acceptable salary given my
experience and background.

I am looking forward to discussing my situation with you. I
will be calling in the next few days to get your input.

Sincerely yours,

Gregory A. Hatfield
RR#2 Box 237A
Terrance, Indiana 47390
(317) 584-7475

Paul H. Gutknecht
11374 Quivas Way
Westminster, Colorado 80234
(303) 465-1236

May 18, 19--

Ms. Marilyn Henry
1238 Oak Creek Drive
Littleton, Colorado 80121

Dear Marilyn,

While continuing the search for a full-time job, I wish to add some new consulting assignments. I hope that you can help me in that regard.

A partial list of things that I can do for clients is enclosed. Please take a few minutes and think about friends, or customers, or problems where my talents and intelligence would be useful.

I'll call next week to hear your ideas.

Very truly yours,

Paul Gutknecht

PG/

Enclosure

Steven R. MacDonald
11285 Admiral Road
Albuquerque, New Mexico 87112
(505) 821-4420

February 3, 19--

Mr. Jeffrey D. O'Toole
Vice President
Deloitte, Haskins & Sells
2000 East Randolph Drive
Chicago, Illinois 60601

Dear Mr. O'Toole:

I know what it takes to make a profit in the consulting
industry because I have been there--as a Managing Partner in
a large consulting engineering firm (Dames & Moore), as
President of a mid-size consulting firm, and as Founder and
President of a multi-discipline firm.

I am interested in a firm that has growth and/or
diversification goals and needs an executive manager who can
assume both P&L and marketing responsibility and, eventually,
an equity position.

I know the consulting industry. I know that it takes an
innovative and unique marketing strategy to produce a top
line, and it takes decisive management to meet chargeability
goals--I can provide both.

In addition, I have the financial experience to manage and
analyze accounting information and negotiate with bankers and
other financial groups with respect to long and short-term
borrowing, letters of credit, payroll arrangements, etc.

I would like to meet to see if an association would be
beneficial to both of us, and I'll call you early next week.

Very truly yours,

Steven R. MacDonald

SRM/btk

Enclosure: Fact Sheet

♥

T. Craig Lincoln

Mr. Bill Frank   July 20, 19--
CareerLab
7700 East Arapahoe Road, Suite 275
Englewood, Colorado 80112

Dear Mr. Frank:

Usually when you call in an artist, that's exactly what you
get. An artist. Good art, but questionable business
understanding.

When you hire me you get a "business artist". Someone who is
a professional design artist. And someone who understands
business.

-- I am a one-person design team. Very small. Very personal.
-- With over 25 years of experience in business art.
-- I designed and implemented the corporate identity program
   for Old National Bank of Washington which saved them
   $7,500.
-- I designed and produced a capabilities proposal for the
   Dravo Corporation. As a result, they were awarded a
   $35,000,000 engineering and construction project.

I could quickly achieve the same results for you.

        USE ME FOR . . .

        1. Corporate design of all printed materials.
        2. Industrial and architectural graphics.
        3. Interior space planning.
        4. Industrial and vocational education design.
        5. Corporate advertising and marketing communications.

Let's meet. Let's talk. Let's do some business that will
put you out front and keep you out front in your market.

At your earliest convenience, please contact me if you would
like to hear and see more. During the day you can reach me
at 303-745-0250.

Sincerely,

T. Craig Lincoln

JULIE NORMAND
Business Writing Services   (303) 744-7559

October 14, 19--

Mr. Mark O. Goodman
Texaco, Inc.
440 South Fox Street
Denver, Colorado 80223

Dear Mr. Goodman:

From time to time, your company may need well-written
publicity or other business writing that you don't have the
time or personnel to handle. How would you like to have a
good business writer on call without adding to your permanent
payroll?

Introducing Julie Normand Business Writing Services.

As a free-lance copy writer specializing in publicity and
business writing for small companies, I have had experience
with a wide variety of products and services. Attached is a
partial client list.

My specialties are:

* Brochure and catalog copy

* Company and marketing newsletters

* Press releases

* Correspondence, form letters, direct mail letters

* Training manuals, employee handbooks

Because I'm not affiliated with any agency and my overhead is
low, my rates are very reasonable. I also have word-
processing equipment that enables me to provide quick
turnaround on rewrites.

Whether you have an extensive project or simply a one-time
"impossible" letter to write, I can help you. Please give me
a call at your convenience.

Sincerely,

Julie Normand

COMPUTERIZING THE LAW OFFICE
Rory Donaldson Software
320 South Vine Street
Denver, Colorado 80209
(303) 777-7068

February 8, 19--

Mr. Robert D. Bennett
200 Colorado State Bank Building
1775 Broadway
Denver, Colorado 80202

Dear Mr. Bennett:

I specialize in helping small law offices (1-15 attorneys)
get the computer systems they need--be it a stand-alone
microcomputer or a complete network; basic word-processing
through legal billing and timekeeping; file sharing through
Lexis research.

Because I do not sell either hardware or software, or
represent any vendors whatsoever, I am not required to sell
you a particular line of products. I recommend solutions
that will work best for you, be it IBM PC and compatibles, or
MacIntosh hardware and software. I then negotiate with a
variety of vendors to get you the best price, service
contracts, installation and guarantees of performance
available.

My services are straightforward:

     - To help you analyze what you want to do, recommend the
       most cost-effective solutions, and the best providers
       of service. To help you negotiate the best prices I
       am only paid by my clients. I accept no fees or
       commissions from any vendors or companies.

     - To supervise all purchases, delivery and installation,
       advising you when to "accept delivery."

     - To help with attorney training.

     - To help with staff training and conversion.

     - My fee is $75 per hour.

In short, I save you time and money by insuring that you get
the quality, products and service you require, quickly.
During the 10 years I've been in the computer business I have
never had a client who didn't save far more than the cost of
my fee by avoiding jargon, frustration, wasted hours,

Mr. Robert D. Bennett
February 8, 19--
Page two

inappropriate hardware and software choices and incomplete
service contracts.

There is no charge for my first hour of consultation. During
this hour you and I will be able to tell if my services are
appropriate for your firm. If I am unable to help, perhaps I
can recommend someone who can. I look forward to talking
with you about how I can be of service. Give me a call
today.

                    Sincerely,

                    Rory Donaldson, Owner

P.S.   Phone 777-7068 to set up a free consultation. Ask for
       me personally.

T H O M A S   W E S T O N   &   A S S O C I A T E S

One Financial Tower
1800 Broadway, Suite 3500
Denver, Colorado 80202 /303-692-2950

May 5, 19--

William S. Frank
President
CareerLab
7700 East Arapahoe Road, Suite 275
Englewood, Colorado 80112

Dear Mr. Frank:

Your clients face a variety of uncertainties: job, location,
longevity, and income. The counseling benefits you offer
address many of their concerns.

We would like to be a part of your network. We can offer a
wide range of personal, unbiased financial services--from
individual consultations to group workshops.

Enclosed is information to help you assess our firm's
capabilities. Please do look it over.

We will call you in a few days to ask if you would like to
talk about the possibility of a relationship with us.

We look forward to meeting you.

Sincerely,

Thomas Weston, CPA

Certified Financial Planner
Admitted to The Registry of Financial Planning Practitioners

SIGMA GROUP INC.
717 Seventeeth Street
Suite 1440
Denver, Colorado 80202-3314
(303) 292-6720

July 9, 19--

Mr. William S. Frank
President
CareerLab
7700 East Arapahoe Road, Suite 275
Englewood, Colorado 80112

Dear Bill:

Thank you again for the opportunity to meet you and to discuss mutual business interests. I hope we have the opportunity to work together in the very near future.

When I refer potential clients to you, I will normally call you first to alert you to the fact that I have made a referral. Please do not feel obligated to assume a client relationship if it does not seem to make sense. Be assured, these referrals will only be senior people. At the same time, I would also appreciate the same courtesy.

Again, thanks for your time this week as I appreciated the opportunity to become personally acquainted.

Best wishes,

George L. Reisinger
Managing Partner

William S. Frank

May 27, 19--

Mr. Norman E. Weatherman
Sherman & Howard
2900 First Interstate Tower North
633 Seventeenth Street
Denver, Colorado 80202

Dear Norm,

Thank you for your referral to High Technology, Inc.
I met with them today and we are mapping out a strategy
for helping the eighteen supervisors who will be leaving
the company.

I am recommending two days of workshops--a couple
half-days now, and one full day nearer the date of the
plant closing. (By the time you get this letter, everything
might have changed.)

I would also work individually by the hour with
supervisors obviously needing extra help after the
workshops are completed.

Thank you for this referral. It was kind of you
to think of me. I will keep you posted on all new
developments, and I will certainly return the favor to
you at the earliest opportunity.

As I told you on the telephone, Tim Silva did a
superb job in his presentation to my personnel friends.
They were more than impressed, and knowing them, I'm
certain you will be seeing some new work coming out of
our joint marketing effort.

Call if you need me.

Sincerely yours,

William S. Frank

Paul H. Gutknecht
11374 Quivas Way
Westminster, Colorado 80234
(303) 465-1236

February 23, 19--

Robert C. Evans
Controller
Firestone
234 Union Avenue
Memphis, TN   38112

Dear Bob,

As you know, my consulting business has been fun and
interesting. However, I prefer to have the responsibility
and authority to make things happen. I want to move back
into the corporate world and make another ten-year
contribution to a company's success.

Management, financial and accounting skills are valuable to
any industry, and some of my consulting has been outside the
petroleum industry, but the oil business is still my first
love. Similarly, Mary and I like Denver very much, but we
would cheerfully relocate for the right opportunity.

Please take a few minutes to think about possible needs among
your friends and associates for a man of my talents. You can
either give them the enclosed copy of my resume, or give me
their names so that I can follow through.

Any assistance or advice you can give me is greatly
appreciated. Thank you.

Sincerely,

Paul H. Gutknecht

PHG:kam

Enclosure

Build Business Relationships

One of my most successful entrepreneurial clients explained his success this way: "I create relationships. The relationships create the jobs."

In the marketing of personal services (that is to say, job-hunting), relationships are everything. Take every opportunity to build goodwill for yourself in the community.

April 4

Dear Bill,

Congratulations on the article "Job Hunters Beware." Did you place that? You really do a great job! And I love the artwork the newspaper provided — really eye-catching

Best Wishes. Talk to you soon.

Sharon Kennicott

August 25, 19--

Mr. Michael T. Simmons
Director of Administration
Prudential Real Estate Group
1800 Broadway, Suite 1800
Denver, Colorado 80202

Dear Mike,

I was extremely pleased to learn that you've gotten happily re-established in human resources and administration.

I'm also glad you stayed in Denver. I appreciate your friendship, and would have felt a loss had you left.

In addition, you're a great resource to the community.

Congratulations!

William S. Frank

THE WEST REAL ESTATE COMPANY
Box 20 Keystone, Colorado 80435
(303) 467-2011

January 18, 19--

Mr. Jory L. Laine
2700 Julian Street
Denver, Colorado 80211

Dear Jory:

I am pleased and excited about your good news.

There was no question in my mind that it was just a matter of finding the right slot and correct niche for this thing to finally come together. When an individual possesses the talent and capabilities you have so clearly demonstrated and the approach you used in looking for new opportunities, it was simply a matter of timing.

I hope your new position offers you a tremendous challenge and fulfillment in addressing those challenges. We look forward to a good 19-- and hope you will continue to keep in touch and drop by anytime you are up in this area.

Very truly yours,

Todd L. Hansen
President

TLH/jd

June 29, 19--

Ms. Ann T. Richardson
Benefits Coordinator
Regal Corporation
350 Inverness Drive West
Englewood, Colorado 80112

Dear Ann:

I hope this book catches you at a time when you need a good
laugh about business.

There are some great Human Resource jokes in here, and I hope
they brighten your day.

Warm regards,

William S. Frank

WSF:bl
Attachment

April 7, 19--

Mr. Richard D. North
Regional Employee Relations Manager
Connecticut Mutual
300 South Parker Road
Aurora, Colorado 80014

Dear Rich:

Denver Business recently interviewed me about outplacement
and the nation's retirement epidemic.

I thought the article was interesting and timely and wanted
you to have a copy.

I would enjoy hearing your thoughts and ideas after you have
had a chance to look it over.

Wishing you all the best.

Sincerely,

William S. Frank

WSF:kam
Attachment

*

BRUCE D. ROBERTSON
4325 Buffalo Road
N. Chili, New York 14514
(716) 594-2766

Many exciting things are happening in my life since I wrote
you last spring. First, I have become a facilitator for The
Management Roundtable (TMR).

TMR, a national organization headquartered in Denver,
Colorado, consists of groups of 10-15 CEO's or Senior Level
Managers. I like that TMR provides such a great opportunity
for these individuals to meet monthly for issue resolution,
management development, enrichment/education, and mutual
support. I am organizing TMR's first group in Rochester,
New York. CEO's will start meeting early next year.

I have just begun my second year of teaching at Roberts
Wesleyan College. My favorite courses last year included
Strategic Planning, Managerial Accounting and Motivation,
Money and Banking, and Income Tax. This fall I initiated a
job-search workshop class for all business seniors. Each
student develops and manages his own MBO's for resume
preparation, job network-building, and practice interviewing.

This summer, I spent a month visiting Colorado and western
New York. In Colorado, I was again part of the Breckenridge
Music Institute's choir workshop. We premiered a two-piano
piece by Berger based upon Psalms 118 & 119. Rafting down
the Colorado River was my risk-excitement for the summer.
In New York, my sons and I visited many parks. We found the
waterfalls in the western New York area fantastic. Brian
loved Niagara Falls. (Sorry, Colorado, nothing close to
these beauties in Colorado.) Our trip to Cooperstown, New
York--the Baseball Hall of Fame--was a highlight for my son
Brett. He is a real baseball aficionado, especially of the
Boston Red Sox.

As to the future, the first meeting of The Management
Roundtable in Rochester will be held January 20th. In
addition, my parents and I are planning a business/pleasure
trip to Europe, May & June. I will also be offering a new
course this spring entitled International Business. With my
special interest in international affairs, I am really
excited about this new offering.

May you all have a blessed and successful fall and winter.

Bruce D. Robertson

C O L O R A D O   B A N K I N G
2400 Broadway, Suite 3400
Denver, Colorado 80202
(303) 325-4883

July 2, 19--

Mr. William S. Frank
CareerLab
7700 East Arapahoe Road, Suite 275
Englewood, Colorado 80112

Dear Bill:

Thank you for the book; it was delightful and definitely made my day. Your thoughtfulness is very much an exception.

I look forward to an opportunity to work together. Be assured when Colorado Bank experiences a need for your career consulting services, I will be in touch.

Once again, I can't tell you enough how much the book was of value to me. We share the same sense of humor.

Most sincerely,

Madeline P. Carson
Vice President Human Resources

MPC/sw

17

Promote Yourself In The Media

Job-seeking is much like running for political office, in that it's important to be seen in public. Employers can't hire you if they don't know you exist, so use every avenue at your disposal to gain visibility. Write articles for newspapers, magazines, and professional journals. Give talks and appear on radio and television. Make certain you are seen, noticed, and hired.

✌✳

February 12, 19--

Ms. Jane Diethl
Managing Editor
<u>Up The Creek</u>
2038 South Pontiac Way
Denver, Colorado 80224

Dear Jane:

Thanks for discussing my story idea on <u>the brighter side of
unemployment.</u>

Yes, Denver's economy is suffering, but there are some
"tricks of the trade," some simple ways to be <u>creative and
innovative in the job market.</u>

Fifty-five-year-olds don't have to be unemployed for 6 to 12
months and they don't have to work delivering pizzas.

Let's talk about it.

Sincerely,

William S. Frank

WSF/bk

Bill Frank & Associates

July 28, 19--

Mr. David Black
General Manager and Vice President
KSTV Channel 8
2300 Broadway, Suite 5200
Denver, Colorado 80202

Dear David:

I have been watching the exciting things you are doing at
Channel 8.

You appear to be always reaching out, risking, looking for
the new angle--the new idea--the new gimmick to benefit your
viewers (and glue them to the set).

How would you feel about doing a brief weekly segment related
to jobs and career--a very timely, HOT topic these days!

You might show such things as:

1. The <u>excitement</u> in the career market (not the 3.6
    percent that aren't employed, but the 96.4 percent
    that <u>are employed</u>--and specifically the very few
    that <u>love their work.</u> The success stories. How
    they got there. The challenges they faced.

    Their advice!
    Their ideas!
    Their enthusiasm!

2. Community resources and information.

3. The Denver market: Where it's <u>HOT</u> and where it's
    <u>NOT</u>.

4. How to choose the right job.

5. How to get a job fast--and so forth.

I would like to help you put these ideas together--and <u>here's
why you would benefit:</u>

1. The public needs this information, wants this
    information--it's timely.

2. Companies are cutting from the top and no one is
    "secure" anymore. People are running scared.

3. The job market is in a turmoil, changing faster and
    faster, and that's not going to stop.

4. No one else is doing this.

I would be a good person to help you because I am a
professional career planner--that's all I do. I have
contacts and resources. I know the Denver job market inside
out, <u>but most of all, I am</u> . . .

-   Great at getting people excited.
-   Great at getting people talking about themselves.
-   Great at getting people <u>involved.</u>

Does this sound workable? I have lots of ideas--and I'm sure
you do too! Let's get together and talk.

Enthusiastically,

William S. Frank
President

Enclosures

William S. Frank
President
CareerLab
7700 East Arapahoe Road, Suite 275
Englewood, Colorado 80112

January 25, 19--

Ms. Dottie Wahl
News Reporter
KCWB Television
2000 Bellaire Drive
Los Angeles, California 90046

Dear Dottie:

I'm excited about getting to meet you. I think we will have
fun together--and job-finding is a very timely topic. To
help you prepare, I am going to tell you a little about
myself and suggest some topics for discussion. OK? Please
use this as a guideline and call me if you need to!

Highlights of My Training:

    -- M.A. in philosophy, 1969, Colorado State University.
    -- Studied psychology, 1965-1990.
    -- Studied psychotherapy with Warner A. Baker, M.D.,
       a Denver psychiatrist.
    -- Studied with Dick Bolles, the country's leading
       career expert, the author of <u>What Color is Your
       Parachute?</u>
    -- Was Vice President for the country's largest
       outplacement consulting firm.

Profile of the People I Work Best With:

    -- High level business executives and professionals.
    -- People going through a major life transition (such as
       divorce).
    -- Age groups 30 to 55.
    -- People in confusion about how it all "fits together"-
       -especially, right-brain, creative, intuitive types
       that don't necessarily <u>fit into a "slot"</u> in our left
       brain, detail, fact, figures, and data-oriented
       culture.
    -- Professionals (dentist, lawyers, doctors) seeking to
       build successful practices.

How I Work

My special talent is to help people sort through confusion _quickly_ (sometimes in as little as one hour) and come to a point of _clarity_ about exactly who they are and exactly where they're going. We try to resolve this at a deep level--for the long term, not just for "now."

My chief tool is to ask questions. Knowing _which_ questions to ask is one of the key things I do. (Someone once said that the best therapist is one who can say "absolutely nothing" at exactly the right moment.) And I think this is what I do.

I also use written exercises, and standardized tests when they are appropriate.

Suggested Topics for Discussion:

1. Why do people have trouble deciding which job they want?

2. The media is painting a very _black_ picture of unemployment. What are some of the _positive_ things happening in the world of work? (Well, for one thing, there's a _revolution_ going on in job-finding.)

3. What can this unemployment now teach us? (For one thing, it is a preview of the future. "Job security," working 40 years for a company is practically a thing of the past. It is no longer possible to take a job and "forget about it." In the future people may change jobs four to five times in a lifetime. Therefore, we must be ready, plan, pack our parachutes, and be ready to jump.)

4. How has job-hunting changed?

5. Why is job-finding a sales job--and how do you do it?

6. What are some of the helpful community resources? (Like books, job networks, community college courses, and organizations.)

I hope this helps, Dottie. See you soon!

Bill Frank

18

Prevent Termination or Leave Gracefully

A poor performance evaluation, especially after many years of good ones, can mean that your company is setting you up for termination. If possible, stand up for yourself and get the poor evaluation off your record. Write a letter contesting any claims you feel are unfair. Substantiate your position with facts and figures.

If you decide to leave, or if you are forced to leave, negotiate a fair severance package and get it in writing. If you do leave the corporation, leave on good terms. Don't burn bridges. There's a very good chance you'll need these people later for a reference, perhaps even years later. Future employers often check references as far back as ten years. Don't lose a valuable job offer because you once left a company on bad terms.

DATE: January 15, 19--
   To: Michael Bond

   CC: David Johansen
         Kathy Richardson

FROM: Barbara Howard

SUBJECT: My contributions to Silicon Valley, Inc.

I have completed in-depth discussions with the people you recommended, and I would like to summarize what I've heard and realized, my beliefs about what I need to do, and evidence of constructive actions taken since my poor performance review. Please consider these factors in the decision whether outplacement is appropriate.

Issues for improvement noted by manufacturing managers:

1.   Excessive analysis or "perfecting", leading to low productivity.

2.   Errors in prioritizing goals and conflicting inputs.

3.   Inadequate communication with team members and supervisor.

My realizations and convictions following recent interviews:

In 19--, my contribution to Silicon Valley, Inc. was not acceptable either to me or to you. I need to:

1.   Take the initiative to identify changes which will make a tangible difference in the product line;

2.   Be tenacious in causing these effects to be realized in a minimal time period;

3.   Create closer linkage with our team and management, to achieve a consensus about priorities and my agenda;

4.   Focus my 15 years of experience on judging the shortest path to effective results; and

5.   Avoid unnecessary diversions from the key commitments.

What I have addressed and changed since my last review:

1.   An example of productivity and avoiding "perfecting" is four completed Engineering Change Order releases of all KKD, Checkout, and Product Acceptance procedures of SEMI and T-Systems, as the products have evolved through trials, controlled release, and first Production. These

were on-time, easier to use, and have credibility with the checkout Technicians because they were heavily involved in the development. There were few errors noted in recent audit.

2. Toward improving communication and prioritizing, I initiated "Ontarget" objective tracking, as well as weekly "defect resolution" meetings with Checkout and team engineers/designers. Defect diagnosis and elimination, training, and cooperation are the goals.

3. In the area of responsiveness to varied inputs, my role as Product Engineer for review and classification of all SEMI-2 Engineering Change Orders has been executed with quick turn-around times and concise recommendations to originators.

There is no doubt of my error in failing to confront the issues of my review more widely. Whereas I consulted only Jim Thomas, Bill Randolph, and certain SEMI-2 team members, I would have done better to work with you and the managers recently interviewed. However, the issues have been addressed in earnest over the last six months and I feel that substantive corrections have already begun. Based on recent candid feedback from my teammates and manager, I feel comfortable in recommending their opinions to you as evidence of improved contribution.

My ability to change certain behaviors:

Some course corrections have occurred, Mike, but we both know that behavioral changes are evolutionary and progress slowly, if they happen at all. However, I'd like to offer some evidence of meaningful change which came unexpectedly in the recent interviews. In discussing some positive attributes, a number of the managers used words like "personable", well-liked", or "easy to get along with." This was good news to me because a key Area-For-Improvement in my early years at Silicon Valley, Inc. was "interpersonal skills." I'm suggesting that this behavior has been altered enough to be no longer an issue.

In summary, Mike, I believe that my level of contribution has improved visibly this year and that most members of my team would agree. I hope you will consider recent performance in your decision.

Sincerely,

Barbara Howard
Project Engineer

```
TO:      T. Randolph Edwards
FROM:    Robert Wolfe
DATE:    April 18, 19--
SUBJECT: Outplacement, Director of Finance
```

This memo is a follow-up to our meeting of April 12th in which we discussed the arrangements necessary for me to make a smooth transition from Worldwide Manufacturing to another company. Here are the ten points we covered:

1. My employment as Director of Finance will continue at my current salary level through January 2nd, and I will be free, at my discretion, to take time off for personal business.

2. I will receive a lump sum severance payment amounting to 12 months' salary (based on my current rate of pay) the day I leave the company.

3. All my benefits (Medical and Dental Insurance, Matching Donations, Thrift Plan) will continue for one year after my departure.

4. All bonuses (gainsharing, executive incentive paid at target achievement level) will be paid for 12 months after my departure, as though I were a full-time employee. Bonuses to be paid when other employees receive their checks.

5. You will permanently remove my recent poor performance review from personnel file, and I will review and approve my personnel records before leaving.

6. Senior management will give my reason for leaving as "Position eliminated by corporate restructuring caused by sale of company."

7. Worldwide Manufacturing will provide me outplacement assistance of $16,500 (15% of annual compensation) within 30 days of joint approval of this agreement.

8. I will vest 100% in pension and 401K plans.

9. Existing stock options will take effect upon my departure.

10. I will be free to cease active employment at any time before January 2nd, if I accept a job offer.

Randy, I have enjoyed our work together, and am sorry to see it coming to an end. I am confident this package is fair to all of us, and that it represents a sound basis for a smooth transition.

INTER-OFFICE MEMORANDUM

    TO   Mike Taggert   **DATE**   November 3, 19--

SUBJECT   Resignation   **FROM**   Dan Goin

_____

This will confirm my resignation as Director of
Personnel and Compensation at City Medical Hospital.

I have accepted the position of Human Resources Director
at a growing operations management company in the Denver
area. I am looking forward to my new position and the
challenges that await me.

My last day of work will be December 31, 19--, which
should provide sufficient time to complete existing
projects and turn over management of the personnel,
benefits and compensation areas. Please feel free to
contact me at any time should you have any questions
regarding my past work. I hope that the transition will
go smoothly for everyone.

The past 15 years with CMH have been rewarding. I
appreciate your trust and confidence in my abilities and
your support. I am grateful for the opportunities and
experience afforded me and for the many friends that I
have made along the way. I wish you and the
organization continued success.

19

Support A Friend In The Job Market

Sometimes it's difficult to know what to say when a friend is having difficulty finding the right job. These letters will help you to encourage your friends and relatives. The "secret letter" (page 314) allows you to help out when someone wants to run a confidential campaign.

William S. Frank

December 15, 19--

Michael Kenner
Vice President Human Resources
IBM
1383 Fountainview, Suite 2300
Houston, Texas 77057

Dear Mike:

I seldom write a marketing letter for someone--in fact I
never have--but this time I'm making an exception, because
there's someone I think you should meet.

I have a personal friend who is still employed and
successful. Mike is stable and not in danger of losing his
job. But he is looking for another position in human
resources, because he has outgrown his present company.

He's the kind of guy who tells it like it is and gets things
done. In fact, he is . . .

        -- Outspoken
        -- An action-taker
        -- Very results-oriented
        -- Also risk-oriented.

In short, he's probably the kind of human resources
professional you'd like to have around.

For nine years he's been an outstanding performer in the oil
and gas and electronics industries--and his strengths are in
O.D., Succession Planning, Compensation and Benefits,
Training and Development, and Wage and Salary Administration.

I NEED YOUR HELP.

1.   Call me if you have some ideas.
2.   Call me if you know of suitable openings.
3.   Call me if you'd like to learn more.
4.   Call me if your friends might know something.

I can be reached at 303/771-4357 and would enjoy meeting you.

Sincerely yours,

William S. Frank

P.S.   If you offer any help or ideas, I will send you a
       current updated directory of all the Executive Search
       Consultants in the country.

Daniel I. Stack
100 East Ninth Avenue
New York, New York 10038

August 2, 19--

PERSONAL AND CONFIDENTIAL

Mr. William S. Peterson
Office of the Chairman
Continental Illinois National Bank
231 S. La Salle Street
Chicago, Illinois 60693

Dear Bill:

My congratulation to the Continental directors and to you on
your new assignment! You will have a full measure of both
challenge and opportunity--you and John should make a great
team.

On seeing the announcement, a former Asarco/Southern Peru
lawyer-executive sensed an opportunity and phoned me to ask
that I introduce him to you. I asked Mr. Ruby to send me a
dossier. It arrived this morning and is enclosed.

The dossier fairly presents Mr. Ruby's experience as I know
it. He worked directly with me during the later stages of
Asarco's Mexicanization exercise and subsequently was a
principal participant in handling the Southern Peru end of
the extraordinarily complex Southern Peru/Cuajone mine
financing. He has had unusually solid hands-on experience
in "making things work" in Latin America.

Mr. Ruby is an intensely creative, smart, energetic,
outspoken bilingual executive. He thinks he would be useful
to Continental in providing fresh insight, ideas, and follow
through in the area of structuring and negotiation work out
of non-performing Latin American loans. My experience with
him suggests he would be a superior candidate for just this
sort of position.

If you or one of your associates would like to talk to me
about any aspect of the enclosed, I would be pleased to
respond. I have a new phone number: (212) 520-3000.

All the best.

Yours sincerely,

Daniel I. Stack

Enclosure

GEORGE L. OCHS
6031 West Rowland Place
Littleton, Colorado 80123
(303) 979-9294 (H)
(303) 629-4567 (B)

May 18, 19--

Mr. Bill Frank
CareerLab
7700 E. Arapahoe Road, Suite 275
Englewood, Colorado 80112

Dear Bill:

Enclosed is a resume from a friend of mine, Russell Murray.
His specialty is corporate communications. He has often
provided me with consulting advice over the past few years in
my work for Prudential in Aurora.

Should you come across any employers who have the need for
someone with Russell's background, I would appreciate your
putting Russell in touch with them.

As you well know, Russell is attempting to make effective use
of the networking technique. Therefore, please keep his
resume on hand for a few months and keep his corporate
communications background in mind when going about your
business.

I've been very busy on a new assignment with Prudential and
have not been able to touch base with you. I apologize for
that and hope to get back in contact with you, perhaps the
second half of August.

Sincerely,

George L. Ochs

GLO/cb
Enclosure
cc: Russell Murray

STATE NATIONAL BANK OF PARK RIDGE

R. William Collins
President

February 10, 19--

Mr. Thomas D. Becker
2028 South Strathmore Drive
Park Ridge, Illinois 60068

Dear Tom:

I have received your letter of February 8, and I wanted you to know that I will do anything possible to assist you in locating a suitable position. As you undoubtedly know, I have the highest personal respect for you, and in my conversations with other banks in Park Ridge, I will keep your availability in mind.

Tom, if there is any other way in which I can be of assistance to you, please let me know. By all means, use my name as a reference should you wish to do so. You did not indicate if you would be interested in a banking position outside of Illinois. If so, please let me know. I am acquainted with a large number of banks throughout the country, and I may be able to assist you in this regard.

Please express my warmest best wishes to your entire family.

Cordially,

R. William Collins

RWC/sjh

PART FOUR

NOTES AND COMMENTS ON SELECTED LETTERS

Notes and Comments on Selected Letters

Involve friends in your job-search, 11

The "friendship letter" penned by Dale Kreeger may be one of the best job-hunting letters ever written, because it can be modified slightly and used by nearly everyone. Dale first sent his letter to friends to look for a "real job." When he decided to go into business for himself, he rewrote the letter to sell consulting services. Many letters in this book borrow words from Dale.

Try to make your letter sound personal, one-of-a-kind, even if it will be mailed to several hundred friends. It takes time to write a "universal" personal, but it's worth it. Don't send letters that sound cold and distant.

Announce new job, 32

It's difficult to sell consulting services to friends. You want their business, but you don't want to impose on them and ruin the relationship. Neil does a nice job of walking that thin line.

Clarify your career direction, 36

Your friends will help you chart your course, but you have to ask. Let them know what you need, and involve them—make it clear how important their ideas and opinions are to you. Most people like to feel valued and needed, to be called upon for advice and information. Give your friends the opportunity to help.

Ask for information, not for a job, 39

When writing to a stranger, it's better to ask for advice and information than to ask directly for a job. Most people don't like to reject others, so they resist speaking to job-seekers at all—and they rarely have a job opening. That's why it's easier to ask for information. Most people are willing to be helpful, if you make it clear you won't be pressuring them for employment.

Arrange informational interview, 42

Bud appealed to my ego, saying that he liked one of my seminars. That kind of opening would probably get anyone a meeting with me—I like sincere praise. But Bud's final sentence *guaranteed* a meeting. He said, "I know your time is valuable so please be assured I won't ask for more than 30 minutes."

If you assure people you won't waste their time, they will be more inclined to see you.

Find part-time work as trainer, 49

Perfect example of a well-planned "problem-solver" letter. Sally obviously spent a lot of time on this piece. She understands what my problems *might be*. Good guesswork on her part. She's sending the right letter to the right person. The letter is extremely persuasive without being hard sell. It says "I'm great" without bragging. If I had a big assignment and needed help, I'd certainly give Sally a call.

Find permanent part-time work, 50

Some people don't ever want to work full time. Clint Jones is one of them. (So is Nancy Thomas, the attorney whose letter appears on page 21.) Clint does a good job of telling his friends exactly what industries he wants to be involved with. Don't leave people guessing what you want to do; target a specific market. Make some decisions about where you belong and communicate those decisions to your support group. It's a big mistake to keep your options *too* open.

Summarize your career in a letter, 54

Great example of a letter that briefly explains a 25-year career. Use this idea when caught without a current resume.

Personalize letters to friends, 61-64

One letter is seldom right for everyone on your list of "friends," so you may want to send tailored letters to various subgroups: One for consultants, another for close personal friends, for family, for former vendors, and so on. The more you personalize your campaign, the better it will work. Doug's four letters are variations on Dale Kreeger's friendship theme.

Renew distant contacts, 65

Don't ignore the past. A contact is *anyone* who might remember you. It's better to write to someone who vaguely remembers you than to a total stranger. One senior executive recently found a job through someone he had barely known in high school! In an earlier letter (page 60), Michael wrote to classmates he had never even met. (He got a lot of good responses, too.)

This letter's appeal is akin to that of the FEI letter (page 72): "We're all members of the same elite group." And most groups *do* think they're elite.

Help from professional organizations, 72

Two of my accounting clients have landed jobs by contacting members of the Financial Executives Institute. The first, Len Kenney, lives in Los Angeles. He wrote to 350 members of the FEI, nationwide. One day he received a call from a recruiter in Chicago who was looking for a controller in L.A., right close to home.

Len won the job and went to work for one of *Inc.* magazine's top 20 small companies. When he asked the recruiter, "How did you find out about me?" the search consultant said, "I called a candidate in Chicago to see if he was interested. He wasn't. But he said 'I have the resume of a *friend* right here.'" Someone who had never met Len considered him a friend. Members of professional organizations tend to feel a sense of kinship with their peers. Paul Gutknecht's letter resulted in a job offer. That's a letter worth writing—think about trying this with your own association.

Help from spouse's friends, 74

Contact your own personal network, but don't forget that your spouse or significant other has a different circle of friends. When the oil field was down, Tom Jacob got a good job through his wife. Her best friend's husband was a senior executive in a major oil company.

Tell recruiters where you fit, 76

This form letter is easy to use; it gives recruiters the information they need. Your resume tells them where you have been, not where you want to be next. They have to figure out where to put you. This letter gives them an idea where you belong: by company size, by geography, by any requirement you care to mention.

It's simple—almost a fill-in-the-blanks letter.

Establish rapport with recruiters and headhunters, 79

Surprise! You have to sell yourself to recruiters just the same way you sell yourself to employers. Recruiters must get tired of letters that say, "I've enclosed my resume for your perusal." This search letter has a bit more zip, it's a "teaser."

Craig says, "I have strong marketable skills in which you would be interested." "What skills?" The recruiter wonders. If the candidate *thinks* he's highly marketable, he probably is. Successful, self-confident candidates are much easier to place; they "show" better. Therefore, recruiters place them faster and earn more commission. They like that.

Craig says what he's selling: a rare combination of business savvy and design expertise. That's a big plus, as many artists are erratic.

Saying "at your earliest convenience, please contact me. . ." conveys a sense of urgency. Although closing with "please contact me" is technically weaker (you generally want to state that you'll call, and give a time), the letter is so forceful and direct that it still feels strong.

Answer want ad, 119

Try to keep want ad letters short. Generally, one page is better than two—but two pages is better than three.

This is a well-written response to a want ad; it's obvious Ken has spent some time on it. A letter like this looks easy to write, but it isn't. It could take five hours to write this kind of concise, warm, friendly, professional letter. Ken shows over and over again that he has really thought through why he fits the job description. Tailor letters *only* to those ads you think fit you perfectly. Otherwise, you waste time, your biggest asset.

Answer important want ad, 127

Rick put a lot of work into this piece, which is more of a proposal than an actual letter. He spent several days writing it, and he had a lot to work with (such as 200 letters of reference from celebrities who had performed in his facilities). Save this kind of in-depth writing for those few jobs that are a perfect fit—your dream jobs.

Draft your own reference statement, 135

Even if you're leaving your company on good terms, it's a good idea to draft a reference statement for your boss to review. Then discuss it with him or her. That way the two of you will be telling exactly the same story. It's not uncommon for bosses to be completely unaware of some of their employees' accomplishments.

Get reference from boss who fired you, 136

It's often hard to get a decent reference from someone who has just fired you. It often helps if you draft ideas for him or her to review, as Charles has done here. He outlines his significant accomplishments, strengths as a manager and employee, reason for leaving, and personal characteristics—a great package.

Let your former boss know what you're saying, and what you expect him to say. Negotiate a story the two of you can agree on.

Don't leave it up to him to say whatever he wants.

Sell your way into a company, 145

This is one of my all-time favorite letters, and it contains two of the best job-search lines I've seen: "Freedom to work more than 40 hours per week," and "Whatever it takes, I can and will do."

Like all great letters, this one reflects the writer's personality: Linda is bright, creative, enthusiastic, *alive*. And she's successful. She mailed thirty letters, got three interviews and one job offer. Linda went to work in computer sales and was immediately fast-tracked. When the job soured, she rewrote her letter slightly, remailed it, and received another job offer. Today Linda is president of The Final Word, her own computer training company in Houston, Texas.

Show your track record, 148

Not all marketing people can write a sizzling letter, but Chris did. First of all, she had a winning headline, which is 90 percent of the battle according to John Caples, in *Tested Advertising Methods*. Although her letter is heavily accomplishment-oriented, it doesn't sound "braggy." It also says exactly what she's looking for, which is rare. (Many job-hunters mistakenly stay vague, to "keep their options open.")

Being a good marketer, Chris wasn't out of work long. She attended two national healthcare conventions and received a job offer immediately.

Sell your attitude, 149

I really love this letter. Judy and I talked about marketing letters, and I sent her home to draft one. Normally, clients return with a few scattered ideas and a hodgepodge of notes, but Judy came back and announced that she had completed a sales letter. I looked at the letter and felt it was really aggressive. I was about to suggest toning it down a bit when she told me she had already sent it to her target companies. I thought, "Oh well, let's see what happens."

What happened was delightful. Judy received a dozen calls, and had several interviews and a few temporary consulting assignments. One interview produced the job she now holds (product manager for a high tech medical company).

During salary negotiations, Judy showed me her offer letter. The president of the company wrote, "We can offer you an exciting and challenging environment in which to work. If you are looking for a chance to step up to the plate and hit another home run (to use your analogy), this is the opportunity for you. We hope you will be the lead-off batter on our championship clinical sales team."

End of story. What a letter!

Sales letter offering help, 150

First of all, "Need Help?" is the perfect headline. I've never seen anything better—who could say "no"? *Everyone* needs help. Scott follows with "I love to repair. . ." I like to hire people who love what they do, don't you? They're fun to work with. Would you seek out a repairman who hates what he's doing?

He's labeled himself a "craftsman"—not a handyman.

Another plus. The word "craftsman" implies quality, perfection, and attention to detail. Then he says he "cares." That's important. Who would prefer someone lazy, undependable and indifferent?

Last of all, he offers "free estimate or advice. . ." Free advice is a very nice touch, the essence of good service.

Scott did not exactly fit the "real job" mold. Creative, an independent thinker, and a "do-it-yourselfer," he loved the idea of working for himself. We created a repair/remodeling company for him, and the "Need Help?" letter was the cornerstone of his advertising campaign.

This piece was used numerous ways: as a letter, a flyer, and as a newspaper ad. It worked so well that within a couple of weeks Scott had more business than he could handle.

This is a good structure for a marketing letter. If you change a few words, *anyone* from an accountant to a vice president of finance can use it. It's short and powerful. Try it.

Appeal to the reader's ego, 162

An appeal to the reader's ego is one of the strongest approaches possible. It can't be beat, but you do have to be careful to keep it honest. Readers will react negatively to praise that sounds casual or insincere.

So, when you really do respect and admire someone, tell them so. If executed properly, appeal to ego is an attention-getter business leaders can't ignore.

Approach favorite company, 171

Craig has a "favorite company," and he said so. His letter told a story and showed honest admiration. Best of all, it worked. He interviewed with Caterpillar over the phone, but their corporate downsizing prevented his being hired. Try this approach with any company you truly admire.

Capitalize on industry growth, 173

When job-hunting, look for growing companies and industries. This letter could be modified to apply to *any* industry. For example, take out "outplacement" and plug in "hazardous waste."

The letter really begins with a disguised question: "Are you growing and expanding? If so, then perhaps my resume will be of interest." "Perhaps" is an important word here, a soft-sell. Many job-seekers come on too strong, telling rather than asking.

"My background covers all aspects from start-up through national expansion" pretty well says it all: This person knows what he's doing.

"I hope to contact you directly . . . to determine whether an exploratory meeting is indicated." Assures that the reader feels in control—Wesley is not going to call and demand an appointment.

You could probably get through to almost anyone using this letter. It's thoughtful and polite, and best of all, it's short.

Introduce yourself, 174-175

Jim is a professional copywriter, so his letters are near-perfect. They are smooth, casual, and easy to read—but also forceful and persuasive. What creative director in their right mind could say "no" to meeting him?

Jim is an interesting person: He has worked for advertising agencies in Denver and New York, and recently completed a Ph.D. in Psychology. That's a rare combination, and it intrigues employers.

Blitz employers, 179

Charles mailed three different letters, in the same order as they appear here. The first one caught my attention with the line, "If your firm has any expansion plans in the Southwest . . .". This person clearly knew what he wanted. I like that attitude, but he didn't offer to call, didn't ask me to do anything. That's a mistake.

The second letter includes a resume. That takes the mystery out of the situation, and could weaken a campaign. It's feels like giving in and going back to the old "cover letter and resume" routine.

The third letter mistakenly says it's the *second*—I was tracking his campaign better than he was. "I solicit your comments" is a good start, but he needs to solicit them more actively. Call the reader, or ask them for some kind or reply. A good effort, but letters by themselves seldom do the trick. If you care about meeting someone, call them and tell them *why*.

Increase response to your letters, 184

This is one of my favorite success stories. Jon Bartoshek worked 13 years driving a semi for Safeway, until a back injury prevented his continuing. He approached me wanting to "go into construction management." It seemed impossible, until we carefully analyzed his background. Thirteen years earlier, Jon had owned a small tenant-finish construction company, the kind that builds out offices in leased spaces.

On the resume, we took his construction background and made it look big on paper, and deleted the truck driving experience altogether.

Then Jon said, "By the way, I'd really like to relocate to Houston." (He was in Denver at the time.) We wrote a marketing letter, designed a reply form, gathered the names of commercial construction firms in Houston, and sent off a mailing.

Jon got three positive responses, took three interviews, accepted a job offer, and relocated his family to Houston. Since then he has relocated four times, and today he is the Project Superintentdent for construction of the newest and largest hotel in Miami Beach. Who says you can't change careers?

Guarantee a reply, 190

Letters have always worked well for me. I love writing them, and love seeing the results.

I've used them for:
    college course descriptions
    proposals
    getting new business
    collections
    thank yous
    getting media attention for myself and others
and many other purposes.

I can always tell when a letter feels right. Everything comes together and it "sings." I just know in my heart it's going to work.

This particular letter was a great one. I was doing freelance PR and marketing for small professional firms— MDs, dentists, lawyers, financial planners—and decided I wanted more business. The letter was directed to medical doctors who are facing increasing competition.

The opening headline "Are you a good candidate for PR?" is ideal. But the bullets that follow are even better—because most of them must be answered, "Yes!"

Take this bullet, for example: "Are you already successful, and desiring more success?" What physician is going to say, "No, I'm not successful. I don't want more success"?

I sent along a reply form, and got several positive responses. This letter could be changed to work for almost any consultant or service provider. Give it a try.

Sell benefits to the reader, 192

Few job-seekers have as difficult a situation as Jim. Laid off in a small rural town when the oil field crashed, he lost both his job and his home. His family relocated to Denver without really knowing what the future would hold. But Jim is an optimist, and for an optimist the future is always bright.

Here's how his letter was created. I asked him to talk about sales: his philosophies, approaches, and values. I recorded everything he said. When he finished, we put his key ideas into a sales letter format. We targeted the letter only to companies in Jim's zip code. For an added bang, we added a response form.

The package worked beautifully. Jim got lots of calls and interviews. Best of all, he found the job he wanted close to his new home.

Use letters as flyers, 201

Something offbeat like this "letter" might work for low-to-mid level jobs. I found it on the information table at a convention. When I saw "Please turn me over" stamped in big black letters on a white sheet of paper, I couldn't resist.

The gimmick was good—I read the letter. Also, it's short, that's a plus. But it sounds a bit too much like "here's what I want, here's what I need." It's too cold; when you're asking strangers to help, you need to be cordial. You need to give them a *reason* to help.

Say thank you for everything, 223

Nothing is too small to warrant a thank you note. Absolutely nothing. One of my favorite tricks is to invite someone to lunch, pay for the meal, then write a thank you to my guest. They love it.

Follow up after conference or convention, 228

Every person you meet at a conference is fair game for a follow-up letter. However, the letter has to offer them something: a thank you, an ego stroke, an article from a recent journal, or something else of interest.

Sell by saying "thanks," 233

A thank you note is just a sales letter in disguise. On the surface, you're writing to say "thanks." But underneath, you want something: a job, a consulting assignment, a media placement, another meeting. Really *use* the thank you note to sell. "I had almost forgotten how stimulating business luncheons are" translates to the reader as "you are a very stimulating person to be around."

Jory summarizes his life's work in *one paragraph*! He defines the market he's looking for

(smaller organizations) and asks for referrals in a soft-sell way. He ends strongly ("I will call you.") and signs off cheerfully.

Send a thank you letter to *every person* who offers you any kind of assistance in your quest for success. All the job-hunting books say to do so, but few job-seekers ever do.

Act on want ad replies, 245

Susan is a go-getter. She's always enthusiastic, and this letter shows it. Here's the situation: She answers a want ad for a job that fits her beautifully. So when the company merely acknowledges they have received her resume, she seizes the opportunity to do more selling. That's the way to do it. Don't put these replies in manila folders and file them— not until you've taken action!

Keep selling after turndown, 251

In marketing, "no" doesn't mean "never." It means "not right now, maybe later." Use a turndown as a public relations opportunity—an opportunity to build good will. Respond in such a positive way that the company actually feels bad for not hiring you. (Don't show anger and make them feel glad!) It's a long shot, but sometimes the person who got the offer doesn't work out. Then they call you.

Show your enthusiasm, 254

All of Brad's letters reflect the person behind them. Brad is full of life and energy, and his letters are "hot"—full of excitement and enthusiasm. This letter ultimately resulted in a job offer—Brad is now a science writer for The University of Colorado Health Sciences Center, dealing with the local and national media.

Show how you fit, 258

When following up after a telephone call, don't just write "It was nice to talk to you, and I'll look forward to hearing from you again soon." Sell them something. Here Tom shows similarities between his last job and the new job—very important. Employers often can't see the similarities for themselves. The burden is on you to show them. If you don't show them how you fit, someone else surely will.

Remind friends to help, 260

It's good to let your friends know you're in the job market. But after a month, they usually forget it. If they haven't heard from you, they assume you've found something. So, if you haven't, remind them.

The best reminder letter I ever saw was in the form of a newsletter. The job candidate, a CPA, sent a humorous monthly newsletter, filled with anecdotes, to all his friends and supporters. It was well written and great fun. There was only one problem. He got a job after two months, so the newsletter ended.

Show persistence, 263-264

Don't take no for an answer, because "no" doesn't mean never. No means "not right now." Keep all your options open. Never close a door on yourself. Just remember, marketing is:

1. working magic;

2. actualizing, making things happen;

3. finding out what people *think they need* and giving it to them (not making them need what you've got);

4. a pleasant "can do" attitude; infectious enthusiasm ("I like you . . . I like your carpet, etc.);

5. keeping all the doors open . . . never closing a door, never being rude, curt, or unkind— no matter how disappointed;

6. trying all the avenues;

7. making it a job; working your buns off (with part-time efforts, you get part-time results);

8. knowing what you want . . . having written goals;

9. meeting as many people as possible in as short a time as possible (visibility);

10. always following up;

11. not accepting rejection;

12. not making excuses;

13. staying busy;

14. not quitting until you reach your goals.

Make a second effort, 266

Persistence is the name of the game, and it's especially good to let employers know that you're extremely busy, having a great time, and about to be snatched up by the competition.

Close the sale, 267

How do you rush someone without seeming pushy? You want to seem interested and excited, not desperate. Michael's letter succeeded—he is one of the rare senior executives who is a talented writer. His campaign was full of well-worded letters, many of which appear in this book.

Tell them you'll call, 268

Great letter, weak close. When you put the time into drafting a wonderful letter, don't leave the outcome to chance. Executives are notoriously busy, so don't wait for them to call you—often, they won't. Not because they don't want to, but because they simply don't have time.

When you tailor a letter to an important contact, end it strongly. In this case, "I'll call you to see if there might be something to talk about in this suggestion."

Ask for the job, 271

Michael has a way with words. He crafts the "thank you letter" beautifully, addressing three key issues:

1. The people. He says, in effect, "I like you and I like your people. We'd work well together."

2. The employer's objections: the job's not big enough, not "hands-on" enough.

3. The closing. He says "I want to work here," and asks for the job. And he keeps it short. "I really want this job" letters can drag on for three or four pages if you let them. Be sure you don't.

List your capabilities, 275-276

Employers are not only concerned about the past (what you have done), but about the future (what you will do). A list of your capabilities shows them what you *can* do, not what you have done. Many hiring managers find a list like this more interesting than a standard resume.

Approach consultants, 280

Greg tells me where he got my name. That's a good idea, because it makes the letter seem like less of a shot in the dark as well as letting me know that my advertising is working.

Greg writes a well-worded, well-organized, low-pressure letter. He covers a lot of ground in a short space: family situation, summary of strengths, job targets, and salary questions.

I would gladly have spoken with Greg, but unfortunately, he never called. (This is a serious mistake! If you promise to call, do so. If you fail to call, you convey the impression that you don't keep your promises. That can work against you. You don't want to develop a reputation in your network for lack of follow-through.)

Sell consulting services, 285

This is a warm letter that "sells hot." It's an example of an extremely persuasive sales letter that doesn't *sound* like a sales letter. The format could be used by any consultant, or by almost any job-hunter.

Leave consulting for a "real job," 291

It's difficult to leave consulting and return to a conventional job. Employers often view you with suspicion ("If you're so great, how come you didn't make it as a consultant?"). The best way to handle this is to approach it directly, as Paul does here. Here are some valid explanations for leaving consulting:

1. I'm a team player, not a soloist.

2. I like to make things happen, not watch them happen.

3. I like to stick around to see that my recommendations are carried out.

4. I've proved I can do it alone.

5. Long-term relationships are important to me. I don't enjoy jumping from job to job.

6. I'm a manager, not a guru.

Congratulate your friends, 294

Delightful example of a well-written note. Short and to the point. If your handwriting is beautiful, as Sharon's is, quick thank-you notes are definitely the way to go.

Stay in touch with your network, 299

After you've received a job offer—or while you're happily employed—it's easy to let your network grow cold. As I've said many times, that's a mistake—75 percent of good jobs come from friends. This newsletter is designed to help you keep in touch, even if briefly. It could be improved by being personalized with the recipient's name and address, and a salutation.

Get media attention, 302, 303

I once owned a small PR and marketing firm, and worked for professionals—lawyers, dentists, financial planners, and the like. My competitors claim I've always gotten more than my fair share of media attention . . . and it's true.

During a recent recession I got tired of the press dwelling on the problems in Denver's economy. I thought that "the brighter side of unemployment" would be an interesting story idea. I called the editor of a local weekly newspaper, explained my idea, and sent this short follow-up. The idea resulted in the story called "Job Hunters Beware," and made me some new friends.

I also contacted all the television stations in Denver (page 303). That letter was one of my best—it netted me four television appearances and a long-term relationship with one station in particular.

One key to successful media appearances is briefing the interviewer; explain your background and suggest questions for them to ask. This reduces the chance that you will have to answer off-the-wall questions.

Offer assistance to job-hunting friends, 317

Job-hunters need a lot of emotional support, and this letter offers it without being too sweet or condescending.

Epilogue

Mail your letters

In the early 1980s, I worked with my first oil and gas geologist. Randy's background was solid, but he had a very negative attitude. He was full of reasons why things wouldn't work.

Randy *did* put a lot of energy into writing a sales letter, and it came out very well. Then he put a lot of time and effort into collecting a list of names to mail that letter to. Surprisingly, after all that work, he never mailed his letters. I'm not sure why. Maybe he was afraid they wouldn't work.

Direct mail is an interesting business. You never know what the results will be until you mail the letters. Guesses as to what will happen are often wrong. So don't second guess yourself. Mail your letters.

Update For Next Edition

Wanted:
Your advice, ideas, and suggestions

Dear Reader,

This book is not a one-time event. It is a process, not a product. It is a networking and communications tool, and as such it is never completed. It is always being changed and improved.

If you have job-search letters which you think would help others, please send them to us. If we use one, you will receive a free copy of the next edition containing your ideas.

Best regards,

William S. Frank
CareerLab
7700 E. Arapahoe Road
Suite 275
Englewood, CO 80112

P.S. Be sure to include your name, address, and telephone.

Index
To The Examples

S

ACKNOWLEDGEMENTS AND CREDITS

Thanks to:

My two mentors: Richard N. Bolles, author of *What Color Is Your Parachute?*, and Joe Sabah, author of *How to Get the Job You Really Want*. And to T. Craig Lincoln, one of the country's leading graphic designers, the one person who kept nudging me to get this project done.

My wife, Beverly, who supported me when I spent nights, weekends, and holidays working on this.

The clients and friends who shared their ideas, comments, and letters:

Allan Ake, Patrick Allen, Sharon Almirall, Darrel Ankeny, John Antony, Bob Bales, Tom Barrett, Jon B. Bartoshek, Brad and Wendy Bawmann, Rud Bergfeld, Karen L. Bewley, Don Bloom, Pat Boylan, Barbara Brannen, Jim Brodie, Brandon Broga, Jane E. Buck, E.J. Carr, Dan Casaccia, Shirley Chambliss, Karen Clark, Ted A. Clark, Ronald L. Conrad, Herman Doering, Rory Donaldson, Christine Ewy, Ron Fox, Candy Gabarbi, Daniel J. Goin, Douglas Gragg, Judy K. Griffith, Kenneth W. Grove, Ken and Carol Grunkemeyer, Paul H. Gutknecht, John Haag, Steven L. Hargreaves, Ken Hargrove, William H. Heck, Rich Hegsted, Bill Holley, A.J. Hughes, Rick Ingalls, Bud Inzer, Thomas K. Jacob, Judy Jackson, Clinton D. Jones, Steven D. Jorgensen, James D. Julius, Karen Karvonen, Juanita Keeler, Leonard A. Kenney, Christine Klotz, Dale M. Kreeger, Bobbi Laubhan, Robert M. Lee, Jr., Bob Lee, T. Craig Lincoln, Bill Lowe, Robert E. Lundy, Charles F. Mankus, Chuck McDonald, Alana Majors, Jean M. Marshall, Dan Martinez, James W. Miers, Pat Mills, Jack Mooney, Larry Moore, Samir Y. Naguib, Norman A. Newton, Julie Normand, John H. Norris, George L. Ochs, Susan Ottinger, Richard and Jolene Polson, James J. Precup, Jim Rasmus, Gary W. Rawson, Bill Rector, Sandy Reed, George Reisinger, Matt Reyer, Bruce D. Robertson, Richard P. Ruby, Bob Sanford, W.J. Scheu, John Schlegel, Denny Schroeder, Robert H. Schulz, Jr., Jim Sexton, Tutch Shirane, Fran Sincere, Dick Smith, Sharon Smith, Star Snell, Jim Sonnier, Ann Stack, Neil B. Stein, William A. Steinhour, Ralph W. Stevens, Mark Sullivan, Dick and Laurie Thomas, Mike Trontell, Linda Turnbaugh, Rob Umbreit, Bruce VanDeventer, Colleen Verna, Claire Villano, Stan Warnick, Janice L. Weger, Ann Welsch, Roy J. Wilson, and Les Woller.

The professional writers who edited my work and gave me newer, better, more creative ideas: Eunice Carnal and Gary Provost.

Special thanks to Mariah Bear at Ten Speed Press.

Amy Ottinger, a high school senior, who sat at the keyboard for an entire month to input data. Amy, you showed up at exactly the right moment. And to Gwen Grant who kindly printed the final manuscript on her laser printer.

Those friends who took the time to encourage me at the very beginning when I was least sure of myself, especially Pat Reid, Pat Buchanan, Bernie DiFalco, Jeff Shafer, Anne Salisbury, Ron Oyer, Virginia Hughes, Lee Struck, Linda Tietjen and Kay Nichols. And to those of you who helped me later by asking, "How's the book?"

Those who kindly critiqued, reviewed, and reshaped the manuscript as it was being written, especially Brad Bawmann, Bob Calvert, Ken Cole, Jim Ford, Brad Frank, Alan Gersten, Fritz Ihrig, Bob Jones, Bob Junk, Dick Kline, Bob Lundy, John Mohr, Larry Moore, Gary Rawson, George Reisinger, Denny Schroeder, and Fran Sincere.

Kay Tubbs and Star Snell, who jump-started me by marking every page of the manuscript with helpful suggestions. Without you, I might have stopped.

Jory Laine, my friend, fellow consultant, and business advisor. Thank you for everything you do—and for everything you are.

ABOUT THE AUTHOR

William S. Frank, M.A., is President of CareerLab, a national career consulting firm based in Denver, Colorado. He has been an advisor to the employees and senior executives of more than 100 major U.S. corporations since 1970, including Ampex, AT&T, Coors, Honeywell, Kaiser-Permanente, Pentax, Schlumberger, Sears Roebuck & Company, and TRW.

His articles have appeared in publications including *The Rocky Mountain News* and *The Wall Street Journal's National Business Employment Weekly,* among others.

Mr. Frank is a Board Member of The Colorado Human Resources Association—an organization for personnel directors—and he makes frequent guest appearances in the media as an expert on career advancement.

CareerLab is a small group of business experts who provide career advice to individuals and outplacement counseling to corporations. Corporations hire CareerLab to make sure departing executives are reemployed quickly—whether through a traditional job-search, or by starting or buying businesses or becoming consultants. CareerLab's individual clients are typically high-level business executives or professionals, such as engineers, lawyers, and CPAs. Their corporate clients span all industries and all geographic locations.

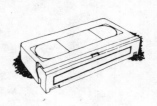